The Abusive Customer

Breaking the silence around an all-too-common problem, this book offers insights into the triggers of customer aggression against service employees, explores its consequences, and provides practical advice for handling abusive customers and mitigating the damage they inflict. Today, more than half of the world's population is employed in the service sector. This fundamental economic shift is accompanied by heightened attention to customer service and the 'customer is always right' paradigm. But when customers act aggressively, everyone pays a price: frontline employees, their families, their companies, and even the abusive customers themselves. Unlike breezier titles on the subject, this book is based in academic research — exploring the 'why?' and 'when?' behind abusive behavior — that underpins its practical approach, illustrated with real-world stories from professionals on the front lines of customer service. The book's useful tools include a sample anti-customer abuse policy and management process, a cheat sheet of practices that work for handling its consequences, a summary of effective service recovery processes and practices, and abuse-handling training list and curriculum templates. Managers and workers in customer-facing roles, in industries such as retail, hospitality, tourism, banking, and contact centers, will welcome this essential resource as part of their efforts to stop aggressive customer behavior, and improve employee morale, job satisfaction, and engagement.

Ivaylo Yorgov is a customer experience and analytics leader with over 15 years of experience in the domain, integrating business and academic research to offer evidence-based insights to his clients. He is the author of *The New Customer Experience Management* (Routledge/Taylor and Francis), which urges companies to evolve to a new mode of working with their customers: proactively supporting customers to create more value after the purchase, and offers examples, recommendations, and a roadmap for achieving this. Ivaylo is currently the Managing Director of a customer analytics company (GemSeek), overseeing its customer success teams.

The Abusive Customer

Breaking the Silence Around Customers'
Aggressive Behavior

Ivaylo Yorgov

Routledge
Taylor & Francis Group

NEW YORK AND LONDON

Cover image: © KTStock / Getty Images

First published 2024
by Routledge
605 Third Avenue, New York, NY 10158

and by Routledge
4 Park Square, Milton Park, Abingdon, Oxon, OX14 4RN

Routledge is an imprint of the Taylor & Francis Group, an informa business

ISBN: 9781032515069 (hbk)
ISBN: 9781032515007 (pbk)
ISBN: 9781003402565 (ebk)

DOI: 10.4324/9781003402565

Typeset in Optima
by codeMantra

Contents

Introduction

Writing this book has been a distinctively sad experience. Of course, I knew sometimes customers can be difficult, to say the least. I have clients, too, and I have also witnessed what angry customers can do in a variety of places – from bars, through bank branches, to airplanes. Derogatory language, interruptions, rudeness, yelling, unreasonable demands, insulting comments, even physical aggression – all of this and much more is part of the repertoire of many more customers than we would like to see or admit. If I am honest, I also know that I'm not exactly innocent of some of the behaviors we'll talk about here. Indeed, I can easily recall more than a handful of occasions in which I have not treated customer service employees in a way I am especially proud of. Never as extreme as in these examples, luckily:

> "F**K THAT! IT'S NOT THERE, OKAY?! YOU NEED TO F**KING GET ME WHAT I ASK FOR!"
>
> (excerpt from a story shared on https://notalwaysright.com, 2008a)

> **Customer:** "Stop f***ing socializing and do your g**d*** job!"
> **Employee:** "Sir, please don't be abusive. I'm just checking our other loc–"
> Angry Customer: "I don't care! DO YOUR JOB!"
>
> (excerpt from a story shared on https://notalwaysright.com, 2007)

> Employee: "Sir, your coupon is expired."
> Customer: "WHAT?! What do you mean it's expired? You f***ing b****, you're just trying to steal my f***ing money! You're trying to rob me! You and this f***ing company are trying to steal my f***ing money!"
>
> (excerpt from a story shared on https://notalwaysright.com, 2008b)

There is always an excuse, of course. The employee is wrong. She is a b.tch, he is a d..k. They looked at me the wrong way. The company sucks big time and wants to rob me. Fair enough, these things might be true. Maybe the

DOI: 10.4324/9781003402565-1

circumstances are against us; maybe we are having a bad day; maybe the employee made a mistake. The question remains though, and I think it is a question we need to seriously ask ourselves: "Does this justify wreaking havoc in a bank office or in a restaurant, or in a hospital?"; "Does it justify the price all these employees will pay when we treat them like punching bags?"; "Does it justify the stress we cause other people?"

As we will see later, it is indeed very often the low quality of customer service and poor customer experience that trigger customers' aggressive behavior. For things to escalate, there is typically a sequence of events involving low customer satisfaction and/or service recovery gone wrong. But tell me, what has the employee done wrong in this occasion:

> I guess one of the worst experiences was waiting on this family. The father was mean to his children and treated me like I was his slave. We have a three drinks maximum at the restaurant and he wanted a fourth drink. I told him I had to get a manager because I am not allowed to serve four drinks to one customer. He then went off on me. He told me that I was stupid because the customer is always right and if I want a tip at all I should be kissing his ass, not telling him off.
>
> (Korczynski and Evans, 2013, 778)

Or what has the flight attendant on a journey to LA done wrong to make a passenger yell at him "I will find your name, date of birth, and address! I will know your social security number before I get off this plane!" (*The Guardian*, 2021). As far as one can tell from the video recorded by Alexander Clark, a passenger on the same flight – absolutely nothing.

Yet, on both occasions, employees suffered significant cognitive and emotional consequences, hurting not only their job performance but also their private lives; the other customers suffered as well, and the company, too! In what can only be described as an utterly meaningless act of value destruction, customers ruined what would have otherwise been a casual, business-as-usual consumption or service exchange.

Writing this book has also been an odd experience for me. All my career, I have been working in the customer experience domain, helping companies design and deliver the best possible experience for their patrons. In a lot of ways, this involves gathering and transmitting the voice of the customer to organizations, thus allowing the latter to address the needs and demands of the former. In this process, I have become convinced that customer experience makes or breaks companies. The ones who are successful in giving their clients what they want succeed and the rest suffer. Implicitly or explicitly, I have been an advocate for customer-centric culture and decision-making more times than I can count, and I am still convinced this is the right way to do business.

Yet, in this process of becoming customer-centric, we somehow tend to forget that what organizations deliver to their clients, especially in the service domain, is made possible by people who communicate with clients on a minute-by-minute basis – their frontline employees. Luckily, this has begun to change, and in the recent years, we are also witnessing a sustained interest in what is known as employee experience.

According to most conceptualizations, customer and employee experience are the two sides of the same coin; the saying that happy employees make happy customers sums it up well. Consequently, we would do well if our efforts to deliver excellent customer experience align with our efforts to deliver excellent employee experience, and companies should consider the latter as high a priority as the former. This is a development one can only appreciate. All businesses are people businesses – if there were no employees, all the computers and algorithms and machines of this world would not be worth a dime. As a result, business consultants ask companies to improve their customer service and to have a look simultaneously also at what happens in the kitchen and improve the way employees feel working for the company. What I believe we often miss, though, is to have an honest look at one of the strongest destroyers of employee experience and motivation – customer abuse.

In a lot of ways, and to this day, it seems strange for me to say it, but the customer is not always right. Customers are not right when they steal. They are not right when they cheat. And, on the topic of this book, customers are not right when they act aggressively toward your employees, fellow teammates, and very often – friends. Customers' abusive behavior lurks beneath the surface of the "Customer is King" paradigm, and the intention of this book is to shed light on it. When customers act aggressively, everyone pays a price – first and foremost frontline employees, and in an unfortunate chain of events, also their families, the companies, even the abusive customers themselves. A host of research shows that when customers act aggressively, they have a detrimental impact on employees' emotional and cognitive states, and cause negative affect, stress, burnout, and emotional exhaustion. These, in turn, lower employees' morale, job satisfaction, and job engagement, ultimately lowering job performance, increasing turnover intention, and even aggressive behavior toward customers.

It is with a heavy heart that I read dozens of stories, and went through hundreds of scholarly articles researching the triggers and consequences of customer aggression. I had no clue how widely spread customers abuse is, and I had never considered the toll it takes on employees. The more I researched the topic, the more convinced I became that we need to break the silence around customers' aggressive behavior.

If I'm allowed to make a call to action, it would be this: let's work together to try to eradicate customer abuse. Its spread is mind blowing.

One study revealed, for example, that bus drivers were subjected to a wide range of violence, including

physical (20.2%; e.g., being spat on or punched, threatened at gun point, sexual harassment, etc.), verbal (35.8%; e.g., intimidation, insults, death threats, etc.), both physical and verbal (24.8%; e.g., being spilled hot coffee on the lap with insults), verbal aggression with physical aggression towards objects (13.8%; e.g., damaging the bus with insults).

(Zhou, Boyer, and Guay, 2018, 256)

Another study, conducted in the United Kingdom, shows that "employees directly involved with customers suffer from verbal abuse every 3.75 days, threats every 15 days and acts of violence every 31 days" (Antonio, Espartel, and Perin, 2019). And, in the United States, "almost 25% were victims of psychological and/or physical aggression from customers" (Patterson et al., 2009, 6).

No organization working directly with end customers is safe. Customer abuse has been shown to impact sectors as diverse as contact centers, retail, hospitality (hotels, restaurants, bars), tourism, banking and insurance, airlines, public/government services, transportation, real estate, education, professional service and more broadly, business-to-business companies; even healthcare employees, the people who save our lives, feel its impact.

In an ideal world, we would be successful in our mission to eradicate customer abuse once and for all, and no customer would ever treat an employee badly. Realistically, it is unlikely that we will succeed in this, simply because no human behavior is fully within our control. We might design the best systems and policies we can think of, and yet fail to reach 100% success rate.

We need a second-best option, then, and it is to prepare for the worst. My second call to action, then, is to help employees deal better with abusive customers as their interaction unfolds, and to help them mitigate the negative consequences of these interactions.

We, as business leaders, need to take a stance. I understand all too well the rationale behind "The Customer is King" approach; I also admire the efforts to create a better employee experience. What happens, though, when the two clash? How do we solve this riddle? How do we react when customers act aggressively toward employees? This destroys employees' experience, but we also have a business to run so we can't just fire every customer who raises his or her voice, can we? And vice versa – we cannot tolerate customers' aggressive behavior if we want our employees to be happy, creative, and productive. I believe it is in clashes like this that we have an opportunity to show leadership and to take decisions that shape our companies' future.

The book is designed to help business leaders and people working in customer service roles alike, as I believe we all need to step up and fight customer abuse. From C-level positions, through middle management, to service representatives, we can eradicate customer abuse only if we act in unison. What managers will find here is insights on the causes of customer aggression and its consequences, and ways in which they can act to prevent it or to support their employees in handling the consequences. Customer service reps will discover important tips on handling difficult conversations with customers, as well as data-backed insights on how to best alleviate the damage aggressive customers do.

The rest of this book is organized as follows. Chapter 1 takes an in-depth look at what is customers' aggressive behavior and how widely spread it is. First, it outlines two major motives for customer deviant behavior – economic and noneconomic – and gives examples of both. Second, it pays special attention to noneconomically motivated customer deviant behavior and defines it as one linked to presenting unreasonable demands or breaking established norms of conduct verbally or physically. Third, this chapter also explores how widely spread customer abuse is.

Having defined customer abuse and established its proportions, Chapter 2 gives an overview of the findings related to the consequences of customer abuse for employees. By now, these are very well documented and include stress, emotional exhaustion, cognitive costs, negative emotions, burnout, anger, and lower job satisfaction and engagement. In addition, customer abuse also has serious consequences for employees' off-work well-being and behavior, such as overeating, impulsive buying, mobile phone overuse, more family conflict, and poor sleep.

Chapter 3 continues the exploration of the consequences of abusive customer behavior by reviewing its organizational impact. The business effects include, for example, lower employee service performance, higher turnover intention, lower work engagement and on-task withdrawal, service sabotage and customer-directed deviant behavior by employees, and lower service evaluation by customers, especially because of observing customer abuse.

Chapter 4 then has a look at what drives customer abuse. It presents insights for the psychological, situational, and societal nature of customer aggression and lays out the foundation for practices that help prevent it or at the very least mitigate its consequences. The psychological drivers of customer abuse are found in narcissism and one of its milder (psychologically) manifestations in consumption – customer entitlement. The strongest situational drivers, as we will see, are poor customer service and especially poor customer service recovery, i.e., mishandled customer complaints. The societal factors that give rise to customer abuse are mostly linked with the 'The customer is always right' mantra and the weak position of labor, which creates a social status distance between customers and employees opening a space for customer abuse to exist.

Building on the insights presented so far, Chapters 5–7 deep dive into the ways of handling customer abuse. Chapter 5 looks at ways to prevent customer abuse and points out to the need for companies to provide better customer experience, especially in the case of service recovery (e.g., appropriate apology, compensation, and recovery process), to be proactive in managing customer experience, and to manage the environment in such a way that makes customer abuse less likely (e.g., lower noise levels and use third-person images).

Chapter 6 then presents insights on managing customer abuse as it unfolds. This includes implementing appropriate policies and systems for identifying and tracking abuse customers, and training employees on coping and problem-solving skills.

Chapter 7 offers insights into what management and employees can do to mitigate the consequences of customer abuse. On the management side, it outlines practices such as employee empowerment, social support, employee participation in decision-making, offering employees opportunities to voice their needs, corporate social responsibility, and appropriate leadership practices. On the employee side, it suggests practices such as developing emotional intelligence skills, sleep practices, taking short breaks, developing resilience, and practicing mindfulness as effective safeguards against the consequence of customer abuse.

The last chapter summarizes all the insights presented thus far and makes a call for action to increase the awareness of customer abuse, to clearly mark it as an unacceptable behavior, and to implement practices for preventing it or at the very least for helping employees deal with its consequences.

I look forward to a world in which customers and employees treat each other fairly, and collaborate to create the highest possible value for both clients and businesses. I look forward to a world in which transactions happen in a civil, polite manner. And, I look forward to a world in which we as business leaders pay attention, create the environment, and implement the interventions needed to build this world. We might never get there, but we can try. At the very least, we can equip our employees with the tools and skills to manage aggressive customers and the dire consequences they cause. I stand against customer abuse, and I hope you join my pledge.

References

Antonio, P., Espartel, L. B., & Perin, M. G. (2019). Dysfunctional customer behavior and service employees tactics. *Revista De Administração Da UFSM*, 12(2), 302–316. https://doi.org/10.5902/1983465924984

Korczynski, M., & Evans, C. (2013). Customer abuse to service workers: an analysis of its social creation within the service economy. *Work, Employment and Society*, 27(5), 768–784. https://doi.org/10.1177/0950017012468501

Not Always Right (2007). We Need One Of These In Every Store. https://notalwaysright.com/we-need-one-of-these-in-every-store/67731/, last accessed on January 10, 2023

Not Always Right (2008a). Paging Leonidas to the Front Desk. https://notalwaysright.com/paging-leonidas-to-the-front-desk-2/68741/, last accessed on January 10, 2023

Not Always Right (2008b). https://notalwaysright.com/a-good-ol-fashioned-a-whoopin/68662/, last accessed on January 10, 2023

Patterson, Paul G., McColl-Kennedy, Janet R., Smith, Amy K., & Lu, Zhi (2009). Customer rage: Triggers, tipping points, and take-outs. *California Management Review*, 52(1), 6–28. https://doi.org/10.1525/cmr.2009.52.1.6

The Guardian (2021). Nobody ever put hands on me before': flight attendants on the air rage epidemic. https://www.theguardian.com/us-news/2021/oct/17/flight-attendants-air-rage-epidemic-coronavirus-covid, last accessed on January 10, 2023

Zhou, B., Boyer, R., & Guay, S. (2018). Dangers on the road: A longitudinal examination of passenger-initiated violence against bus drivers. *Stress Health*, 34(2), 253–265. doi: 10.1002/smi.2779

Chapter 1

What Is Customer Abuse and How Many Fall Victim to It?

We often hold the assumption that the simple fact of knowing something is enough for us to change our behavior. You can see this thinking and the resulting failure in practice everywhere you look. Smokers are smokers not because they think cigarettes are healthy – they know perfectly well they are not. We have one drink too many not because we do not know we'll feel awful the next day; I doubt anyone drinking this last round (or five) of tequila holds any illusions about it. And we know working out is good for our health, yet we often prefer the comfort of our couch to running in the park or training at the gym. Most of the time, it is not lack of knowledge that stops us from doing the things we should do.

This might very well be true, but it does not make ignorance a bliss. Knowledge itself might not be enough, but it is a vital first step in changing our behavior. One of the best advices I have heard, for example, when it comes to increasing one's emotional intelligence is being able to name our emotions, to put a label to them[1]. Merely saying that we feel well or terrible does not cut to the chase. To be able to truly start working on and with our emotions we need to develop a dictionary rich enough to encompass their specifics. For example, it is a completely different story to feel desperate or depressed, and it is a completely different story to feel anxious or scared, even though these emotions seem similar at a first glance.

Similarly, being able to recognize and call customer abuse by its name is fundamental for being able to fight it. We need to differentiate it from other ways in which customers break established rules or go against the socially accepted norms of behavior. Indeed, this might appear at first sight to be an exercise too theoretical or too abstract; yet, consider Abraham Lincoln's words "Give me six hours to chop down a tree and I will spend the first four sharpening the axe." Planning, understanding the issue at hand, preparing – these are the things that allow us to solve issues with efficiency and ease.

So, what, then, is customer abuse? To narrow down to it, we need to have a look at the bigger picture first and to start with an (unfortunately) unsurprising fact: customers are first and foremost people, and there are a lot of ways in which they engage in what is known as deviant behavior – actions

DOI: 10.4324/9781003402565-2

that go against the generally accepted norms of behavior, or outright illegal acts. The most practical way to think about customers' deviant behaviors is to split them into two very broad groups.

Profit-Driven Customer Deviant Behavior

Some of the deviant consumer behaviors are clearly economically motivated. Think about shoplifting for example, or piracy. Both are typically conducted for economic reasons and yield economic benefits for the perpetrators. Buying contraband, buying counterfeit goods, and failure to report billing errors also fall in this category. Albeit less explicit, these behaviors still cause harm to companies by indirectly depriving them of revenues.

A major subgroup of economically motivated customer deviant behavior is related not so much to stealing as to lying. Think about de-shopping. This is the practice of buying products without the actual intent of keeping them but to use them once or twice and then return them to the seller. It is a huge issue for retailers – by a 2012 estimate it was costing US retailers 16 billion dollars per year[2]. Here is what an interviewee of Dr. Tamira King and Dr. Charles Dennis shared with them when they explored the practice of deshopping:

> I wanted a dress but mum wouldn't lend me the money, I liked the dress so I wore it and then came back next morning and took it back with my friends.
>
> (King and Dennis, 2003, 158)

Or have a look at this example:

> I have done it once because I had worn it and did not like it that much. … I wore it two to three times then picked seam, as a reason to go and give it back. I was excited to get my money back and get rid of top.
>
> (King and Dennis, 2003, 157)

While the motivation in both cases is different, at the end of the day there is still a significant economic impact on the company.

We can add easily add more practices to this list; consider, for instance, making false claims and evoking guarantees, fraud, especially in the domain of insurance, and simpler things like switching price tags. Harris and Reynolds, in a seminal article about what they call 'jaycustomers', share remarkable stories of employees witnessing such economically motivated deviant customer behavior, such as this:

> Because they know, they write a letter and they receive $100 back from headquarters. One letter claimed that the smoke from the fajitas

we served made their jacket smell of smoke and they wanted us to compensate them for a new one.

(Harris and Reynolds, 2004, 345)

And this:

On checking in to a hotel I noticed that they had a '100% satisfaction or your money back' guarantee, I just couldn't resist the opportunity to take advantage of it, so on checking out I told the receptionist that I wanted a refund as the sound of the traffic kept me awake all night. They gave me a refund, no questions asked. These companies can be so stupid they need to be more alert.

(Reynolds and Harris, 2005, 326)

One cannot help but be tempted to think that wherever there is an opportunity, there will be a way in which consumer try to trick the system and cheat. What all these acts – from shoplifting through de-shopping to altering tags have in common is that they all have a fairly direct economic impact and they are directed at the business itself, and not at its employees.

Non-Profit Driven Customer Deviant Behavior

While economically motivated deviant behavior is widely spread, there is a whole class of norm-breaking acts that might fall below our radar because they are not driven by a desire for monetary benefits. This non-economically driven customer misbehavior is substantially different depending on its target.

When Customers Target the Company

On the one hand, customers might direct their actions towards the company itself. Such is the case, for example, of acts of vandalism against a company's property. Very often, but far from all occurrences, this happens when customers are under the influence of different substances (read: customer are drunk), like in these cases:

We had a group of 30 guys on a bachelor's weekend and they just picked up all the fire extinguishers and had a brawl in the middle of the corridor, that cost us $600 in repairs (bar manager, six years' experience).

(Harris and Reynolds, 2004, 347)

People have parties … we had a room left with the furniture smashed to pieces, cigarettes and empty bottles smashed everywhere, feces and cigarette butts smeared on the walls, blood all over the sheets, it was the utmost ruin of a room that you have ever seen (hotel receptionist and housekeeper, two years' experience).

(Harris and Reynolds, 2004, 347)

In addition to vandalism, some authors include behaviors such as brand boycott, brand retaliation, and negative word of mouth in this group of company-directed non-economically motivated deviant behavior as well. These are actions customers take to get even at companies for what they perceive to be unjust interactions, i.e., they have been treated badly, or have in some way been cheated by the company.

Given my background in customer experience analytics, I am cautious to include these in the 'deviant' behavior group. After all, sharing a negative experience you had with a company does not exactly seem like something violating the norms of conduct, and customers are fully within their right to do it. Same goes for brand boycott – at the end of the day, if I as a customer am so unhappy with a company that I decide to never again use its products or services, that seems like a legitimate response. The issue with these types of behaviors stems from the proportion in which they are executed. Very often customers exaggerate their experiences when sharing them with others or launch vendetta campaigns against companies. Again, there might be some good reasons for avoiding a brand or sharing negative word of mouth and that is all fine; it stops being fine when it gets out of proportion or when customers share outright lies.

When Customers Target Other Customers

The second group of non-economically driven customer deviant behaviors is one I am sure we can all relate to – these are actions that are directed towards other customers. Clearly, it could happen that we all do things that break norms of proper behavior in consumption context inadvertently. I myself did that the other day when I jumped a queue because I did not notice a customer (it was raised to my attention and yes, I apologized profusely).

Often, though, it seems that our fellow customers do these things on purpose or without any sign of remorse. In one of the first explorations on the topic, a group of researchers[3] developed a typology of customer-to-customer deviant acts including seven types of behaviors: 'Inattentive parents with naughty kids', 'Oral abusers', 'Outlandish requesters', 'Hysterical shouters', 'Poor hygiene manners', 'Service rule breakers', and 'Ignorant customers'. The names are rather self-explanatory, and taken as a whole these categories paint a bleak picture of the ways in which other customers can ruin otherwise good experiences.

Who among us had not been on the receiving end of this story for example? You and I both know that often all reasoning and talking is futile when a kid decides to scream, yet we also cannot help but feel the pain of the customer:

> I once saw a stupid kid standing there in the middle of the restaurant I was at, standing next to his dad who was sitting stuffing his face, and the kid was bawling at the top of his lungs non stop for whatever reason. Instead of telling the kid to shut up, the father just watched him scream-ing the entire time like his kid was a fascinating science experiment, not saying a single word.
>
> (Gursoy, Cai, and Anaya, 2017, 2349)

From minor acts like cutting a queue to people who dismiss service procedures considered common sense by most of us and show complete disrespect to the needs of fellow customers, other people have a significant impact on our consumption experiences. Inadvertently or not, all these acts can break a good, functional customer experience and cause companies at the very least reputational damage. The thing is, when we experience this as customers it is often just a momentary episode and importantly, we can often escape from it – either leave the specific scene or avoid the place in which it happened in the future altogether. There is though one group of people that is disturbingly often at the receiving end of customer deviant behavior and that cannot escape it – service employees.

When Customers Target Employees

Arriving at the final form of deviant customer behavior, and the core topic of this book, we face customers' non-profit driven deviant behavior directed towards employees. Welcome to the world of customer abuse:

> I guess one of the worst experiences was waiting on this family. The father was mean to his children and treated me like I was his slave. We have a 'three drinks maximum' at the restaurant and he wanted a fourth drink. I told him I had to get a manager because I am not allowed to serve four drinks to one customer. He then went off on me. He told me that I was stupid because the customer is always right and if I want a tip at all I should be kissing his ass, not telling him off.
>
> (Korczynski and Evans, 2013)

> He swore at me, saying I was stupid and retarded. It made me feel very bad [...] He should talk more politely to me than this. He didn't respect

me. I am a human like him. If he was a salesperson and was scolded by a customer, how would he feel?

(Akkawanitcha et al., 2015, 272)

Two customers (a mom and her daughter) came to the public relations department. The mom asked me to give her money back. She claimed that she had bought sausages 4 days before that were rancid [...] I made a call to the fresh food department. The staff member in that department asked me how the sausages were. I said that they were normal and did not smell that bad. The daughter heard what I said and became very angry and shouted. She asked me if I thought it was rancid or not, then she shoved the sausage into my mouth and said to me "eat it." I was very frightened and I couldn't control myself. I pushed her hand out of the way and the sausage went flying into her face unexpectedly. This made her get even angrier.

(Akkawanitcha et al., 2015, 272)

For the purpose of our discussion in the remainder of the book, we will use the term customer abuse to mean a deliberate (non-accidental) violation of social or consumption norms committed by customers while interacting with service employees and/or directed at them. There are a couple of important points to make here before moving forward.

First, unlike acts like stealing and committing fraud, customer abuse, as we will use the term here, does not involve any economic benefit for the customer. In fact, customers often lose when they act abusively, as a plethora of studies show that when mistreated employees perform their tasks less effectively which ultimately worsens customers' experience. There are cases in which the customer might benefit from making aggressive demands, of course, but this is merely a by-product of their behavior and not its primary goal.

Second, unlike vandalism, customer abuse is directed at other people instead of property. Vandals surely cause companies a lot of money as they destroy objects and ruin the physical environment. What abusive customers do though is far worse – they hurt the very flesh and blood of a company – its employees.

Third, unlike customer-to-customer deviant behavior, which can often be attributed to inadvertent reactions, customer abuse is overt and deliberate. This is not to say that customers wake up in the morning and start thinking how to be aggressive towards the cashier in the local café – I'm not saying that customer abuse is a rationally planned behavior. I am merely pointing out to the fact that when a customer calls an employee stupid this does not happen by accident (the way jumping a queue can). It is a clearly deliberate act.

The concept of norms plays a critical role in understanding customer abuse, and is also the reason why sometimes it might not be very clear whether a certain behavior is abusive or not. Most researchers working on the topic broadly agree that it involves some kind of violation of the accepted norms of behavior. For example, in one of the first conceptualizations of customer misbehavior, Fullerton and Punj define it as "behavioral acts by consumers which violate the generally accepted norms of conduct in consumption situations, and thus disrupt the consumption order." (Fullerton and Punj, 1997) A similar definition is used by two other researchers who have contributed a lot to our understanding of it: "deviant customer behavior ... is deliberate acts by customers that violate widely held norms." (Daunt and Harris, 2006, 101) Pointing slightly more towards the interactional element of service encounters, still others consider customer mistreatment to be "low-quality interpersonal treatment employees receive from their customers" (Wang et al., 2011, 315). And finally, Kang and Gong define dysfunctional customer behavior as "customer actions in service settings that deliberately violate the generally accepted norms of conduct for how to treat employees" (Kang and Gong, 2019, 626).

No matter how they call it – deviant customer behavior, customer misbehavior, customer incivility, customer aggression, customer abuse, or aberrant customer behavior – all researchers agree that it involves acts that go against what we deem acceptable, i.e., as violating the social norms or those imposed by the company itself.

Norms play an important role in defining customer abuse because to judge the acceptability of our own actions, we usually view them from two aspects: whether the people who are important to us perform these kinds of behavior, and whether a person or a group that is important in some way to us would approve or disapprove the behavior[4]. The former is called descriptive norms, and the latter – injunctive ones.

Descriptive norms refer to what in our daily lives is aptly summed up in the saying "Monkey see, monkey do", and to the way children often excuse their actions: "But, mom, everyone is doing this!". They refer to what other people do. Injunctive norms, then, enter the picture in the role of the 'mom' in the last example. If she does not approve of the behavior, she is evoking the concept of injunctive norms. Injunctive norms are about whether people who are important for us will approve of what we are doing. Kids are clearly often stuck in between these two types of norms, when they want to do what their friends are doing but their parents do not allow them to.

Back to the topic of interest for us here, the term customer abuse, then, denotes behaviors that deviate from social norms of conduct on one or both of these aspects. While some people can indeed act like a..holes most of the time, the majority of us don't go about our days constantly yelling at people or threatening them, so even based on descriptive norms alone, these actions would classify as abusive. And even if for some reason such aberrant behavior becomes widely spread, I believe we need to constantly ask ourselves whether this is the world we want to live in, i.e., whether those close to us would approve of our actions and more importantly, what social environment are we creating when we abuse employees. If there the answer is 'No', then they also violate injunctive norms and are thus unacceptable.

Now, of course norms change and we can have an almost endless discussion about what is morally right or wrong. Yet, I strongly believe that there is a common, almost universal baseline of socially acceptable communication norms. I'm not even talking about saying 'Please' and 'Thank you' here, although that would certainly make our moms proud. I think even with norms changeability in time, we can all agree that yelling and shouting at other people, calling them stupid, swearing, and arguing forcefully is not acceptable. And clearly, pounding fists on counters, slamming phones down, and shoving sausages in people's mouths is also not OK.

Having said all that, what would be examples of behaviors we can classify as abusive? How can we describe and more importantly, how can business leaders and service employees recognize customer abuse?

There are two basic forms customer abuse might take: verbal and physical. In both its manifestations, these are acts that offend employees or threaten their dignity or safety.

Acts of **verbal abuse** include, but are not limited to, for example,

customers using condescending language[5], customers yelling at employees[6], making insulting comments, shouting, cursing, speaking rudely, speaking with sarcasm, speaking with a strong voice, arguing forcefully, sexist comments (both explicit and implied), racist comments (both explicit and implied), irrelevant personal remarks (e.g. about your appearance), threats (e.g. I'll have you fired), intimidating silence, accusations of various sorts (e.g. Calling you a racist), comments about your competency, knowledge, dedication[7].

It is a long list and dark list, I know. Unfortunately, the list of **physical acts of customer aggression** is not any shorter… Included in this group are behaviors like:

standing in your personal space, starting at you (long eye contact), table pounding, throwing things, leaning over you (using height advantage), fearsome facial expressions, loud sighing, pointing, other offensive gestures, shoving of personnel, slamming a phone down, attacking employees, unwanted physical contact[8].

Basically, any physical action that is used to intimidate employees and any unwelcome physical contact constitutes an act of physical customer aggression.

As you can see, customer abuse spans quite a broad range of behaviors, some of which might be considered borderline cases (like loud sighing or intimidating silence). Yet, I believe these lists give us a good starting point for building almost a checklist for recognizing customer abuse. At the end of the day, if we go back the discussion of what is deemed acceptable (i.e., a social or a consumption norm), I hope we all agree on is that none of the behaviors listed above is acceptable in neither personal, nor public settings. It is not OK to shout at service employees, it is not OK to call them words, it is not OK to argue forcefully with them. I do not think there is even a need to point out that throwing things at people is also not OK, just like attacking them or making unwanted physical contact. I think we, as business leaders, as employees, and most importantly – as humans – need to be very firm on these points. Abusive behavior in any form is degrading and dehumanizing, and customer abuse is no exception. The fact that some people are paid to deliver a service does not and should not include tolerance towards abrasive behavior.

At this point, you might be thinking, just like I did when I started working on the topic: "Surely this kind of behavior cannot be too widely spread. I know some people do it but they are the exception rather than the rule". Research says you and I are wrong. Customer abuse is widely spread and impacts thousands of people daily. Let us have a look at the data.

Customer Abuse Takes Epidemic Proportions

According to the World Bank, 2019 marked the first time in human history in which more than half of the world's population is employed in the service sector. In markets such as US, UK, and the Netherlands this share reaches more than 75%.

Think about it for a second. If you live in the US, the UK, or the Netherlands, 4 out of every 5 people you know will have a service-related job; in other countries this proportion might be closer 3 out of 5 – still a very considerable share. These people could be any of, for example, healthcare workers, bank tellers, through lawyers, hotel employees, restaurant managers, copywriters, photographers, business coaches, bus drivers, or one of the many other professions providing services to customers. Our ability to produce what we need to sustain our lives more easily and with less human involvement than ever means that less and less of us are involved in producing products and more and more are involved in delivering services. Changing business models, such as the trend towards turning products into services (such as software as a service) further boosts this trend.

What this means is that half of us worldwide, and more than three quarters in US and Western Europe, are exposed to direct communication with clients. What this also means is that all these people are exposed to work situations which might potentially involve customer abuse. People working in environments in which emotions loom large are especially vulnerable. These service situations have been appropriately called emotionally charged service encounters (ECSEs)[9] and research has identified four types of services that are especially prone to such interactions.

First, you have the negative services, "e.g. medical service encounters such as when a patient with a cardiovascular disease meets her physician" (Delcourt et al., 2017, 85–86) These are interactions in which almost by default we anticipate negative news or at the very least an unpleasant experience. Consequently, such encounters are inherently loaded with negative emotions, such as fear, anxiety, and feeling threatened.

Next, there are the "complex and high-involvement services (e.g. when a young couple meets a real estate agent to purchase their first house)" (Delcourt et al., 2017, 86) These include all situations in which we are exposed to something we haven't experienced before or don't experience very often, something which is important or with significant consequences, and that involves a rather complex process. For sure, purchasing a house is one such thing, and by extension for most people any case in which a lawyer is involved would count as an emotionally charged service encounter as well. So would probably purchasing our first car, opening a mortgage loan, relocating to a different country, filing our taxes or any other situation in which we simply don't know how to solve a problem. There is no shortage of business-to-business encounters that are complex and high-involvement as well. However experienced one is, deciding to open a new factory or launching a new ad campaign is still a complex decision that might cost millions.

A third group of emotionally charged service encounters includes "services for which bad news is often delivered to customers (e.g. a repair technician who must tell customers that an appliance is beyond repair)" (Delcourt et al., 2017, 86) In short, all cases in which a company or a person needs to do service recovery, i.e. fixing something broken, are ridden with emotions.

And last but not least, you have the "services subject to frequent failures (e.g. a restaurant delivering cold food to a customer)" (Delcourt et al., 2017, 86); transportation services fall squarely in this group as well. This group included interactions with less impactful outcome, compared to the complex and high-involvement services, but these can happen more often and as in all other cases, we have very limited control over the outcome. In fact, as we will see later, the third and the fourth group of emotionally charged service encounters represent the bulk of situations in which customer abuse is likely to occur, as they are both inherently full of negative emotions.

I hope it took you less time than it took me to see one very important point that is implicit in this framework: this list covers virtually all types of service exchanges: any and all service interactions hold the potential to become emotionally charged with all the negative consequences. Even a simple bank branch interaction can go south if there is a failure or if negative news is delivered to the customer. Healthcare work is inherently emotionally charged. Airplane crews are frequently subjected to customer abuse because there are frequent failures and bad news is delivered to customers. In retail settings customers are also very often driven by emotions, and can get emotionally aroused be it with positive emotions or negative ones. The list can go on and on to cover pretty much any service you can imagine. When working at the frontlines with clients there is never a certainty that the interaction wouldn't enter a negativity spiral.

So how exactly often does customer abuse happen? Here is what we know:

- As early as 2002, Carol Boyd[10] reported that three out of four airline and railway cabin crew were subject to verbal aggression from passengers once a month or more often, in most cases sarcasm, condescending remarks and swearing, and almost two in three have experienced physical abuse.
- In a seminal article in 2004, Harris and Reynolds (Harris and Reynolds, 2004) reported that 92% of hospitality employees have service personnel have encountered oral abusers at the workplace in the last six months, 49% – physical abusers, and 38% – sexual predators.
- In a call center study in 2004, researchers discovered that about 15% to 20% of the total volume of calls per day involved customer aggression, and more than half of the call center employees said that they have already experienced such in the week the study was conducted[11]. To make this easier to digest, that is approximately one customer yelling or calling you names per hour.
- In 2005, in a study among social workers close to two thirds of them "reported they had been victims of physical or psychological assault and 14% reported they had committed such an assault on a client within the past year" (Ringstad, 2005, 305)
- In 2006, a survey conducted in the US discovered that about a quarter of all interviewed have been on the receiving end of psychological and/or physical aggression by customers[12].
- In 2007, two researchers, Gettman and Gelfand, reported that "Sexist hostility was the most common form of CSH (client sexual harassment) ..., having been experienced at least once by 86% of the women

surveyed. This was followed by sexual hostility, which was reported by 67% of the participants; unwanted sexual attention, reported by 40% of the participants; and finally, sexual coercion, reported by 8% of the women surveyed." (Gettman and Gelfand, 2007, 763). In a word, two out of every three women you know working in the service sector has been a subject of sexual hostility.

- In 2012, a team of researchers discovered that in the Swiss general hospital in which they conducted their investigation, half of the staff has been a victim of patient aggression in the previous 12 months, and a tenth in the last week[13].
- In 2013, a study conducted among healthcare staff in Wales showed that in the preceding four weeks, more than 80% had been subject to verbal aggression, 50% had received threats, and about 63% had been assaulted[14].
- In 2017 homecare workers reported being on the receiving side of each the following in the last year: "verbal aggression (51.5%), workplace aggression (27.5%), workplace violence (24.7%), sexual harassment (27.6%), and sexual aggression (12.8%)." (Glass et al., 2017, 641)
- In 2018 a study among bus drivers showed "a wide range of violence they experienced at work, including physical (20.2%; e.g., being spat on or punched, threatened at gun point, sexual harassment, etc.), verbal (35.8%; e.g., intimidation, insults, death threats, etc.), both physical and verbal (24.8%; e.g., being spilled hot coffee on the lap with insults)" (Zhou, Boyer, and Guay, 2017, 256)
- In 2021, a study by One Fair Wage reported that almost 40% of restaurant employees consider leaving their job because of concerns of customer harassment and abuse[15].
- If anything, things seem to have escalated during the Covid-19 pandemic. The annual "Freedom from Fear" survey by the UK Union of Shop, Distributive and Allied Workers (USDAW) shows that 90% of service workers reported verbal abuse in 2020 and 2021, up from about 65% in the preceding three years; and in 2021 12% of the workers said they have been physically assaulted by customers, up from about 4% in the 2017–2019 period. Another alarming insight from the study is that almost two thirds of employees do not feel confident that reporting such incidents will make a difference (with about a third being very certain it will not!).

Another dark list. From bus drivers, restaurant employees, call center personnel, to what I would not consider imaginable – the very people who take care of our health! – are subjected to verbal or physical abuse disturbingly often. These are not rare occurrences of acts committed by dysfunctional customers. This is the everyday reality of your friends, family, and fellow employees. And, assuming that it's not one and the same customer visiting restaurants, calling contact centers and buying in shops and abusing employees, then these are behaviors the majority of us – me, you, our friends and family – conduct and/or fall victim to.

What Did We Discuss in This Chapter?

What we saw in this chapter is that there is a host of ways in which the customer is not always right.

- First, customers may be acting in a deviant manner for economic reasons: they shoplift, use pirated software, or de-shop, to name just a few.
- Second, there is a large class of customer deviant behavior that is non-economically motivated. It can be directed at the company (vandalism, for example), other customers (jumping queues, insults), or service employees.

Customer abuse (towards service personnel) is a subclass of the latter, and can be thought of as the deliberate (non-accidental) violation of social or consumption norms committed by customers while interacting with service employees and/or directed at them.

There are two basic forms of customer abuse: verbal and physical:

- Verbal abuse includes but is not limited to *customers using condescending language, customers yelling at employees, making insulting comments, shouting, cursing, speaking rudely, speaking with sarcasm, speaking with a strong voice, arguing forcefully, sexist comments (both explicit and implied), racist comments (both explicit and implied), irrelevant personal remarks (e.g. about your appearance), threats (e.g. I'll have you fired), intimidating silence, accusations of various sorts (e.g. Calling you a racist), comments about your competency, knowledge, dedication.*
- Physical abuse includes but is not limited to *standing in your personal space, starting at you (long eye contact), table pounding, throwing things, leaning over you (using height advantage), fearsome facial expressions, loud sighing, pointing, other offensive gestures, shoving of personnel, slamming a phone down, attacking employees, unwanted physical contact.*

Perhaps surprisingly, customer abuse is actually widely spread among a large variety of service job: healthcare workers, call center personnel, bus drivers, restaurant employees, shop personnel, homecare workers, and one would imagine a host of other roles that have not been studied yet – are all frequently subjected to customer abuse.

Having established these foundations, it is time to move on to an exploration of the consequences of customer abuse. In the next chapter we will have a look at how abusive customer behaviors impact employees' mental and physical health and well-being.

Notes

1 See for example HBR Guide to Emotional Intelligence, p. 35.
2 King and Balmer (2012).
3 Gursoy, Cai, and Anaya (2017).
4 Ajzen and Schmidt (2020).
5 van Jaarsveld et al. (2015).
6 See van Jaarsveld et al. (2015).
7 I'm indebted to Robert Bacal's insightful book 'If It Wasn't For The Customers I'd Really Like This Job: Stop Angry, Hostile Customers COLD While Remaining Professional, Stress Free, Efficient and Cool As A Cucumber.' For the majority of the item on this list, bar the first two of them. Bacal's book is one of the first comprehensive treatments on the topic of customer aggression, and provides an excellent overview of it.
8 The majority of this list is compiled following Robert Bacal's book (see Bacal, 2011).
9 Delcourt et al. (2017).
10 Boyd (2002).
11 Grandey, Dickter, and Sin (2004).
12 Patterson et al. (2009).
13 Hahn et al. (2012).
14 Lepping et al. (2013).
15 One Fair Wage (2021).

References

Ajzen, I., & Schmidt, P. (2020). Changing behavior using the theory of planned behavior. In M. Hagger, L. Cameron, K. Hamilton, N. Hankonen, & T. Lintunen (Eds.), The Handbook of Behavior Change (Cambridge Handbooks in Psychology, pp. 17–31). Cambridge: Cambridge University Press. doi: 10.1017/9781108677318.002

Akkawanitcha, C., Patterson, P., Buranapin, S., & Kantabutra, S. (2015). Frontline employees' cognitive appraisals and well-being in the face of customer aggression in an Eastern, collectivist culture. Journal of Services Marketing, 29(4), 268–279. https://doi.org/10.1108/JSM-12-2013-0328

Bacal, Robert. (2011). If It Wasn't For The Customers I'd Really Like This Job: Stop Angry, Hostile Customers COLD While Remaining Professional, Stress Free, Efficient and Cool As A Cucumber. Bacal & Associates. Kindle Edition.

Boyd, C. (2002). Customer violence and employee health and safety. Work, Employment and Society, 16(1), 151–169. https://doi.org/10.1177/09500170222119290

Daunt, Kate, & Harris, Lloyd. (2006). Deviant customer behavior: An exploration of frontline employee tactics. The Journal of Marketing Theory and Practice, 14, 95–111. doi: 10.2753/MTP1069-6679140201

Delcourt, Cecile, Gremler, Dwayne, De Zanet, Fabrice, & van Riel, Allard. (2017). An analysis of the interaction effect between employee technical and emotional competencies in emotionally charged service encounters. *Journal of Service Management*, 28, 85–106. doi: 10.1108/JOSM-12-2015-0407.

Fullerton, R., & Punj, G. (1997). What is consumer misbehavior? In Merrie Brucks & Deborah J. MacInnis (Eds.), *NA – Advances in Consumer Research* (Vol. 24, pp. 336–339). Provo, UT: Association for Consumer Research. https://www.acrwebsite.org/volumes/8065/volumes/v24/NA-24

Gettman, H. J., & Gelfand, M. J. (2007). When the customer shouldn't be king: Antecedents and consequences of sexual harassment by clients and customers. *Journal of Applied Psychology*, 92(3), 757–770. https://doi.org/10.1037/0021-9010.92.3.757

Glass, N., Hanson, G. C., Anger, W. K., Laharnar, N., Campbell, J. C., Weinstein, M., & Perrin, N. (2017 July). Computer-based training (CBT) intervention reduces workplace violence and harassment for homecare workers. *American Journal of Industrial Medicine*, 60(7), 635–643. doi: 10.1002/ajim.22728. Erratum in: *American Journal of Industrial Medicine* 2017 Sep;60(9), 840. PMID: 28616887.

Grandey, A. A., Dickter, D. N., & Sin, H.-P. (2004) The customer is not always right: Customer aggression and emotion regulation of service employees. *Journal of Organizational Behavior*, 25, 397–418. https://doi.org/10.1002/job.252

Gursoy, D., Cai, R.(R)., & Anaya, G. J. (2017). Developing a typology of disruptive customer behaviors: Influence of customer misbehavior on service experience of by-standing customers. *International Journal of Contemporary Hospitality Management*, 29(9), 2341–2360. https://doi.org/10.1108/IJCHM-08-2016-0454

Hahn, S., Hantikainen, V., Needham, I., Kok, G., Dassen, T., & Halfens, R. J. (2012 Dec). Patient and visitor violence in the general hospital, occurrence, staff interventions and consequences: A cross-sectional survey. *Journal of Advanced Nursing*, 68(12), 2685–2699. doi: 10.1111/j.1365-2648.2012.05967.x.

Harris, L. C., & Reynolds, K. L. (2004). Jaycustomer behavior: An exploration of types and motives in the hospitality industry. *Journal of Services Marketing*, 18(5), 339–357. https://doi.org/10.1108/08876040410548276

HBR Guide to Emotional Intelligence (HBR Guide Series) (2017). Harvard Business Review Press. https://store.hbr.org/product/hbr-guide-to-emotional-intelligence/10112

Kang, Min, & Gong, Taeshik. (2019). Dysfunctional customer behavior: Conceptualization and empirical validation. *Service Business*, 13, 625–646. doi: 10.1007/s11628-019-00398-1.

King, T., & Balmer, J. (2012). When the customer isn't right. Hbr.org, https://hbr.org/2012/02/when-the-customer-isnt-right, last accessed on January 10, 2023.

King, T., & Dennis, C. (2003). Interviews of deshopping behaviour: An analysis of theory of planned behaviour. *International Journal of Retail & Distribution Management*, 31(3), 153–163. https://doi.org/10.1108/09590550310465558

Korczynski, M., & Evans, C. (2013). Customer abuse to service workers: An analysis of its social creation within the service economy. *Work, Employment and Society*, 27(5), 768–784. https://doi.org/10.1177/0950017012468501

Lepping, P., Lanka, S. V., Turner, J., Stanaway, S. E., & Krishna, M. (2013). Percentage prevalence of patient and visitor violence against staff in high-risk

UK medical wards. *Clinical Medicine*(London), 13(6), 543–546. doi: 10.7861/clinmedicine.13-6-543. PMID: 24298096; PMCID: PMC5873651.

One Fair Wage, Why Restaurant Workers, Particularly Mothers, Are Leaving the Industry, and What Would Make Them Stay. (2021). https://onefairwage.site/wage_shortage_not_a_worker_shortage, last accessed on January 10, 2023

Patterson, Paul G., McColl-Kennedy, Janet R., Smith, Amy K., & Lu, Z. (2009). Customer rage: Triggers, tipping points, and take-outs. *California Management Review*, 52(1), 6–28. https://doi.org/10.1525/cmr.2009.52.1.6

Reynolds, K. L., & Harris, L. C. (2005). When service failure is not service failure: An exploration of the forms and motives of "illegitimate" customer complaining. *Journal of Services Marketing*, 19(5), 321–335. https://doi.org/10.1108/08876040510609934

Ringstad, R. (2005). Conflict in the workplace: Social workers as victims and perpetrators. *Social Work*, 50(4), 305–313. doi: 10.1093/sw/50.4.305. PMID: 17892240.

USDAW, Freedom from Fear. (2022). https://www.usdaw.org.uk/freedomfromfear, last accessed on January 10, 2023.

van Jaarsveld, D. D., Restubog, S. L. D., Walker, D. D., & Amarnani, R. K. (2015). Misbehaving customers: Understanding and managing customer injustice in service organizations. *Organizational Dynamics*, 44(4), 273–280. https://doi.org/10.1016/j.orgdyn.2015.09.004

Wang, M., Liao, H., Zhan, Y., & Shi, J. (2011). Daily customer mistreatment and employee sabotage against customers: Examining emotion and resource perspectives. *Academy of Management Journal*, 54, 312–334. doi: 10.5465/AMJ.2011.60263093

World Bank, Employment in services (% of total employment) (modeled ILO estimate), https://data.worldbank.org/indicator/SL.SRV.EMPL.ZS?end=2019&start=1991&view=chart, last accessed on January 10, 2023.

Zhou, B., Boyer, R., & Guay, S. (2017). Dangers on the road: A longitudinal examination of passenger-initiated violence against bus drivers. *Stress Health*, 34(2), 253–265. doi: 10.1002/smi.2779

Chapter 2

Customer Abuse Hurts Employees

The examples of customer abuse we discussed previously might seem to some like minor irritations. I mean, sarcasm hurting someone, really?!? Intimidating silence? Loud sighing? Seriously? How much of a consequence can such small acts have?

A study after study after study gives an answer to this, and it is an unequivocal: huge! As Warren Bennis notes, "These events are more than little hurts, irritations; they're more like little deaths." (Porath and Pearson, 2009, Introduction).

At first, employees who are exposed to customer abuse experience increased stress, which manifests itself in emotions like anger, nervousness, fear, anxiety, and emotional dissonance, and feelings of worthlessness, humiliation, and lower self-esteem.

Like every stressful encounter, customer abuse requires employees to manage themselves and their emotions (i.e., self-regulate) so they can, on the one hand, manage the specific situation, and on the other – cope with the consequences of it. In the case of facing aggressive customer behavior this task is significantly more difficult because employees are stuck between a hammer and a tough place. The conflicting demands of keeping the customer happy and at the same time managing the threat leads to emotional dissonance, which exacerbates the situation.

One of the biggest issues is that these efforts employees, and all of us really, spend to self-regulate, to manage our emotions and behaviors, are not free. Quite the contrary – they require the expenditure of significant amounts of time and energy, which leaves one and all emotionally and cognitively exhausted. This dynamic, in turn, unlocks a negative spiral, in which it is even more difficult for employees to self-regulate when they are depleted, and they often resort to less-than-optimal strategies for coping with customer abuse, which in turn leaves them even more exhausted. In the long run, this can easily lead to a condition that has taken epidemic proportions in our societies – burnout – with all its negative consequences.

DOI: 10.4324/9781003402565-3

Ultimately and inevitably, this results in dire consequences for the organization itself, as we will see in the next chapter. Before we get there, though, let us unpack the chain of consequences that customer abuse causes on a personal level.

Self-Regulation

How and Why Do We Act?

To be able to understand and fully grasp the impact of customer abuse on employees, we need to have a look at the bigger picture first, and try to answer the question, "Why do we do the things we do?" Why am I writing this right now? Why are you reading it? Where did we get our common interest in this topic from? How did we come to stages in our professional lives we are at? What about our personal lives? Why did we go by car to work today? Why have this third cup of coffee? The answer to these questions is important, as they represent kind of the "normal," default almost way of living our lives. To understand how events like customer abuse disrupt it, we first need to chat a little bit about the principles guiding our behaviors.

To do this, we will turn to one of the most impactful and widely applicable theories of human behavior that was put forward in the late 1990s by two psychologists, Charles Carver and Michael Scheier. Little known to the wider public, in their book "On the Self-Regulation of Behavior" (Carver and Scheier, 1998), they lay out the principles of a cybernetic theory of human behavior that is striking in both its simplicity and insightfulness.

In the cybernetic-inspired view, human behavior is seen as a "continual process of moving toward, and away from, various kinds of mental goal representations, and that this movement occurs by a process of feedback control." (Carver and Scheier, 1998, loc 513). In simpler words, any human action is driven by a goal, we act to achieve them, and we use information about the environment and the impact of our actions on it to guide our behavior. This is called a feedback loop, and it operates similarly to the one used by a thermostat as we will see further in this chapter.

The feedback loop has four elements with distinctive and tightly interrelated functions: there is goal or standard or reference value, a comparator, an output function, and an input function. Bear with me, it is simpler and more insightful than it sounds.

The goal is the value the system is controlling for; what is it that the feedback loop is after. For practical purposes, we can think of it as the reference value that the system uses to judge whether it should instigate an action. This could be anything really, from whether you and I have enough energy to go on (are we hungry), through being loved, to leaving a mark in the world.

The input function is simply a sensor. It provides information where we stand on the goal or the reference value we have. For example, in a system that monitors how hot or cold it is in a room, this would be the thermometer.

These two inputs then combine in the comparator, which does exactly what its name suggests – it compares the two and provides a signal as to whether a corrective action is needed or not.

If there is a discrepancy between the reference value and the input, then an action will be instigated (lest for the cases in which to correct for the difference it is better not to act), which is then the output function. The latter, our actions, will then have an impact on the world.

There is an important element sitting between our actions and the impact on the world – we can think of it as disturbance, although it implies that it only has a detrimental impact on our efforts. In fact, it simply refers to the fact that there are many other things going on in the world and our actions are not the only thing that impact it.

This effect of our actions on the world will once again be monitored via the input function, which, together with the reference value, will feed in the comparator, which will instigate (or not) an action and so on.

The prototypical example of a feedback loop is provided by the air conditioning system. When you set the AC to maintain the temperature in a room at a certain level, you are simply providing the device with a reference value or a goal. It would then receive input from a thermometer, and these two values will be compared to each other. If the temperature deviates from the goal, an action will be put into motion, and the air conditioning will start blowing either hot or cold air. This will then impact the air temperature in the room, but it is important to note that there might also be a disturbance in the system – for example, if you want the room temperature to be 24 degrees Celsius and it is currently 22, the air con will start blowing air with temperature pre-defined for these kinds of situations. If all of this happens on a cold winter day and you open the door to the garden, cold air will come in and despite the air conditioner's initial efforts, the room will get colder. Therefore, it is important for the feedback loop to be a loop really. At its second iteration,[1] the sensor (the thermometer) will now receive the combined input from the effect of the initial efforts and the disturbance; the latter two will sum up to provide a new input value for the system, which will then be compared against the reference value, and so on.

To give a more human example, this is also, schematically, how your body monitors for physiological needs, such as thirst and hunger. You and I have an internal system dedicated to monitoring the amount of energy available in our bodies (the reference value). If the input the brain received from the rest of the body indicates a lower value, the comparator will flag this and you and I will feel hungry or thirsty, and we will get an impetus for action. We then eat, drink, etc.; the sensors again send this new value to the comparator, and we either continue to eat or stop.

And finally, a less prosaic example. Imagine that you are cooking dinner. The reference value in this case could be simply a yes or a no – is the dinner cooked or not. In the beginning, you do not need the input value as you are at zero point – nothing is cooked yet. As you progress, you will start receiving constant input from the sensor, in this case your sight (does this lasagna look gold-brown) and smell (who among us cannot recall the pleasant smell of lasagna in the oven?). At one point the input and the reference value will match, and an action – stop the oven and get the lasagna out – will be instigated. Unless there is a disturbance of some sorts, you will do that and voila, dinner is ready.

Summing up what we discussed so far, we have goals and which goals we get active in pursuing (getting a glass of water, becoming a CEO) and how do we pursue them is a function of a feedback loop. We have a goal, we get input which says how far we are from achieving it; if there is a difference between the two, we act, and we get further input as to whether we were successful in minimizing (or maximizing, if the goal is to avoid something) the gap between the goal and the current state. This, then, is the process that lies behind all our actions and their outcomes, i.e., behind both our successes and our failures.

But this process is not free. With every action we take we invest part of our, by definition, limited resources, which naturally means that a key part of everything we do is manage them. What exactly are those resources and how do we do this management? This is what we move on to next.

It Is All a Matter of Resources

To understand how the resources we all have come into the picture, we need to add one more framework to the mix – the so-called Conservation Of Resources theory (in the remainder of the book referred to as COR) that was advanced in the late 90s by Stevan Hobfoll, a renowned psychologist specializing in the treatment of stress and anxiety.

The basic assumption of the framework is that people "actively engage their environment in order to increase the chances of obtaining positive reinforcement" (Hobfoll, 1989, 516). We strive to do well in life and to receive positive things – pleasure, enhancement of ourselves, achieving our goals, you name it.

Critical to the COR theory, as the name suggests, is the concept of resources – things that "have instrumental value to people, and second, they have symbolic value in that they help to define for people who they are…" (Hobfoll, 1989, 517). Hobfoll suggests there are four basic groups of resources: object, condition, personal characteristic, and energy.

- Objects are basically our material possessions, such as cars, houses, and hair dryers.
- Conditions are states that we value and want to achieve, such as marriage or tenure.
- Personal characteristics, which includes for instance our personality traits and skills.
- Lastly, energy refers to time, money, and knowledge.

What we do in life, then, is that we invest objects, conditions, personal characteristics, and energy to achieve desired outcomes (once again, a desired outcome could also be the avoidance of a certain state). We have goals, we receive or create input, we compare the two and decide whether an action is needed or not. Depending on the resources we have (knowledge, money, objects, personal characteristics), we chose one or another course of action, and then we monitor if what we did had the desired impact, i.e., were we successful or not. So far, so good.

According to COR, there are two key principles that guide people's behavior when it comes to resource management, and four corollaries of those. It's very much worth going through these, as we narrow the discussion down toward the consequences of customer abuse.

The first principle of COR is The Primacy of Resource Loss: "resource loss is disproportionally more salient than resource gain" (Hobfoll, 2001, 343). This is a principle popularized by the research and work of authors such as Daniel Kahneman and Amos Tversky, and its basic meaning is that losing 10 dollars feels worse than finding 10 dollars feels good. We feel worse when we lose than we feel happy when we win.

The second principle of COR claims that "people must invest resources in order to protect against resource loss, recover from losses, and gain resources" (Hobfoll, 2001, 349). This idea also refers to the fact that resources are interchangeable, albeit not completely. For example, we invest time in exercise so we can be healthy, and we invest money to attend a course to gain knowledge and experience.

What follows from these principles are four corollaries:

1 "… those with greater resources are less vulnerable to resource loss and more capable of orchestrating resource gain." (Hobfoll, 2001, 349), and vice versa. Because of their interchangeability, those with a higher net amount can summon more resources to protect themselves against loses or to benefit in the future.

2 "... those who lack resources are not only more vulnerable to resource loss, but that initial loss begets future loss" (Hobfoll, 2001, 354). If you are someone with limited resources and if resources can be used to protect or gain more of them, a loss of resources means you have less power to protect yourself against future loses, which opens a negative spiral.

3 In a similar way, the third corollary of COR states that for those with more resources, an initial gain starts a positive spiral; resource availability begets further resource gains. Corollaries 2 and 3 are also known as the Matthew effect – he who has more will be given more and he who doesn't will be taken away from. The Matthew Effect has been shown to exist in a variety of areas in life, such as number of friends and wealth. It basically suggests a pattern in which those who start from an advantageous position accumulate more advantage in time and those who start from a disadvantageous position become even more disadvantaged in time.

4 And finally, COR also claims that people who experience a lack of resources are more likely to engage in a defensive position to preserve what little they have. This is perhaps not unexpected – if you don't have much, every unit of resource becomes more valuable and there is little to invest in growth, so you focus on protecting what you have. This also opens interesting avenues for thinking about passive-aggressive behaviors, but that's a topic for another discussion.

What we know about human behavior so far, then, is that it is driven by goals, and we invest at least part of the resources we possess (objects, conditions, personal characteristics, and energy) in every action we take. Naturally, we prefer not to lose these resources and invest in protecting them. This is all a very normal process occurring thousands of times a day.

To give this a bit more flesh, let us talk about Sarah.

Sarah is 33, happily married to Mark, with him she has a 2yo kid, Jessica. She lives in a small but cozy place near a park which she loves visiting for a run or a walk with her child. Sarah works nearby at a retail store.

It's a nice spring day in May. Sarah wakes up to the sound of her kid crying. Luckily, it turns out it's nothing major – Jessica was playing with her favorite toy which she dropped and broke; Sarah pampers her and makes a mental note to get her a new one on the way back from work.

Time for the morning coffee, finally! A shower, a breakfast for Jessica, and she is off to drop the kid at the kindergarten and continue her way to work. Arriving at work, she gets her second coffee of the day and chats with her colleagues Sam and Rebecca; she loves these moments when they can just be themselves, talk about the small pains and pleasures of life, and share important moments. The day goes well and without major troubles. Like always, there is the grumpy old man murmuring something about the inflation and all, and the occasional group of teenagers making awful noise, but hey, that's the charm of life.

Sarah leaves work when she is supposed to, grabs Jessica from the kindergarten and enjoying the summer sun, goes on a whim and gets ice cream for both of them. She just loves the strawberry flavor! A nice dinner and a glass of wine with Mark once Jessica is asleep, and Sarah can focus on studying – she's attending this exciting marketing course online, looking to upskill and change jobs soon. After an hour or so, her eyes become heavy, so she calls it a day. And a good one at that! She kisses Jessica, snuggles with Mark, and goes to sleep.[2]

This is of course a made-up example, which I hope helps us see the dynamic we just outlined in action. One thing to note, for instance, is Sarah's reaction when her kid is crying. The goal Sarah has, one imagines, is for her child to be happy or at the very least – content. The crying sends a clear signal – there is something wrong. The comparator, then, instigates an action, and Sarah pampers Jessica. Jessica stops crying and the episode is quickly forgotten.

A similar situation happens at work. The group of teenagers is noisy, so Sarah notices them (input). She compares this signal with the goal of having a calm, business-as-usual day, and becomes slightly annoyed – just enough for her to remember it, but not enough to make her anxious, for example.

And finally, Sarah wants to change her job (goal). She has probably gotten some input before and realized that with her current skill level she is unlike to land the job she wants, so Sarah decides to take action and attend an online course.

Notice, first, that we are not saying that Sarah is right or wrong in wanting these things. Neither are we saying that she consciously thinks them. What we are merely observing is that Sarah does these things on purpose. Second, we are not saying that she has made the best choices from the repertoire of actions that is available to her. It might happen, for example, that the online course is no good and does not in fact help her land this position. That we cannot know, in any case in advance. I do not think Sarah knows it either. What is important for our discussion is that feedback loop between a goal and an input, a comparator, and actions is clearly visible.

Looking at this from a resource perspective, it is also fairly easy to see how many of them Sarah uses throughout the day. Money is one for sure; she spends some on that ice cream she gets with her daughter. Time is another one – for example, she spends time to attend the online course in the evening, or to chat with her husband. But Sarah is not only spending resources. That course, for example, is creating a resource for her in the shape of certification and skills, and the time spent with her friends at work creates social support, which is also a resource. Finally, perhaps less visibly, the fact that she successfully calms Jessica in the morning surely contributes to Sarah feeling she's doing a good job as a mother, thus strengthening her identity in this domain. All in all, during the day, Sarah both spent and created resources, and we can imagine she did not feel a lot of stress.

But what happens when something disrupts this flow? What happens when the input suddenly shows a value so low that we feel threatened? How do we feel when we take actions but achieve no result?

The short answer is: stress and negative effect, and a lot of them. This is where customer abuse begins to take its toll on employees.

When Things Get Messy: Customer Abuse Causes Stress and Negative Emotions

Imagine Sarah going with her day pretty much the way we just described it, but instead of having a business-as-usual afternoon, a man approaches the reception and asks to check out. You start the process, and then this happens: "I take out the invoice and everything, and then he starts telling me, 'But you're too stupid…you can't write! … Then he starts saying, 'Fuck you!'…terrible insults, such as 'Bitch'. He threw everything at me…" (Rouquet and Suquet, 2021, 2086)

How does this make you feel and what is the impact of this episode on your day? What if this happens three times during one shift? What if it happens three times per shift, three times a week?

For one thing, we would probably feel distressed[3]. This is one of the most consistent findings in the customer abuse research literature – when customers act aggressively, employees experience significantly higher level of negative stress.

Stress

Have you had trouble sleeping recently? Fatigued? Upset stomach? Headache? Thinking almost obsessively about the troubles in your life? Money? The kids? Felling as though you could cry? Nervous? Irritable?

You are not alone.

According to stress.org, three in four Americans experience physical or psychological symptoms caused by stress (Stress.org (a)); in fact, US businesses are estimated to lose up to 300 billion dollars per year as a result of workplace stress (Stress.org (b)). That is slightly more than the GDP of Finland; if the costs associated with stress in the United States alone were used to create a new country, it would have the 44th biggest economy in the world in 2019.

In the United Kingdom, according to mentalhealth.org, in 2018 three quarters of the people have at some point felt so stressed out that they have felt overwhelmed or incapable of coping. One analysis estimates that in the United Kingdom, nearly 14 million work days are lost every year due to stress.[4] That is 37,534 years, approximately, or 500 human lifespans, calculated with a life expectancy of 75 years. Expanding the geographical scope, a survey by Gallup discovered that approximately a third of people in the world experienced stress, worry, or anger in 2019[5]. In Australia alone, stress is reported to cost 14.2 billion dollars in lost productivity per year[6]. This is the equivalent of giving everyone, woman, man, children, in a country with the population of, say, Spain 300 dollars.

So, clearly, a lot of us feel stressed and this has tremendous impact on our health. But what exactly is stress?

Stress Is Caused by a Loss of Resources

We feel stressed, a number of academic research suggests, when we either lose what we have, are threatened to lose it, or we don't advance when we expend resources. This follows directly from the two frameworks we outlined above – the cybernetic theory of self-regulation and the CORs theory. Remember that in both of these, we pursue goals, be they related to achieving or avoiding different states or conditions. To achieve them, we invest resources, defined broadly as these things that help us in this.

What we don't want to happen is for our progress toward our goals to be disrupted, and for our resources to be threatened, lost, or inefficiently used[7]. If this happens, we experience stress: a "reaction to the environment in which there is (a) the threat of a net loss of resources, (b) the net loss of resources, or (c) a lack of resource gain following the investment of resources." (Hobfoll, 1989, 516). We feel stressed when we separate from someone we love or when we lose them. We feel stressed when there is inflation, leading to loss or at least a threat of a loss of. We feel stressed when there is inflation, leading to loss or at least a threat of a loss of our income and savings. This list can go much further.

The threat of these things happening is also enough to cause stress. Think about a presentation you are about to give in front of an audience. You might feel anxious, according to COR, because there is a threat of losing face. Or you might feel stress during important negotiations because of the threat of losing an important deal. None of these need to be actual threats, as long as we see them as such, and as we will see later on, reappraisals of these situations are one of the key ways of tackling stress.

Finally, and this also happens often enough in our daily lives for us to relate to it, we feel stress when we do stuff and get nothing in return. Working on projects with all our hearts but constantly stumble upon challenges beyond our control? Stress. Going to the gym three times a week and not seeing a visible progress? Stress. Spending time and effort to date someone you like without any effect? Stress.

How Does Customer Abuse Relate to Stress?

> The stress can be too much. You can really feel your heart rate racing. I mean, this is real stress – physical, felt stress – not just a bit of 'oh, I've too much work to do. ' Real, tangible stress, that's all down to some damn guy pushing his weight around – trying to be the 'big man', the 'top dog'!
>
> (Harris and Daunt, 2013, 285)

So how does customer abuse relate to stress? Why does it make employees stressed out? Well, following what we discussed so far, there are at least three ways in which customer abuse diminishes or threatens employees' resources. First, dealing with abusive customers depletes employees' resources directly by making them spend time, energy, and company money, on top of what could otherwise be a business-as-usual transaction. We will talk more about exhaustion and burnout latter in this chapter.

Second, customer abuse poses a serious threat to service employees' view of themselves, which can be considered one of the basic types of resources that we possess[8]. This includes, for instance, whether other people see ourselves the way we see us, the degree to which we believe we are capable, important, and worthy if you will as team members, our beliefs about our own competence and ability to perform our jobs well, our self-esteem. All of these are elements of how employees see themselves, and one might say – the very foundations of their self-view and sense of worthiness – get severely shaken when customers act abusively. This has been shown to be the case in a variety of countries and employment roles[9], so there's no cultural element in it or a group that is especially likely to feel this way. When customers behave aggressively, they disrupt our very core beliefs about ourselves.

Third, in addition to threatening existing resources, customer abuse also makes it harder, if not impossible, for employees to gather additional resources by investing time and energy, which according to the COR s framework is one of the key sources of stress. Employees' efforts in doing their job simply do not yield any benefits for them, or at the very least the required investment to making the customer happy becomes much higher. This is not to mention the opportunity costs involved in managing these negative emotions – after all, every drop of energy spent on dealing with the consequences of customer abuse is energy that is not spent elsewhere, for example, with spouses, kids, and friends.

The evidence that customer abuse causes acute stress to employees is overwhelming; virtually all studies that I know of consistently report a strong relationship between the two. In some ways, it might be stating the obvious or preaching to the converted, yet I feel that there is a need to be very explicit about it so that we can keep these findings at the top of our minds.

First, and perhaps most disturbingly, in a seminal article investigating the consequences of customers' dysfunctional behavior, Harris and Reynolds describe this story shared with them by a bar manager:

> He just smashed a glass on the floor and then held it to my throat. That was scary. You do worry about it. There as a thing in the film 'Trainspotting', and the one guy puts a glass into someone's face, and there is a horrific crunching noise-I can't watch that bit of the film, I have to switch it off.
>
> (Harris and Reynolds, 2003, 149)

This scene and the effects the employee describes are "typical symptoms of post-traumatic stress disorder [PTSD], alarmingly indicating that extreme dysfunctional customer behavior may lead to significant long-term psychological harm." (Harris and Reynolds, 2003, 149), the authors explain. The memory of this episode left such a deep mark on this bar manager, that even only reminders of it in presumably safe settings are enough to trigger his fight, flight of freeze response, i.e., stress.

PTSD symptoms after customer abuse were also uncovered by a study among bus drivers. The authors report that:

> Half of the participants met the diagnostic criteria for acute stress disorder within the first month following the index event. Majority of them experienced at least moderate levels of post-traumatic stress disorder (PTSD) problems over the 1-year span. About 9.3% of participants showed a delayed onset of PTSD 6 months after.
>
> (Zhou, Boyer, and Guay, 2018, 253)

But customer abuse does not have to take such extreme forms like being threatened with a piece of glass to your throat to cause increased stress. In 2007, two researchers, Hilary Gettman and Michele Gelfand (2007), published the results of a study they conducted among almost 400 women in the United States working in professional services such as law, human resources, sales, and others. The authors wanted to know what drives sexual harassment from clients, and more pertinent to our topic – what are its consequences. Their findings are crystal clear: the more sexual harassment they experienced at work, the higher the stress level of women, with all the downsides of it. In this particular study, the higher stress levels lead to employees psychologically withdrawing from clients, which could ultimately impact their ability to work with them and possibly hurt their careers.

The results from another study, this time with more than 1,200 home-workers in Oregon, United States, corroborate these insights. Experiencing any form of customer abuse, be it verbal aggression, workplace violence, or sexual harassment increased employees' stress levels significantly, and was also associated with depression (Hanson et al., 2015).

Now, technically speaking, stress is neither a disease, nor a condition. Stress is better thought of as a response – the fight-or-flight-or-freeze decision our bodies make in a split second. It gets activated when something our brain interprets as threatening or overwhelming occurs in the environment. By this definition, as you can imagine, there is a host of things that can cause stress – from the state of the economy, through how our kids are doing in school, to a dog suddenly starting to bark at you.

Stress is also not necessarily a bad thing to experience. If it is in the right proportions, it can put us in the right state to be able to tackle what is coming our way. Our hearts start beating faster, our muscles become tense, our breath quickens. In short, our bodies prepare to fight or fly from the situation. Viewed from this perspective, stress looks suspiciously like good old excitement. The problem with stress does not lie in the fact that it happens. Once the stressors are gone, our bodies return to their "normal" states and all is well.

This is not what happens in the vast majority of customer abuse though. Instead, the stress experienced in these situations causes predominantly negative emotions, and this is one of the most consistently reported findings in the customer abuse literature. It is to the negative affect experienced during or after customer aggression episodes that we turn our attention next.

Negative Emotions

When working at the front desk, a customer was rude and complained about a room that smelled bad. When I went to check on it, there did not seem to be anything wrong. Then the guest called me incompetent and told other guests they should ask someone else for help since I did not know how to do my job.

(Baker and Kim, 2021, 4486)

One time I was screamed at by a customer for not having their food ready right away. I comped his purchase, but he still continued to yell at me and spit in my face.

(Baker and Kim, 2021, 4486)

The second thing that happens when employees face similar customer aggression is that they experience negative emotions such as anger, frustration, anxiety, and fear. Indeed, a second widely reported finding in the customer abuse research literature is that when customers act aggressively, employees experience a host of negative emotions. A study after study[10] show that employees subjected to customer aggression report significantly increased negative emotions such as anger, fear, anxiety, cynicism, rage, wish to retaliate, disappointment, sadness, embarrassment, and a plethora of others.

In a study among nurses, for example, the researcher found out that the most widely shared emotions after patient abuse were "anger, fear or anxiety, post-traumatic stress disorder symptoms, guilt, self-blame, and shame. These main effects occurred across most countries and nursing domains." (Needham et al., 2005, 283). Negative emotions as a result of customer abuse were also reported among people with waitstaff experience in Canada (Fisk and Neville, 2011), public service employees in Germany (Dudenhöffer and Dormann, 2013), call center employees in the United States (Park and Kim, 2019), and employees in a grocery chain in Hong Kong (Tan et al., 2020).

There is nothing cultural or industry vertical specific about the way customer abuse leads to negative emotions among employees; quite the contrary, the relationship between the two is ubiquitous and universal. But why does this happen? To answer this, we will go back to Carver and Scheier's model of self-regulation. As a reminder, the model states that our actions are controlled by a feedback loop – we have goals and a comparison between them (where we want to be) and input (where we are) kickstarts or not actions. What is the role of emotions in this?

Suppose, for a second, that there is not one, but two feedback loops. The first one does the job we just described – we will call it, after Carver and Scheier, a monitoring loop; it monitors our progress toward our goals. The second loop is kind of a meta one and monitors the work of the first loop. More specifically, it checks how quickly the first loop is closing the discrepancy it has encountered (how quickly we are moving toward (or away) from what we want to achieve (or avoid)). What is interesting in this conceptualization is that emotions appear to be a result of the rate of achieving our goals – if we advance in an acceptable rate, we would feel good; if we advance too slowly or do not advance at all, we would feel bad.

This might sound counterintuitive at first, but you can easily find very good examples in your daily life. Think about a project of yours at work, say, developing an app. One day you learn that the developers have made a mistake which sets your delivery date two months back. Quite naturally, you would feel frustrated, but why so? Well, you already know that you have not yet finished the project, so goal accomplishment in itself is not the issue. The problem is that you are facing a significantly slower rate of progress than expected, as suggested by Carver and Scheier.

It is like running 10k with a specific tempo in mind. If at 5k you are on track, you would likely feel confident and strong, maybe relieved; if you are lagging, you might experience frustration and desperation. You have probably gone the full distance before so running 10k is not the problem. It is the rate that is causing you trouble.

So far, we saw that people have goals and our actions are controlled by a feedback loop – we start acting if there is a discrepancy between where we want to be and where we are. This self-regulation process requires resources, be they emotional ones, cognitive, financial, or social, or simply energy. Customer abuse interrupts or makes the process more difficult and causes stress because it threatens the amount of resources employees possess. In addition, aggressive customer behavior halts or slows down employees' rate of progress toward their goals, which leads to negative emotions such as frustration, anger, anxiety, and desperation.

As if this is not enough, there is one other factor that makes customer abuse even more stressful and difficult to handle. It is called emotional dissonance, and this is what we turn to next.

Emotional Dissonance

> I got really upset. We get taught that the guest is always right, but there are boundaries, and I did not think that she was allowed to make personal comments. It may have been little but it upset me ... of course I told the mangers and they did not care, that made me even more mad ... Managers are supposed to back us up ... so I started crying, it made me feel a little bit better, but the manager still did not say anything to the woman, it's personal comments are going to make you upset ... it was still wrong to say that about me and I had a right to be angry ... even if management thought I should just blow it off.
>
> (Korczynski and Evans, 2013, 780)

> all part of the job, and you will hear managers say, 'Right, if you can't put up with this, you shouldn't be doing the job...', and that's it, and that's a widely held view these days...
>
> (Bishop and Hoel, 2008, 355)

To understand what emotional dissonance is, it is worth going back to Sarah's story and the goals she has and make some fairly reasonable assumptions. For the purpose of the discussion, let us accept that Sarah is a dedicated employee who wants to do a good job and advance in her career, whether inside her current job or not. She is diligent, professional, treats customers politely and with respect.

If that's Sarah's goal, then her input, in the feedback loop model, would probably be something along the lines of assuring customer satisfaction is high at all times. This should, presumably, lead to opportunities for her to advance, salary increases, and bonuses. I know it does not always happen, but let's assume that she's working for a company that appreciates its employees.

Sarah might not call it like that, but she is engaged in what is known as emotional labor. In her seminal book, *The Managed Heart*, the sociologist Arlie Hochschild describes a fundamental shift in what is required by us as employees in our jobs as our societies transition toward a service economy model. If previously the major strain for employees was a physical one, in service economies this shifts toward what she calls "emotional labor." This type of work

> requires one to induce or suppress feeling in order to sustain the outward countenance that produces the proper state of mind in others.... This kind of labor calls for a coordination of mind and feeling, and it sometimes draws on a source of self that we honor as deep and integral to our individuality.
>
> (Hochschild, 2012, 7)

Virtually all employees are well aware of emotional labor. All the requirements that say we need to smile while working with clients, be nice, be helpful, try to help them, show empathy, care for them – all of these display rules require us to manage our emotions at work in a way never experienced in such a scale and with such intensity in our history. And while managing our bodies to execute voluntary actions, such as moving our hands or legs, is rather effortless, managing our bodies to show an emotion that is completely different from what we are actually feeling is one hell of a difficulty, as anyone who has tried to work on their emotional intelligence can testify.

So even her business-as-usual days require Sarah to do a large amount of emotional labor. She might not be feeling up to the task of smiling and proactively trying to help customers, but if she wants to be successful in her job, she needs to do it.

Now, what happens when a customer acts abusively toward her? All of a sudden, the typical flow of activities is interrupted as a major stress factor is included in the model. If before Sarah only had the goal of achieving high customer satisfaction, now she has two goals: dealing with the stress and negative emotions from the customer's aggression WHILE trying to increase customer satisfaction as much as possible. She may want to escape or to fight the customer, but she cannot because the second goal interferes with this. She may want to make the customer happy but she cannot because she's under attack. This is exactly what emotional dissonance looks like – experiencing two competing, unreconcilable feelings at the same time, or in the context of customer service, the clash between what you feel and what you need to show to conform to what you are expected to show[11].

In a lot of ways, emotional dissonance always lurks beneath the surface of customer service, but becomes much more clearly visible and acute when a customer acts aggressively. For example, in a study[12] of 4,000 employees working in areas as diverse as travel agency employees, flight attendants, sales clerks in shoe stores, educators, bank assistants, call center employees, police officers, and hospital staff, researchers found out that first, experiencing verbal aggression and other customer-related stressors leads to negative emotions, and second, that there was a significant relationship between customer aggression and emotional dissonance, i.e., the more they perceived customers to be aggressive toward them, the more they felt torn by their feelings. A plethora of other studies[13] confirm these findings.

So far, we saw that customer abuse is a major stress factor in employees' lives, sparks negative emotions, and creates an emotional dissonance. Experiencing these states is bad enough on its own. The problem is their impact does not stop here. To manage both the customer in front of them and the impact of their abusive behavior on themselves, employees need to invest additional resources, which are by definition limited. Ultimately, customer abuse leads to emotional and cognitive exhaustion, which is one of the symptoms of the modern-day pandemic called burnout.

Emotion Regulation

Put in a situation in which they need to handle aggressive behavior directed at them, which as we saw is further exacerbated by the job demands to keep or make the customer satisfied, employees need to further engage in a resource-extolling process of dealing with the situation. Unless they try to manage the emotions looming large, employees face the threat of being fully encapsulated by them, thus risking to engage in behaviors like striking back at the customer, and continuous feelings of fear, anxiety, rejection, shame, and even depression. In short, lest they are put under control, emotions can quickly lead us to escalate the situations we are in further, and all the more so the stronger the emotions are.

To tackle situations in which we need to control our feelings, all of us engage in emotion regulation, which is "the processes by which individuals influence which emotions they have, when they have them, and how they experience and express these emotions." (Gross, 1998, 275). The interesting question, though, is not whether people try to manage their emotions, but rather how do they do it. Research has identified five steps people engage in while trying to manage their emotions, and it's worth going through these to paint a more complete picture of what employees experience when customers act aggressively. In short, the five steps are as follows:

- Choosing to select (or avoid) situations which are less (more) emotionally charged
- Changing the situation
- Switching our attention elsewhere
- Changing our thoughts about it
- And controlling our responses resulting from the emotion

Situation selection is pretty self-explanatory. Simply put, we try to avoid places and people that create negative emotions. If you frequently pass through an area, which is rather shady and makes you feel edgy, you'll probably chose to avoid it. Similarly, if some people make you feel bad by telling offensive jokes or being rude, you are likely to try to avoid them. This option, unfortunately, is not available to service employees, which as we saw often creates emotional dissonance. Now, of course, an employee can simply walk out of the interaction, but in most cases that would also mean they are not doing their job, which is likely to have undesired consequences.

Next, we can try to change or modify the situation to the best of our abilities. At this stage, we focus on the problem at hand and try to remove it so we do not feel the associated emotion. In the case of customer abuse, this is easy enough to see. Employees may try to calm down the customer, to solve the issue they are facing so as to reduce their emotions, or, if need be, to employ additional resources, such as calling in a supervisor or other support, for example. All of the elements included in this last sentence either are or require resources: the supervisor, from the perspective of this situation, is a resource; so is the company policy for dealing with abusive customers; the time and energy spent on calming the customer are also resources, and so is, for example, the compensation an aggressive customer may receive. Successful or not, changing the situation at hand is costly.

Switching our attention to something else is another strategy we can employ to manage our emotions. Broadly speaking, there are three things we can do: distract ourselves, concentrate, and ruminate or worry.

- When we distract ourselves, we are not coping with the situation at hand but retreat from it instead, and that is not necessarily a bad thing!. We may engage, for example, in recollections of happier times, or we may simply avert our gaze to look elsewhere. This strategy can only have a limited positive impact when dealing with abusive customers. Distracting ourselves by doing something else, for example, is not much of an option when the customer is standing in front of us, although there are some tricks employees can apply. And reminding ourselves of our last holiday might work, but then again, how feasible is to do this and keep talking to someone in front of you?

- Concentration is somewhat similar to distraction and refers to engaging our thoughts in something different than the stressor, i.e., the abusive customer. This is a rather long-term strategy, as it involves having a hobby, from example. Gardening or doing photography may help indeed but not in the case in which we face an aggressive customer.
- Rumination and worry, in their extremes, are both considered maladaptive emotion regulation strategies. When we ruminate, we go back again and again and again on the causes and consequences of distress, that is, repeatedly thinking about customer abuse, for example. Worry is similar to rumination, but is directed toward the future – we think about what is likely to happen and how we will react, and what will the consequences be, and so on. The vast majority of research suggests that we need to avoid both of these strategies, but the problem is they come to us quite naturally. We'll return to these points when we talk about the strategies of handling customer abuse.

Further down the process of emotion regulation, we may try to change our thoughts about them. The problem is not whether we should think about emotions or not. The issue is rather what we think about them or how we think about them. Included in this group are both adaptive (do-more-of-these type of strategies) and maladaptive (do-not-go-near-them) strategies, such as:

- Denial: refusing to accept that what's happening is happening
- Downward social comparison: choosing to compare ourselves to people who are doing worse so we can appear and feel better
- Cognitive reframing, which "may be a particularly potent form of cognitive change, such as when one experiences failure with respect to one goal but reframes this as a success—or at least a nonevent—with respect to another goal ...." (Gross, 1998, 284). Examples of this include, positive reappraisal – coming up and focusing on a positive aspect of the experience and decentering – shifting the focus from the specific episode to the bigger picture
- Self-distancing, or the practice of adopting a third-person perspective toward the situation, has been shown to be super effective in dealing with emotions
- Humor is a brilliant cognitive change strategy

As a final resort against the impact of negative emotions, we have the option to try and directly affect our responses – that's what is colloquially known as managing one's emotions, but as we saw we in fact use a lot more strategies than this. A host of things that we do fall under this umbrella. Drug use, smoking cigarettes, indulging in food consumption (including overeating), but also exercise, sleep, and relaxation are all actions we take to alter our responses to stressors. A major sub-strategy here includes inhibiting the expression of our negative emotions or even faking their opposites. Somewhat ironically, this is not a brilliant strategy to employ, as research shows that the expression of our negative emotions in fact makes the feeling slightly stronger[14].

This is all very good, but there are a number of issues that employees face when having to regulate their emotions, especially when dealing with abusive customers.

- First, a major challenge is that they need to select the right strategies, i.e., management of our emotions (or emotion regulation) requires knowledge and skills. Not all of what was described about is a good approach to handling our emotions, and let's face it – we are all often times not taking the best decisions in this regard.
- Second, even if successful, this process is not cost-free, especially when done repeatedly, and often leads to emotional and cognitive exhaustion.
- Third, because of lack of skills or knowledge or when they are exhausted, employees may resort to, mildly put, less than ideal strategies, such as striking back or engaging in surface-acting.

The first issue is super critical and we will talk about it in more detail in a later chapter when we discuss how employees can learn to cope better with customer abuse, and the third one is the topic of the next chapter. Here, we will focus on emotional and cognitive exhaustion and the personal consequences it leads to.

Customer Abuse Leads to Exhaustion and Burnout

I felt like I was no longer a person but rather an object of the customer's imagination. I wanted someone else to take these customers so I didn't have to look him in the eyes and smile like everything he was saying was okay.

(Baker and Kim, 2021, 4487)

Have you become cynical or critical at work? Do you drag yourself to work and have trouble getting started? Have you become irritable or impatient with co-workers, customers, or clients? Do you lack the energy to be consistently productive? Do you find it hard to concentrate? Do you lack satisfaction from your achievements? Do you feel disillusioned about your job? Are you using food, drugs, or alcohol to feel better or to simply not feel? Have your sleep habits changed? Are you troubled by unexplained headaches, stomach or bowel problems, or other physical complaints? These are all questions the Mayo Clinic suggests to ask ourselves to spot burnout.

If you are experiencing the above, you might very well be suffering from a burnout, and as with stress, you are far from being alone in this – in fact, burnout is taking pandemic proportions.

Some quick stats:

- According to a Gallup survey among more than 12,000 full-time workers, three out of four experience burnout at least sometimes[15].
- Similarly, research by Deloitte reports that 77% of workers have been affected by burnout[16].
- A study among 1,500 US workers by Indeed.com reported that one in every two experienced burnout in 2021[17].
- In a meta-analysis of studies among physicians, 67% reported experiencing overall burnout, 72% – emotional exhaustion, 68% depersonalization, and 63% low personal accomplishment[18].

But what exactly is burnout? The World Health Organization (WHO) describes burnout as

resulting from chronic workplace stress that has not been successfully managed. It is characterised by three dimensions:

- feelings of energy depletion or exhaustion;
- increased mental distance from one's job, or feelings of negativism or cynicism related to one's job; and
- a sense of ineffectiveness and lack of accomplishment.

(World Health Organization, 2022)

What this means is that when we experience burnout, we lose practically all interest in our work and in being successful in it. We are so drained, cognitively and emotionally, that our brains refuse to function any more, especially in a work environment. We close ourselves and detach from work; it's almost like we are placing a barrier between us and the job so we can protect our self. Whatever we achieve gives us no pleasure, almost like in the stories in which someone is enchanted and loses all sense of taste – they eat but everything tastes like ash. In the vivid words of Wenche Fredriksen, Human Capital & Diversity Lead at Accenture for more than a decade,

> The burn out phase was a night mare which lasted for over a year. For many months, I could not handle sound, light or movement. I could not focus or handle information. I could not eat, sleep or cry. I was totally exhausted. Making cereal felt like making a 5-course dinner. I was going to pick up my kids, but had to return without going out of the car, because I could not move my legs. Taking a shower was overwhelming. I could not make appointments, because I could not handle any kinds of expectations. At the lowest point, I was convinced that I would never work again.
>
> (Fredriksen, 2019)

This is echoed by Michael Stephens, ex-Virgin Atlantic Creative Director of Marketing:

> It manifested in subtle ways to begin with. I had insomnia, and I self-prescribed medication for that, which meant I could sleep, but eventually I realized I couldn't sleep without the pills. Then other symptoms crept in and became more prominent – IBS and eczema. Gradually my neck started to hurt. One day I woke up and couldn't move it. I had to go to the GP. And she immediately told me that I needed to take time off. I told her, "Ok. I just need to go in today and make four people redundant."
>
> (Orlebarbrown.com)

All these effects and many more are by now well-recognized in psychological research. The plethora of studies unequivocally give credence to officially including burnout as a disease, which happened in the 11th revision of the International Classification of Diseases by WHO. A review of 36 studies conducted in 2017 produced an unfortunately long list of major physical, psychological, and occupational longer-term consequences of burnout. To give you just a flavor, these include among others (based on Salvagioni et al., 2017):

- Obesity
- Type 2 Diabetes
- Cholesterol
- Coronary heart disease
- Hospitalization for cardiovascular disease or musculoskeletal disorder
- More pain (overall, but also neck–shoulder pain, backpain, headache)
- Mortality below 45 years
- Insomnia

- Depressive symptoms
- Hospitalization for mental disorders
- Absenteeism

Clearly, burnout has severe implications for both our personal and work lives. And while there is evidence that burnout can be caused by a wide variety of things, such as workload, perceived lack of control, lack of reward, and lack of supportive community[19], as a specific burnout trigger few things are as "effective" in leading to burnout as customer abuse.

In fact, the relationship between customer aggression and burnout has been well documented in a wide variety of service contexts, such as among drivers, personnel caring for residents living in homes for the elderly, hospital staff, call center employees, restaurant employees, bank tellers, and hotel employees[20]. For example, in a survey among people who work or have recently worked in the tourism or the hospitality industry, Melissa Baker and Kawon Kim (2021) found strong evidence that customer mistreatment leads to cynicism and depersonalization. In fact, experiencing customer mistreatment makes it almost 20% more likely for an employee to become cynical and makes them 30% more likely to treat customers in a depersonalized way.

There is also plenty of evidence that customer abuse leads to emotional exhaustion. For example, in a series of studies among retail, restaurant, and call center employees, van Jaarsveld and her collaborators discovered that "customer interpersonal injustice relates positively to employees' negative emotions, [and] employee negative emotions are positively associated with emotional exhaustion" (van Jaarsveld et al., 2021, 301). In the case of restaurant employees, for instance, an increase of 1% pt on an imaginary customer injustice scale, leads to 0.4 decrease in emotional energy, that is, customer injustice can easily account for half of the energy employees spent per day.

Similarly, a study among customer-facing employees in hotels in Nigeria (Alola et al., 2019) discovered that the more customer incivility employees experienced, the more emotionally drained they felt. And as a final example, a study among 215 call center employees in the United States showed strong support for the fact that "higher levels of problematic customer behaviors, abusive and unreasonably demanding behaviors ... lead to higher emotional exhaustion in customer service employees." (Poddar and Madupalli, 2012, 554).

A clear picture emerges, then. Customer abuse, be it via stress, negative emotions, and the need to regulate one's emotions, leads to one of the most widely spread diseases in the modern world – burnout – with all of its dimensions: exhaustion, depersonalization, and cynicism, and a sense of inaccomplishment.

And once burnout sets in, it unlocks a myriad of consequences for employees going beyond the work environment, such as impaired memory, overeating, poor sleep quality, and more family conflicts. As if feeling stressed and exhausted isn't enough, customer abuse has acute consequences for employees spilling over to their personal lives. These have been well-documented in the literature on the topic. For example, Liu et al. (2017) conducted a study among 110 employees of a Chinese telco company; they reasoned that customer mistreatment would put employees in a negative mood (which was indeed the case in both this and other surveys), and wanted to know if it leads to "maladaptive behaviors," i.e., we think that things we all do sometimes help us, but in reality, they do not. In this specific case, the researchers were interested in whether customer abuse makes employees overeat in the evening. Indeed, it did. The authors explain: "...when employees experienced more customer mistreatment during the whole workday, they were likely to experience more negative mood in the afternoon before they left work and subsequently engaged in more overeating behaviors in the evening." (Liu et al., 2017, 1247).

Customer abuse also affects how well employees sleep at night, thus further exacerbating the effect of emotional exhaustion by not allowing them to recover from the stress. A group of researchers analyzed the part of the Korean Working Conditions Survey concerning workplace victimization, i.e., abuse from coworkers, supervisors, and customers, for four years – 2010, 2011, 2014, and 2017. As the authors conclude, "Victimization was found to be negatively correlated with sleep quality in each year." (Chu, Lee, and Kim, 2021, 7) Similar results were reported among homecare workers; on a 0–100 scale, those who experienced verbal aggression scored 14.4 points higher on sleep problems compared to those who did not (Hanson et al., 2015).

The evidence for the next negative consequence of customer abuse we'll discuss comes from China. Zhang et al. (2022) asked 57 employees in a call center providing tax service support to keep a diary for five days, noting things like customer mistreatment, self-control capacity, negative emotions, and level of relaxation. What they discovered is that customer abuse impairs self-control capacity and subsequently leads to impulsive buying and mobile phone overuse – employees buy more things we probably don't need and we stay more on our phones, instead of spending time with our families and friends when customers mistreat them.

Talking about family life, customer abuse has been shown to have a direct detrimental effect on it as well. Three researchers – Zhu, Lyu, and Ye (2021) – reasoned that by virtue of being a significant stressor, customer abuse would make it more difficult for employees to fulfill expectations at home, and negative emotions experienced at work will also spillover to the home domain, thus also potentially leading to uncivil behaviors at home. That was indeed the case, and employees who felt mistreated at work tended to report higher levels of work-to-family conflicts, which ultimately lead to behaviors such as hostility and apathy toward family members.

As you can see, there is a whole plethora of unfortunate consequences that unfold from customers' aggressive behaviors. Stress, negative emotions, emotional exhaustion, burnout, and all the negative effects they bring to our lives – this is what happens to service employees when they face customer abuse.

What Did We Discuss in This Chapter?

This chapter has been quite a bleak journey. We had a look at customer abuse from the perspective of employees and saw the tremendous stress it causes them; following the COR s theory, we also conceptualized stress as a loss or a threat of loss of resources, or unfairly small gains for our investment and discussed why customer abuse is such a strong stressor. Consequently, customers' aggressive behavior is linked to strong negative emotions such as anger, anxiety, frustration, and desire to retaliate.

As with any stress reaction, when they experience customer abuse employees need to put in time and energy to manage themselves in order to cope with the specific situation and to somehow alleviate these negative feelings. Their task is made more difficult in order of magnitudes by the fact that they are stuck between the "customer is always right" philosophy and the abusive customer without many options for action. This is causing them emotional dissonance, which is an unstable, unsustainable state.

All of this is extremely taxing, both emotionally and mentally, and ultimately leads to burnout – feelings of emotional exhaustion, cynicism, sense of lack of accomplishment – and impaired cognitive functions, such as memory. In turn, this dynamic makes it even more difficult for employees to self-regulate, unlocking a negative spiral that continues on unless we make efforts to prevent it.

Logically, given that all businesses, but especially service ones, are people businesses, these consequences do not stop with the employees. Companies suffer significant costs because of customer abuse, and it is to these that we turn now.

Notes

1 I am calling this an 'iteration' for simplicity – in the air con example this would be a close to non-stopping process.
2 Excuse the unengaging prose.
3 Distress is the term for stress which has negative impact on us; there is also eustress, which has a positive one. Because the broader term 'stress' has become more popular publicly, I will use it in the remainder of the book as a synonym of 'distress'.

4 See Recoverytree.com
5 See Ray (2019).
6 See Medibank.com.au
7 Note that a threat or a loss of resources doesn't necessarily need to be objectively true in reality – it is enough for us to perceive such loses or non-gains to feel stressed. Each of these propositions are easy enough to see in practice.
8 See Hobfoll (1989).
9 See for example Amarnani et al. (2022), Pierce and Gardner (2004), Chen et al. (2021), and Akkawanitcha et al. (2015).
10 See for example Fisk and Neville (2011); Bani-Melhem (2020); Dudenhöffer and Dormann (2013); Porath and Erez (2009); Park and Kim (2019); Volmer et al. (2012).
11 See for example Abraham (1999).
12 See Dudenhöffer and Christian Dormann (2015).
13 See Karatepe, Yorganci, and Haktanir (2009); Yeh (2015); Madupalli and Poddar (2014); Goussinsky (2011).
14 See Gross (1998, 285).
15 Wigert (2020).
16 See Deloitte.
17 Threlkeld (2021).
18 Rotenstein et al. (2018).
19 See Saunders (2019).
20 See Yagil, 2021.

References

Abraham, R. (1999). The impact of emotional dissonance on organizational commitment and intention to turnover. *Journal of Psychology, 133*(4), 441–455. doi: 10.1080/00223989909599754

Akkawanitcha, C., Patterson, P., Buranapin, S., & Kantabutra, S. (2015). Frontline employees' cognitive appraisals and well-being in the face of customer aggression in an Eastern, collectivist culture. *Journal of Services Marketing, 29*(4), 268–279. https://doi.org/10.1108/JSM-12-2013-0328

Alola, U., Olugbade, O., Avci, T., & Öztüren, A. (2019). Customer incivility and employees' outcomes in the hotel: Testing the mediating role of emotional exhaustion. *Tourism Management Perspectives, 29*, 9–17. doi: 10.1016/j.tmp.2018.10.004.

Amarnani, R. K., Restubog, S. L. D., Shao, R., Cheng, D. C., & Bordia, P. (2022). A self-verification perspective on customer mistreatment and customer-directed organizational citizenship behaviors. *Journal of Organizational Behavior, 43*(5), 912–931. https://doi.org/10.1002/job.2610

Baker, M. A., & Kim, K. (2021). Becoming cynical and depersonalized: How incivility, co-worker support and service rules affect employee job performance. *International Journal of Contemporary Hospitality Management, 33*(12), 4483–4504. https://doi.org/10.1108/IJCHM-01-2021-0105

Bani-Melhem, S. (2020). What mitigate and exacerbate the influences of customer incivility on frontline employee extra-role behaviour? *Journal of Hospitality and Tourism Management, 44*, 38–49. https://doi.org/10.1016/j.jhtm.2020.05.005

Bishop, V., & Hoel, H. (2008). The customer is always right? Exploring the concept of customer bullying in the British Employment Service. *Journal of Consumer Culture*, 8(3), 341–367. https://doi.org/10.1177/1469540508095303

Carver, C., & Scheier, M. (1998). *On the Self-Regulation of Behavior*. Cambridge: Cambridge University Press. Kindle edition.

Chen, J., Kang, H., Wang, Y., & Zhou, M. (2021). Thwarted psychological needs: The negative impact of customer mistreatment on service employees and the moderating role of empowerment HRM practices. *Personnel Review*, 50(7/8), 1566–1581. https://doi.org/10.1108/PR-06-2020-0489

Chu, Y., Lee, K., & Kim, E. I. (2021). Why victimized employees become less engaged at work: An integrated model for testing the mediating role of sleep quality. *International Journal of Environmental Research and Public Health*, 18(16), 8468. doi: 10.3390/ijerph18168468. PMID: 34444217; PMCID: PMC8393796.

Deloitte, Workplace Burnout Survey. Burnout without borders. https://www2.deloitte.com/us/en/pages/about-deloitte/articles/burnout-survey.html, last accessed on January 11, 2023.

Dudenhöffer, S., & Dormann, C. (2013). Customer-related social stressors and service providers' affective reactions. *Journal of Organizational Behavior*, 34, 520–539. https://doi.org/10.1002/job.1826

Fisk, G. M., & Neville, L. B. (2011). Effects of customer entitlement on service workers' physical and psychological well-being: A study of waitstaff employees. *Journal of Occupational Health Psychology*, 16(4), 391–405. doi: 10.1037/a0023802.

Gallup, Employee burnout: Causes and cures. https://www.gallup.com/workplace/282659/employee-burnout-perspective-paper.aspx, last accessed on January 11, 2023.

Fredriksen, W. (2019). Rising from the ashes – A story about burnout and the way back to life. https://www.linkedin.com/pulse/rising-from-ashes-story-burnout-way-back-life-wenche-fredriksen/, last accessed on January 11, 2023.

Gettman, H. J., & Gelfand, M. J. (2007). When the customer shouldn't be king: Antecedents and consequences of sexual harassment by clients and customers. *Journal of Applied Psychology*, 92(3), 757–770. https://doi.org/10.1037/0021-9010.92.3.757

Goussinsky, R. (2011). Customer aggression, emotional dissonance and employees' well-being. *International Journal of Quality and Service Sciences*, 3(3), 248–266. https://doi.org/10.1108/17566691111182825

Gross, J. J. (1998). The emerging field of emotion regulation: An integrative review. *Review of General Psychology*, 2(3), 271–299. https://doi.org/10.1037/1089-2680.2.3.271

Hanson, G. C., Perrin, N. A., Moss, H., et al. (2015). Workplace violence against homecare workers and its relationship with workers health outcomes: A cross-sectional study. *BMC Public Health*, 15, 11. https://doi.org/10.1186/s12889-014-1340-7

Harris, L. C., & Daunt, K. (2013). Managing customer misbehavior: Challenges and strategies. *Journal of Services Marketing*, 27(4), 281–293. https://doi.org/10.1108/08876041311330762

Harris, L. C., & Reynolds, K. L. (2003). The consequences of dysfunctional customer Behavior. *Journal of Service Research*, 6(2), 144–161. https://doi.org/10.1177/1094670503257044

Hobfoll, S. E. (1989). Conservation of resources. A new attempt at conceptualizing stress. *American Psychologist*, 44(3), 513–524. doi: 10.1037//0003-066x.44.3.513.

Hobfoll, S. E. (2001). The influence of culture, community, and the nested-self in the stress process: Advancing conservation of resources theory. *Applied Psychology*, 50, 337–421. https://doi.org/10.1111/1464-0597.00062

Hochschild, A. R. (2012). *The Managed Heart* (3rd ed.). California: University of California Press.

Karatepe, O. M., Yorganci, I., & Haktanir, M. (2009). Outcomes of customer verbal aggression among hotel employees. *International Journal of Contemporary Hospitality Management*, 21(6), 713–733. https://doi.org/10.1108/09596110910975972

Korczynski, M., & Evans, C. (2013). Customer abuse to service workers: An analysis of its social creation within the service economy. *Work, Employment and Society*, 27(5), 768–784. https://doi.org/10.1177/0950017012468501

Madupalli, R., & Poddar, A. (2014). Problematic customers and customer service employee retaliation. *Journal of Services Marketing*, 28(3), 244–255. https://doi.org/10.1108/JSM-02-2013-0040

Liu, Y., Song, Y., Koopmann, J., Wang, M., Chang, C. D., & Shi, J. (2017). Eating your feelings? Testing a model of employees' work-related stressors, sleep quality, and unhealthy eating. *Journal of Applied Psychology*, 102(8), 1237–1258. doi: 10.1037/apl0000209.

Mayo Clinic, Job burnout: How to spot it and take action. https://www.mayoclinic.org/healthy-lifestyle/adult-health/in-depth/burnout/art-20046642, last accessed on January 11, 2023.

Medibank, Workplace stress costing the Australian economy. (2008). https://www.medibank.com.au/livebetter/newsroom/post/workplace-stress-costing-the-australian-economy, last accessed on January 14, 2023.

Mentalhealth.org.uk. Results of the Mental Health Foundation's 2018 study. (2018). https://www.mentalhealth.org.uk/explore-mental-health/mental-health-statistics/stress-statistics, last accessed on January 14, 2023.

Needham, I., Abderhalden, C., Halfens, R. J., Fischer, J. E., & Dassen, T. (2005). Non-somatic effects of patient aggression on nurses: A systematic review. *Journal of Advanced Nursing*, 49(3), 283–296. doi: 10.1111/j.1365-2648.2004.03286.x.

Orlebarbrown.com, Burnout and me: One man's story. https://www.orlebarbrown.com/blog/michael-stephens-burnout-and-me-blog.html, last accessed on January 11, 2023.

Park, J., & Kim, H. (2020). Customer mistreatment and service performance: A self-consistency perspective. *International Journal of Hospitality Management*, 86, 102367

Park, Y., & Kim, S. (2019). Customer mistreatment harms nightly sleep and next-morning recovery: Job control and recovery self-efficacy as cross-level moderators. *Journal of Occupational Health Psychology*, 24(2), 256–269. doi: 10.1037/ocp0000128.

Pierce, J. L., & Gardner, D. G. (2004). Self-esteem within the work and organizational context: A review of the organization-based self-esteem literature. *Journal of Management*, 30(5), 591–622. https://doi.org/10.1016/j.jm.2003.10.001

Poddar, A., & Madupalli, R. (2012). Problematic customers and turnover intentions of customer service employees. *Journal of Services Marketing*, 26(7), 551–559. https://doi.org/10.1108/08876041211266512

Porath, C. L., & Erez, A. (2009). Overlooked but not untouched: How rudeness reduces onlookers' performance on routine and creative tasks. *Organizational Behavior and Human Decision Processes*, 109(1), 29–44. https://doi.org/10.1016/j.obhdp.2009.01.003

Porath, C. L., & Pearson, C. M. (2009). The cost of bad behavior: How incivility is damaging your business and what to do about it. Portfolio Hardcover.

Ray, J. (2019). Americans' Stress, Worry and Anger Intensified in 2018. https://news.gallup.com/poll/249098/americans-stress-worry-anger-intensified-2018.aspx, last accessed on January 14, 2023.

Recoverytree.com, Stress Facts and Statistics. (2022) https://www.therecoveryvillage.com/mental-health/stress/stress-statistics/, last accessed on January 10, 2023.

Rotenstein, L. S., Torre, M., Ramos, M. A., Rosales, R. C., Guille, C., Sen, S., Mata, D. A. (2018). Prevalence of burnout among physicians: A systematic review. *JAMA*, 320(11), 1131–1150. doi: 10.1001/jama.2018.12777.

Rouquet, A., & Suquet, J.-B. (2021). Knocking sovereign customers off their pedestals? When contact staff educate, amateurize, and penalize deviant customers. *Human Relations*, 74(12), 2075–2101. https://doi.org/10.1177/0018726720950443

Salvagioni, D. A. J., Melanda, F. N., Mesas, A. E., González, A. D., Gabani, F. L., & Andrade, S. M. (2017). Physical, psychological and occupational consequences of job burnout: A systematic review of prospective studies. *PLoS One*, 12(10), e0185781. doi: 10.1371/journal.pone.0185781.

Saunders, E. (2019). 6 Causes of Burnout, and How to Avoid Them. https://hbr.org/2019/07/6-causes-of-burnout-and-how-to-avoid-them, last accessed on January 11, 2023.

Singlecare.com. (2023). Stress statistics 2022: How common is stress and who's most affected? https://www.singlecare.com/blog/news/stress-statistics/, last accessed on January 10, 2023.

Stress.org (a) https://www.stress.org/daily-life, last accessed on January 10, 2023.

Stress.org (b) https://www.stress.org/42-worrying-workplace-stress-statistics, last accessed on January 10, 2023.

Tan, A. J. M., Loi, R., Lam, L. W., & Chow, C. C. (2020). Buffering negative impacts of jaycustomer behavior on service employees. *Journal of Services Marketing*, 34(5), 635–650. https://doi.org/10.1108/JSM-03-2019-0112

Threlkeld, K. (2021). Employee burnout report: COVID-19's impact and 3 strategies to curb it. https://www.indeed.com/lead/preventing-employee-burnout-report, last accessed on January 11, 2023.

van Jaarsveld, D. D., Walker, D. D., Restubog, S. L. D., Skarlicki, D., Chen, Y., & Frické, P. H. (2021). Unpacking the relationship between customer (in)justice and employee turnover outcomes: Can fair supervisor treatment reduce employees' emotional turmoil? *Journal of Service Research*, 24(2), 301–319. https://doi.org/10.1177/1094670519883949

Volmer, J., Binnewies, C., Sonnentag, S., & Niessen, C. (2012). Do social conflicts with customers at work encroach upon our private lives? A diary study. *Journal of Occupational Health Psychology*, 17(3), 304–315. https://doi.org/10.1037/a0028454

Wigert, B. (2020). Employee burnout: The biggest myth. https://www.gallup.com/workplace/288539/employee-burnout-biggest-myth.aspx, last accessed on January 14, 2023.

World Health Organization. (2022). ICD-11 for mortality and morbidity statistics, QD85 Burnout. https://icd.who.int/browse11/l-m/en#/http://id.who.int/icd/entity/129180281, last accessed on January 11, 2023.

Yagil, D. (2021). Abuse from organizational outsiders: Customer aggression and incivility. In P. DCruz, E. Noronha, L. Keashly, & S. Tye-Williams (Eds.) *Special Topics and Particular Occupations, Professions and Sectors. Handbooks of Workplace Bullying, Emotional Abuse and Harassment*, Vol. 4. Singapore: Springer. https://doi.org/10.1007/978-981-10-5308-5_3

Yeh, C.-W. (2015) Linking customer verbal aggression and service sabotage. *Journal of Service Theory and Practice*, 25(6), 877–896. https://doi.org/10.1108/JSTP-07-2014-0146

Zhang, H., Zhou, Z. E., Liu, Y., Shi, Y., & Xiao, J. (2022) Too depleted to control yourself? Effect of customer mistreatment on after-work maladaptive behaviours through self-control capacity impairment. *Applied Psychology*, 71, 27–48. https://doi.org/10.1111/apps.12310

Zhou, B., Boyer, R., & Guay, S. (2018) Dangers on the road: A longitudinal examination of passenger-initiated violence against bus drivers. *Stress Health*, 34(2), 253–265. doi: 10.1002/smi.2779.

Zhu, H., Lyu, Y., & Ye, Y. (2021). The impact of customer incivility on employees' family undermining: A conservation of resources perspective. *Asia Pacific Journal of Management*, 38, 1061–1083. https://doi.org/10.1007/s10490-019-09688-8

Chapter 3

Customer Abuse Hurts Companies

What we discussed so far might seem distant to us as business leaders. It is all too easy to disregard the negative consequences of customer abuse on employees as employees' problems or part of the job. Maybe we think that if employees let aggressive customers affect them so much it is because they are all too sensitive. We would be wrong to think that, and I am not saying this from a moral high ground perspective.

Even if we do not empathize with employees, we need to realize that customer abuse it not only an employees' problem. It is not (only) caused by them, it is not only them who experience its consequences, and it is not something they can solve on their own.

What we will have a look at this chapter is how ultimately, when customers act abusively, companies stand to lose a lot as well, be it directly or through the negative consequences on employees. Higher costs to manage abusive customers, lower employee job satisfaction, higher turnover, lower performance, poorer customer experience, and abuse spreading like a flu are all, as we will see, part of the mix. On to a review of how customer abuse hurts companies.

What Do Employers Expect from Service Workers?

Now girls, I want you to go out there and really smile. Your smile is your biggest asset. I want you to go out there and use it. Smile. Really smile. Really lay it on?

(Hochschild, 2012, 4)

Before we jump into the many ways abusive customers have a detrimental impact on our business via the harm they do to employees, I think it makes good sense to have a look at what gets broken in the first place – what do we want from our staff? This will help us see which elements of the ideal performance are disrupted when customers act aggressively.

DOI: 10.4324/9781003402565-4

Let's go back for a second to Sarah, the hotel receptionist we encountered in the previous chapter. What is she expected to do at work? What skills does she need to have to her job well? The easiest way to answer these questions is to go through a hotel receptionist's job description. Here is one description of Sarah is doing:

As a Hotel Receptionist, you will deal with enquiries and room reservations made on the telephone, online or by email.

Receptionists often use a computerised system to check guests in and out. You issue keys or key cards to guests. You then either provide guests with clear directions to their room, or a Porter will show them to their accommodation.

It is important that you make a good first impression – a warm welcome and pleasant atmosphere in the reception area can help to get guests' stay off to the best start.

You keep accurate records of which guests have arrived at, or left, the hotel. You make sure that any necessary information goes to the housekeeping, restaurant, maintenance, and management departments.

You provide guests with information about local attractions and places of interest. You might provide additional services for the convenience of guests, such as ordering newspapers or taxis, storing valuables and taking messages.

You make sure that guests receive their messages without delay, along with any mail that might arrive for them. Some Hotel Receptionists operate the hotel switchboard, directing incoming calls and helping guests to make external calls.

Hotel Receptionists prepare a customer's account when they leave the hotel. You put together the cost of additional items such as drinks, telephone calls and newspapers, and include them in the final bill. You take payment from the customer in cash, or by credit/debit card. Some Hotel Receptionists might also exchange foreign currency.

Guests might come to the Hotel Receptionist with any queries or complaints – not all of which will be easy to deal with.

Receptionists often need to use their sales skills to persuade guests to take a better and more expensive room, to stay longer, use hotel services such as the restaurant, spa, and leisure facilities, or take advantage of a special promotion to help to increase revenue for the hotel. You might also make reservations and appointments for these facilities.

In the event of an emergency, Hotel Receptionists might have responsibilities such as helping people as they evacuate the building, calling the emergency services, and checking that all guests have reached safety.

Sometimes, Hotel Receptionists might also live in the hotel where they work. In small hotels, you might have other duties such as serving in the bar or restaurant or helping with housekeeping. Some Hotel Receptionists wear a uniform.

Some Hotel Receptionists working a late shift might count up the money that has been taken that day and put it into the safe for the Duty Manager to take to the bank.

(CareersWales.gov.wales)

Here's another one just to be sure we aren't missing anything. The job duties of a hotel receptionist include:

- Greet all guests and assist them with check-in and check-out
- Maintain a positive attitude and friendly demeanor
- Respond to all guest questions and requests
- Answer and forward phone calls
- Manage guest bookings and reservations
- Keep a tidy and orderly workspace
- Assist with administrative and clerical tasks as needed

(Bamboohr.com)

The website setupmyhotel.com goes even beyond, especially in the way they translate these requirements into behaviors:

- Staff well groomed, uniformed, name tag was present.
- Staff did not eat, drink, smoke, or chew gum.
- Staff maintained focus on guest, was not distracted.
- All guests are acknowledged with eye contact and smile within 10 feet, even if the guest is waiting in line.
- Guests are not waiting in line for longer than 5–8 minutes.
- Front office team were staffed adequately and also as per the demand.
- Staff spoke first and greeted the guests with a simile, welcoming comment within 5 feet.
- Staff verified the guest's name and used it a minimum of two to three times during the interaction with the guest.
- Registered guests were not asked for duplicate information.
- Guest was discreetly asked how they would like to settle their account after their personal information was confirmed.
- Details were verified including dates of visit, rate, room type, bed type, smoking preference, email address, and billing method.
- All special requests, relevant procedures were explained either on registration form or verbally.
- Guest correspondence / messages / parcels were discreetly conveyed to the guest.
- Staff are engaging guests in conversation during the check-in procedure.

- Check-in of the guest shown on the property management system (PMS).
- Credit card pre-authorization done and cards returned back to the guest.
- Key card in the jacket was presented, floor level was indicated, and other information within the key jacket was explained to guest.
- Room number was discreetly provided to guest.
- Guest registration procedure accurately completed within 5 to 8 minutes (As per hotel standard or hotel type).
- In case room is not ready, the other options were provided and agent offered refreshment at the coffee shop and also store luggage.
- Front desk agent gave directions to room, and also offered assistance with the luggage.
- Staff spoke last, offered an authentic departure greeting referring to the guest's reason for stay, and thanked the guest.
- Staff did not congregate or engage in personal conversation with other staff, no horseplay.

Now that is already a lot, and surprisingly, I can go on and on listing all the things we expect from service employees. Trust me, it can be an excruciatingly long and challenging list! I did not include all of these to say that companies ask too much of employees; that might be true, but it's not for me to judge. What I wanted to do is make us think about what it takes to do all these things at work, day-after-day, even when we do not feel up to them.

It takes commitment, for one thing. Often, employees will have to go beyond what is written in their job description to "make the customer feel at home." Without commitment, we cannot really expect employees to go the proverbial "extra mile"; they need to be actively engaged in what they are doing, to find it meaningful and in a word (two) – worth pursuing. We would also, ideally, want our employees to be satisfied with what they are doing. It is a job, I know, and professionals are expected to be at their best even when it is hard, but realistically speaking, a happy employee will do a much better job at making each moment matter than an unhappy one.

Furthermore, because of the many items they need to keep in mind, ideally employees will have sufficient, if not extensive, experience in the job, be it in the same company or another. We simply would not like them to leave, as it means we need to train a new employee to do these things. We would also like service employees to participate actively in the company's life, to be supportive to colleagues, to proactively look for opportunities to help others, and to kick-start initiatives that will make the business better.

Now, imagine a Harry Potter magic wand that can bring all of that to rubble in a second. This magic wand exists and its name is customer abuse. What we will see in the remainder of this chapter is the ways in which customer abuse hurts your business either directly or via the damage it inflicts on service employees.

Remember that customer abuse is experienced as a stressful event that causes negative emotions. To cope with this, employees need to invest considerable resources in self-regulation, and especially in emotion regulation, i.e., in managing themselves so that they can manage the situation. Resources are limited though, so unless replenished appropriately, employees run out of them. This leaves them emotionally drained, which is one of the key facets of burnout. When this happens, what do employees do next?

Well, one option, when facing a loss or a threat of a loss of resources, as suggested by the frameworks we discussed earlier, is that employees will react by trying to safeguard their resources. In essence, they will disengage and do their best to cut their losses. The extreme form of disengagement is simply quitting the job, while its milder version is to withdraw, neglect job requirements, and be absent from work more often.

Another option, especially given that employees might not be able to disengage, is to continue to try to regulate themselves and their emotions, but as can be expected, doing so while running on empty is far from ideal. Very often emotion regulation fails and employees engage in actively destructive behaviors directed toward customers and coworkers.

And finally, even if they still want to do their job well and have the motivation for it, because at this point they are emotionally drained, employees might simply lack the capacity and energy to do it, i.e., customer abuse decreases employees' performance.

This is the whole chain of events that ultimately leads to negative consequences for businesses and customers alike. First things first, let us have a look at the concepts of work engagement and satisfaction.

Employees on the Defense

Customer Abuse Makes Employees Disengaged from Work

What is Work Engagement?

Employee engagement might seem as a rather elusive concept at first. We can all recognize an engaged employee when we see one, but how are we to define it? Perhaps, the easiest and most intuitive way to put it is that it is "a positive mental state … in which an individual feels connected to his or her work." (Wang and Chen, 2020, 418). There are three surefire ways to recognize committed, engaged employees. They have a high level of energy at work and are willing to persevere in the face of adversity; they show "dedication, characterized by strong work involvement and senses of enthusiasm, significance, confidence and fearlessness in the face of challenges" (Wang and Chen, 2020, 418); and they are absorbed, fully concentrated at work – the state in which as we all know, time flies.

As you can imagine, employees that exhibit these three aspects of work engagement bring about significant benefits to their employers. After conducting a meta-analysis of 456 studies, Gallup (2020) reported that the leading companies in employee engagement achieved considerably better results than their lagging counterparts. The top companies had 18% higher sales, 23% higher profitability, 64% less safety incidents, and 41% less quality issues, for example.

No wonder that in the recent years we are witnessing a stronger and stronger drive from companies to make their employees more engaged at work and to deliver excellent employee experience. For example, in 2017, the Dale Carnegie Research Institute reported that two out of three of the business leaders they interviewed says employee engagement is a very important part of what they think about, plan, and do every day or at least frequently. The sustained interest in employee engagement is also evident by the size of employee engagement software market, which is expected to reach about 370 USD million by 2026 with compound annual growth of 13.5% over 2020 to 2026[1].

Things do not look that shiny, though, when we look at the actual state of affairs of employee engagement. In fact, it is a grim picture. While increasing from the early 2010s, in 2021 only approximately one in three employees in the United States is an engaged one[2]. And that is still good, given that globally, only one in five employees is engaged in their work[3].

At this point, I was going to say that this widely spread disengagement from work is expensive. That would be an underestimation though, unless we consider the $7.5 trillion in lost in productivity globally[4], which is not a minor sum. This is all extra value not created because companies and managers are unsuccessful in engaging their employees in the job, in giving them a purpose, guiding their development, showing care about their well-being, and simply put, being there for them.

And all of this is further aggravated by customer abuse, which drains employees and makes them disengage from work to save what little precious resources, often in the form of self-esteem, they are left with. Let's briefly review what the research on the topic has to say about customers' aggressive behavior and employee engagement.

Work Disengagement after Customer Abuse

To begin with, a study conducted among 500 hotel workers in China discovered that customer incivility leaves employees emotionally exhausted, which then lowers their sense of professional identity, that is, a person's consistency, perception, and belonging to the profession he or she is engaged in[5]. Professional identity is important as people who score high on this have a good understanding and recognition of their career and act according to what the profession requires. In essence, customer incivility makes people less engaged in the professional path they have chosen, thus making them less likely to engage in performing according to its requirements.

Another study conducted in China[6], this time among gig-workers like food-delivery workers and app-based ride-hailing drivers, found out that negative treatment by customers makes them experience their job as less meaningful, that is, as being less important and having less value. A sad state, when you consider it – can you imagine spending all of your working day in a job that you yourself don't think is important? And all of that because a customer thought that managing their aggressive behavior is part of these people's job.

Furthermore, customer mistreatment also lowers employees' satisfaction with their own ability to do the job well and their need for autonomy[7]. These two, competence and autonomy, are part of the triad of needs that were proposed by Ryan and Deci, as cornerstones of human motivation (the third one is relatedness). Similarly, researchers have discovered that experiencing customer mistreatment leads to emotional exhaustion, which by now we know well, and that drainage of energy ultimately leads to lower intrinsic motivation at work[8]. Employees' willingness to do their job well after they encounter customer abuse? Gone!

To investigate a similar aspect of disengagement further, Greenbaum et al. conducted a study among more than 600 employees and 600 supervisors working in a government agency in the United States. They found out, as in many other studies, that customer abuse leads to emotional exhaustion. What was interesting in this project though is that the researchers also found a relationship between exhaustion and job neglect. Employees who were subjected to customer mistreatment were more likely to "passively [allow] conditions to deteriorate through reduced interest or effort, chronic lateness or absences, using company time for personal business, or increased error rate" (Greenbaum et al., 2014, 1191)

Further to employees' feeling disconnected from work, there is strong evidence that customer abuse also leads to behavioral avoidance, that is, employees not only experience disengagement but also act in such a way. One such example is absenteeism. An article very appropriately titled "The employee as a punching bag: The effect of multiple sources of incivility on employee withdrawal behavior and sales performance"[9] investigated whether experiencing customer and/or coworker abuse would lead to absenteeism (i.e., missing scheduled shifts at work) and tardiness (i.e., being late for work). Both of these turn out to be correct. The more employees perceived customer abuse, the higher the number of times they were late or missed shifts entirely.

Relatedly, when they experience strong stress, even if they are at work, employees simply pull back from putting in a lot of effort. In an interesting experiment[10] conducted in Hong Kong with close to 150 participants, half of them were put in a high stress condition (the other half had the luck to be in the low-stress group). The researchers then asked them to reply to customer (in this case – students) complaints. Participants in the high-stress condition spent nearly half less time answering to complaints compared to the control group – 3.15 minutes vs 5.40 minutes. Everything else being similar, highly stressed people simply didn't take as much time to work on their responses compared to others, indicating, as the authors point out, a depletion effect.

Work disengagement is also visible in another behavior that we often take for somewhat granted – helping others at work. In a very interesting study to which we will return later on, Porath and Erez discovered that being exposed to rude behavior – no matter if "rudeness instigated by a direct authority figure, rudeness delivered by a third party, and imagined rudeness." (Porath and Erez, 2007, 1181) – decreases our willingness to help others. We just don't want to do anything extra beyond the bare minimum.

The last study was conducted in a lab, but a psychological one – no one's life was on the line. Not so in this next research[11]. In a medical simulation in a neonatal intensive care unit, teams who were exposed to rude behavior significantly less often shared information within the team, and significantly less often asked other team members for help; both of these decreased the accuracy of diagnosing the patient (in this case the mannequin) and to conducting the necessary procedure. A scary finding if there was ever one.

Talking about medical teams, I will just give the floor to the researchers who did a review of the findings about the effects of patient (!) aggression against nurses on the latter. No commentary is necessary.

Assaults can affect or undermine the nurse-patient relationship and lead to behaviors such as less eagerness to spend time with residents, less willingness to answer residents' call lights, avoiding patients, or adopting a passive role. ... Nurses' perceptions of their job competency and security at or satisfaction with the workplace may be affected. ... Patient aggression and assault can lead to real or perceived impairments in professional performance, leading nurses to doubt the quality of their work, their competency, or perceive themselves as having failed.

(Needham et al., 2005, 288)

Having been through all of this, it is perhaps out of the question that employees who experience customer abuse would in any shape or form go the extra mile to help customers (or the company itself for that matter). Nevertheless, it's worth reviewing briefly what businesses are missing on when customers abuse their people.

For example, in a study among nurses in the United States, Lavelle et al. (2021) tested an extensive model of the impact of customer abuse on employees. Their study supports the view that we outlined in the previous chapter suggesting that customer mistreatment leads to emotional exhaustion, which then, as we'll see in a minute, leads to employees faking emotions. The latter, in turn, reduces the amount of extra-role behaviors they undertake, or actions such as "Goes out of the way to ensure patients are satisfied," "Demonstrates a strong commitment to patient satisfaction," and "Works hard to keep patients satisfied."

In addition, customer abuse makes it less likely for employees to show such behaviors within the organization as well. Things like "being willing to sacrifice personal interest, caring for colleagues, being loyal to the hotel and generally being responsible,"[12] a study among hotel workers discovered, decreased with customer mistreatment. Finally, and related to the ways in which employees can go the extra mile to help their organizations, experiencing customer mistreatment reduces the amount of effort "to provide information about customer needs and make suggestions to management regarding improvement in service delivery" (Huang and Kwok, 2021, 3380), i.e., what is known as customer-focused voice.

In the very competitive environments, the majority of businesses operate these days, just doing what is expected is rarely enough. With the advent of the customer experience paradigm and the desire to orchestrate every part of the customer journey comes the need for all parts of the organization to be dedicated to going above and beyond to make the customers happy. Everything that we saw in these last few paragraphs suggests that when customers act abusively, employees' willingness to do that diminishes, simply because they disengage from their jobs. They just don't want to spend the effort to work in an environment which drains their resources; instead, they want to, as saw earlier, protect themselves, and this often means simply not giving all you have to achieve the company's mission.

But employees' desire to cut their losses in potentially stressful situations does not stop with limiting the amount of effort they put in or arriving late for work. Often, to preserve themselves, they simply start faking their emotional display, and it is to the so-called "surface-acting" that we'll turn to next.

Customer Abuse Leads to Surface Acting

[It's of] absolute importance not to allow them to get you to 'lose your cool.' You need to remain calm and act as though their behavior is not irritating you.

(Fisk and Neville, 2011, 397)

When we spoke about emotion regulation, we noticed that often times we resort to a less-than-optimal response adjustment strategy, namely, inhibiting the expression of our negative emotions or even faking their opposites. In the research around service jobs and the requirements they put forth, this is called surface acting, as opposed to deep acting. What is very important to note here is that deep acting is not equal to faking; in fact, it is the exact opposite: "When deep acting, the actor attempts to modify feelings to match the required displays. The intent then is to seem authentic to the audience, thus it has been called "faking in good faith" (Grandey, 2003). Deep acting is more akin to putting ourselves in the other person's shoes, to connecting with them, rather than merely displaying the emotions that social norms oblige us to.

Hochschild gives a vivid example of deep acting in our daily lives by telling the story of

the reaction of this young man to the unexpected news that a close friend had suffered a mental breakdown:

I was shocked, yet for some reason I didn't think my emotions accurately reflected the bad news. My roommate appeared much more shaken than I did. I thought that I should be more upset by the news than I was. Thinking about this conflict I realized that one reason for my emotional state might have been the spatial distance separating me from my friend, who was in the hospital hundreds of miles away. I then tried to focus on his state ... and began to picture my friend as I thought he then existed.

Sensing himself to be less affected than he should be, he tried to visualize his friend — perhaps in gray pajamas, being led by impassive attendants to the electric-shock room. After bringing such a vivid picture to mind, he might have gone on to recall smaller private breakdowns in his own life and thereby evoked feelings of sorrow and empathy. Without at all thinking of this as acting, in complete privacy, without audience or stage, the young man can pay, in the currency of deep acting, his emotional respects to a friend.

(Hochschild, 2012, 42)

With surface acting, it's exactly the opposite. We try to *display* what we are expected to display, but we make no effort or we are unsuccessful in our attempt to connect on a deeper level. "In surface acting," Grandey explains, one modifies "the displays without shaping the inner feelings." (Grandey, 2003, 87). Fake smiles, learned, cliched phrases, words spoken without conviction, barely made efforts to solve an issue – all these things that we as customers see often enough are examples of surface acting. The overall impression of someone who is surface acting is that of watching a movie with rather poor actor work.

Of the two ways of approaching customer service situations, deep acting is the more productive one both for the employee[13] and for the company, but it requires quite a bit of work to become well-versed in it, and is consequently disrupted when employees are subject to customer abuse and exhausted. Indeed, a host of research shows that customer abuse leads to surface acting, and the latter, ironically, makes employees even more exhausted.

For example, in 2012, a group of researchers interviewed 309 sales employees from a department store in South Korea to investigate whether customer incivility leads to surface acting. To measure the latter, they asked employees to indicate whether they "Just pretend to have the emotions they need to display for their job" and "Show feelings to customers that are different from what they feel inside." (Hur, Moon, and Han, 2015). What they found out is that employees indicating they experience more customer incivility also resort to surface acting more. In another study[14], this time conducted in Poland, two researchers interviewed 315 retail sales employees to investigate the linkage between customer incivility and surface acting – does experiencing aggression make employees fake emotions? The answer is again a resounding "Yes" – employees who say they experience more customer incivility are 30% more likely to surface-act than the others. And finally, as early as 2004, Grandey et al. conducted a study on this topic with close to 200 call center employees and discovered that "Employees who felt more threatened by customer aggression used surface acting ... while those who were less threatened used deep acting." (Grandey, Dickter, and Sin, 2004, 397).

Customer Abuse Makes Employees Want to Quit

Disengagement from work in the shapes and forms we just discussed before is just one of the ways in which employees try to conserve precious resources when they feel emotionally exhausted. Basically, becoming disconnected means that workers are putting a wall between themselves and their jobs to try and preserve their energy, their self-esteem, their mental state if you will. Going one step further on the "escape" route of dealing with customer abuse, we arrive at the ultimate solution employees can engage with – quitting their jobs.

Employee turnover, or the rate at which workers leave the company, is one of the biggest challenges many businesses face because there is a host of potential costs associated with turnover. Tackling the direct effects first, an employee leaving the organization can lead to lower team productivity, lower team morale, loss of talent and knowledge, and even damage to brand reputation.

Perhaps, it is an employee working with this very important client that leaves or one that isn't that great at performing their duties but does miracles to the team spirit. Perhaps, it is this great team player who is always looking for ways to help, or the employee who had unique knowledge of a certain business area. Whoever it is, it results in the very least in missed opportunities, and in the worst case, in lower productivity, morale, and even in losing more employees due to ex-employees recruiting others.

And then you would need to add the costs for replacing an employee to understand how big an issue employee turnover is. Replacing a single employee in the United States, according to Gallup, can cost anything in the range of 1.5–2.5 times the employee's salary[15]. For a company of 100 people with an average salary of USD 50,000, the total costs for replacing employees per year could easily be in the range of USD 660,000 to USD2.6 million. What is the total amount US businesses are losing per year due to voluntary turnover? The staggering USD 1,000,000,000,000; yep, one trillion dollars per year.

To get an even better view of the challenge employee turnover poses, consider that a fifth[16] to a quarter[17] of the people working in a company one year would be gone the next. On average, that is. Some industries are much more prone to exhibit high employee turnover. Dailypay.com reports that while sectors like finance and insurance, and wholesale trade have turnover rates below 2%, others are not so lucky. I couldn't believe my eyes when I saw these numbers:

- Staffing: 352% (Source: American Staffing Association)
- Hotels: 60%–300% (Source: CHA International)
- Supermarkets: 100% (Source: Small Business Chronicle)
- Retail: 59% (Source: Small Business Chronicle)
- Fast food (or QSR): "Compared to other industries, the QSR industry is said to have the highest employee turnover rate every year, which varies from 50% to 100%." (Workpulse, 2020)

Hundred percent turnover rate means that if you start working in a restaurant now, every single one of your colleagues would have left a year from now, including you. This is huge. Imagine all the hiring efforts, trainings, and administration that go into making an employee productive. One day these give results and the next they are in vain – the employee quits.

There are, of course, a host of reasons for employees to quit their job, and a host of things businesses can do to prevent it. Suggestions include, for example, a better hiring process, making sure that the right employees join the company, and a better onboarding. Given that a lot of employees leave during their first year in the job, it is no surprise that companies with a good onboarding process have new hires retention 82% higher than others[18].

Higher employee engagement and employee training and development opportunities are also found to work miracles for reducing turnover rates. And, as perhaps you can expect, managers play a critical role in the process of keeping employees. In a striking example, Gallup reports that

> Among former employees, 36% were actively searching for a new job for one or more months before leaving their last job. And, yet, more than half of exiting employees (51%) say that in the three months before they left, neither their manager nor any other leader spoke with them about their job satisfaction or future with the organization.
>
> (Gallup (b))

So, companies do want to keep their employees, and for very good reasons. And for that, especially in the recent years, they've invested millions in trying to build practices that increase their retention rates. Yet, there is a relatively underappreciated, yet surefire!, way to retain more employees, and you guessed it – it is to reduce the amount of customer abuse employees are subjected to. One of the most consistently reported findings in the literature about customer mistreatment is that it makes people considerably less happy with their job and considerably more likely to quit.

As early as 2009, three researchers conducted a study among hotel workers in Cyprus to understand how customer verbal aggression impacts employees. Sure enough, they found out that it leads to emotional exhaustion and emotional dissonance, as we discussed in the previous chapter. But following the Conservation of Resources framework, they went further – they wanted to know if exhaustion and dissonance would make employees want to quit their jobs. This not only turned out to be the case, but the amount of turnover intentions that can be attributed to customers' verbal aggression is disturbing – fully 43% of the desire to leave the organization was driven by customer abuse[19].

This relationship was confirmed in a much more recent study conducted among employees of a retail organization in the Philippines[20]. To better understand how customer injustice (a form of customer abuse) relates to turnover, they collected attitudinal, as well as actual turnover data months after the initial study. First, their results offer one more confirmation of the fact that customer abuse leads to negative emotions, which in turn exhaust employees. Second, taking this one step further, the team discovered that emotional exhaustion increases turnover intentions and ultimately leads to actual turnover. In fact, a whole quarter of the actual turnover can be attributed to customer injustice.

In a further examination of the customer abuse–turnover relationship, researchers[21] conducted a study within 139 call centers in Canada, working in a variety of industries like telecommunications, financial services, leisure, and nonprofit, among others. They interviewed managers within these call centers about the level of customer abuse they see in their organizations, and also collected actual turnover data from them. The results found a positive and significant linkage between the two, leading the authors to the conclusion that "establishment-level customer aggression is positively related to workforce quit rate." (Liu, van Jaarsveld, and Yanadori, 2022, 348)

I can continue this list much further; in fact, there is not a single study of which I'm aware that investigated the relationship between customer abuse and employee turnover that didn't confirm this finding – when customers mistreat employees, the latter want to escape to preserve their resources, i.e., to quit.

So far, we had a look at one of the routes employees can take to work through the negative effects of customer abuse they experience – they can try to protect themselves by becoming disengaged and putting in less effort in serving customers, by placing a wall and hiding their true emotions (surface acting), and by simply quitting the organization and the setting in which they face the dire consequences such as negative emotions, stress, exhaustion, and burnout. While it is clear that employees who are disengaged and don't put in their whole selves probably wouldn't fare all too well in their companies, these behaviors are costly for organizations as well, as they are linked to lower productivity and high investments to mitigate them, as in the case of employee turnover.

But these are far from all the costs companies incur when customers act abusively. Even if they don't take the disengagement route and if they want to continue doing their job well, employees might simply not be able to do it because of the emotional and cognitive load customer abuse puts on them. In a word, customer abuse hampers employee performance, and this is what we turn to next.

Customer Abuse Hampers Employee Performance

I felt dead inside. I'd pushed myself too far, for too long. The well was dry, there was no water left to pour, my cup was empty.

(Lynch, 2021)

We saw earlier that customer abuse unlocks a detrimental chain of events for service employees. Aggression threatens to or directly limits the resources they have at their disposal, which creates all kinds of negative emotions like fear, anger, and anxiety, and results in distress. Due to the nature of their work – working on the borderline between the business and its customers – employees face a dilemma. On the one hand, they want to protect themselves, but on the other, business demands require them to try and provide the best customer experience possible. This further exacerbates the effect of customer abuse by creating emotional dissonance. All of this makes it harder for employees to regulate their emotions, thus requiring them to put in even more resources. Ultimately, this leaves them exhausted and burned out. We already saw some of the negative effects of burnout for employees, which include poor sleep quality, more family conflict, lower life satisfaction, and higher propensity to experience major medical conditions.

Aside from these very serious consequences, burnout also has devastating effects on the very core of who we are – our brains. In one study, a neuroscientist, Amita Golkar, and her collaborators recruited 40 participants who experienced "sleeplessness, diffuse aches, palpitations and fatigue, a subsequent onset of irritability, anxiety, memory and concentration problems, feeling of depersonalization, and reduced work capacity" (Golkar et al., 2014) attributable to chronic stress, and 70 people who didn't have these symptoms. They asked both groups to look at different pictures (a mix of neutral and negative ones) and to keep, intensify, or suppress their emotional response to them. This was not the researchers' true intention though. At one point, while people were looking at the pictures, they played a loud sound designed to startle participants – it's the difference between how the burnout and the nonburnout groups react that the researchers were interested in.

To begin with, there were no differences in the so-called startle response between the burnout and the nonburnout groups when they looked at neutral pictures. So far, so good. What is more interesting is that the two groups showed different patterns of when they were looking at negative ones – participants with burnout had a significantly more pronounced reaction compared to the others. In addition, they were also much less successful in downplaying their negative emotions when looking at negative pictures; as the authors point out, "Stressed subjects were less capable of down-regulating negative emotion, but had normal acoustic startle responses when asked to up-regulate or maintain emotion and when no regulation was required" (Golkar et al., 2014). In a word, they had a more difficult time dealing with negative emotions when they experienced them – everything looked bleaker.

The next study Golkar and team did helps explain why this happens. They asked the same participants to come back to the lab the next day for an fMRI measurement – the researchers wanted to see if and how the brain structure and connections differ between participants with and without burnout. The results are startling. Burnout people had weaker connections between the amygdala (the part of the brain that is critical for emotional reactions) and the prefrontal cortex, which is responsible for the executive functions, behavioral control, and the "orchestration of thoughts and actions in accordance with internal goals" (Golkar et al., 2014). The latter was just not able to send strong enough signals to control the functioning of the amygdala – the part of our brains responsible for emotions like fear could go on firing on all cylinders.

And the effect of burnout on the brain is not limited to the number of connections between its different parts. Another MRI study[22] discovered something perhaps even more disturbing. On the one hand, our mPFC (medial prefrontal cortex), part of the prefrontal cortex, wears out and becomes thinner among people exposed to chronic stress. True, this a rather natural process happening with age as well, but stressed-out participants in Savic's study showed an even more pronounced thinning. In addition, the amygdalae of burnout people appeared to be bigger compared to other subjects, indicating overactivation. The latter,

> leads to impaired modulation of the mPFC regions, which then triggers further stimulation of the amygdala — leading to even more activation of the mPFC. As this cycle spirals further out of control over time, neural structures begin to show signs of wear and tear, which lead to cortical thinning as well as memory, attentional, and emotional difficulties.
>
> (Michel, 2016)

Unfortunately, there is plenty of evidence that customer abuse is related to exactly the kind of difficulties Michel points out and ultimately leads to lower job performance. Our first stop in briefly reviewing the evidence for this is a study conducted in Israel of mental capacity we seldom appreciate while it's intact but mourn the loss of when gone – memory. A group of psychologists[23] reasoned that if customer abuse is such an emotional event and such events consume not only emotional but also cognitive resources, then surely mistreatment by customers would also have a detrimental impact on the latter. Employees spent cognitive resources, for example, when they try to rethink the stressful situation to cope with it and when they ruminate, think over and over, about it. It is exactly this logic that researchers set out to test. In their first study, they asked participants to listen to a call between a customer and an employee, half of which involved an aggressive customer. Participants in the study were then asked to recall details about this call, such as what was the issue customer called to talk about, and after about 25 minutes they were asked to do this again.

Sure enough, all participants recalled less details in the second exercise than in the first – that's to be expected. What is more important though is that participants who listened to an aggressive customer recalled less information from the very start. Those in the neutral condition were able to share about 6.0 details when asked immediately after listening to the call; those in the aggressive customer situation recalled a quarter less – merely 4.4 details.

To further verify their findings, in another study, the same researchers asked people to read transcripts of service calls, some of which included aggressive customer behavior. Then, participants completed the so-called Raven test, which is a commonly used method to test working memory[24]. As hypothesized, participants who read the transcript of aggressive interactions fared worse on the test (2.44 on average) than those who read neutral dialogues (3.83 on average). Customer abuse, in short, impairs employees' memory, thus making it more difficult for them to even remember what clients asked for.

In another very interesting set of studies, researchers[25] looked for insights if experiencing rudeness hampers our performance on routine and creative tasks, and whether it makes us less helpful. Using quite an elaborate experiment design, they exposed approximately half of the 100 participants to a confederate who was deliberately acting rudely; with the rest, the confederate was neutral during the interaction. To test people's performance on a rather routine task, researchers asked them to solve ten moderately difficult anagrams. Those who experienced rudeness solved 3.8 on average, while the others solved 5.0, pointing directly toward the fact that rudeness affects our cognitive abilities, even when experienced for a brief period of time.

In addition, the researchers asked participants to come up with as many uses for a brick (yep, the thing used to build our houses) in 5 minutes, which is a task regularly used to assess creativity. They then had independent raters evaluate the quality of responses. On the one hand, participants in the rude condition came up with less uses for a brick; on average, they listed 8.5 ideas, while those in the neutral condition reported 11.8 uses. Not only the quantity was different though – the rated creativity of brick uses among people exposed to rudeness was significantly lower compared to those for which everything was business-as-usual. Interestingly, we don't need to actually experience rudeness to be on the receiving end of these effects even only "imagining a rude incident reduced routine as well as creative and flexible performance" (Porath and Erez, 2007, 1193), the authors found out in another of their studies.

And finally, to measure helpfulness, Porath and Erez did something quite sneaky and ingenious. They could have simply asked people how willing they are to jump in and support others, but that of course would have been an unreliable, self-reported measurement. Instead, they asked their confederates to simply knock over a jar with ten pencils that was on his desk. The researchers reasoned that whether and how many pencils participants picked up would give us a better idea of how helpful they are. Participants in the neutral condition picked up, on average, about eight pencils. Those who experienced rudeness? Two.

We want employees to remember things, to deal well with routine tasks, to be creative? Not going to happen when customers mistreat them. The cognitive and emotional load to deal with the stress is just too high for employees to spend precious resources on, well, doing their job well. They simply don't have them.

Speaking of cognitive and emotional load, let us spend some time with service agents of a large transportation company. What they do, is respond to messages and calls of customers asking all kinds of things – from seeking information to looking to solve an issue. Three researchers, Rafaeli, Altman, and Yom-Tov (2019), reasoned that there might be some very interesting insights lurking beneath the surface of these interactions, so they got their hands on a sample of almost 150,000 customer-agent chats and went to work. To begin with, they created measurements for cognitive and emotional load: the number of words customers use in a message is a good indication of the former, and the latter is well represented by how emotionally charged are the words used by customers.

The results are amazingly clear. To begin with, the more words a customer used, the slower the agent's response time (once we are pass the approximately seven to eight words mark). The relationship is strictly linear, meaning that this is valid for every single word the customer adds; an increase from 10 to 15 words slows agents down as much as an increase from 90 to 95 words. For us as customers this means that if we want faster answer, we'd better explain things briefly.

What about emotional load? Does it slow agents down as well? First, the fastest response times were registered when the conversation included predominantly neutral words. No emotions, fast response time. Perhaps, more interestingly, positive emotional words increased agents' speed of responding two times compared to a neutral conversation. This is odd at first, because we would expect that a positive attitude makes people happier and puts them in a better mood. That might very well be the case, but it doesn't change the fact that emotionally charged words require us to do emotion regulation, which requires resources. But if positive words have that effect, how much would negative affect impact the conversation? Well, add further 50 seconds on top of the positive conversation and you'll know the result. A negative chat, all in all, increases agents' response time threefold – if it takes them about 50 seconds to answer to customers along the duration of a neutral conversation, in a negative one they take up to 150 seconds in total.

Relatedly, research has also discovered that emotional load increases the time it takes for agents to respond, the number of messages needed to handle the customer request, and how long the messages from the agents are. To give us a more intuitive idea of what is the total business impact of these insights, it helps to put things in perspective. The authors explain

> The total throughput time required to handle a "negative" customer is 15.7 minutes (1.32 minutes times 11.9 turns); compared to 11.1 minutes for a neutral customer and 7.6 minutes to handle a "positive" one. This analysis suggests that the total amount of throughput time associated with a negative customer is 42% longer than the one associated with a neutral customer. Many contact centers measure agent performance by the number of calls an agent handles per hour (average concurrency divided by total throughput time). They should be aware that an agent can serve 12.6 neutral customers per hour but only 8.9 negative ones (assuming average concurrency = 2.33).
>
> (Altman et al., 2021)

The impact of customer abuse on employees' cognitive and emotional abilities goes further than this, and there is a plethora of evidence that hampers their in-role performance, more broadly speaking. For example, researchers[26] conducted a study among both nurses and their supervisors in a US-based for-profit hospital to investigate the whole chain of negative consequences customer mistreatment causes. First, they found evidence suggesting that customer injustice exhausts employees emotionally, which then leads them to adopt surface-acting strategies, as we saw earlier in the book. Surface acting, unfortunately, is also not free, and that is one of the reasons why it isn't considered a productive emotion regulation strategy – in fact, it further depletes employees. All of this, the authors reasoned, would further hurt their performance. Indeed, they found out that the more customer mistreatment employees experienced, the less their supervisors agreed that they "adequately complete assigned duties," "fulfill responsibilities specified in the job description," and "meet formal requirements of the job" (Lavelle et al., 2021, 663). In fact, about a quarter of this in-role performance decrease can be attributed to surface acting, which itself is driven by emotional exhaustion.

Quite naturally, all this decreased performance on the side of employees is felt by the customer as well; perhaps, unfortunately though, not by those who acted aggressively but the ones that are served after. Remember the study[27] we briefly spoke about that found out employees spent less time answering customer complaints when they were put under high stress? The same study reported that customer satisfaction with employees' responses was also significantly lower in the high-stress condition – not only employees spent less time, but they ultimately didn't serve their customers well.

In a similar fashion, a study[28] among bank tellers in the United States, investigated the level of customer incivility they experience, their emotional exhaustion, and how do they react (whether they surface-act or not). What is interesting is that while in the previous studies we discussed asked employees and/or their supervisors to rate service performance, in this case the researchers asked customers to do it. Sure enough, given everything we discussed so far, they discovered that customer incivility leads to surface acting, which exhausts employees emotionally. What this ultimately led to is a decrease in service quality scores given by customers – for every three-point increase of customer mistreatment on an imaginary customer mistreatment scale, service quality decreased by one point.

So far in this chapter, we saw that when facing customer abuse, employees sometimes attempt to escape the stressful encounters and either limit their engagement at work and put a barrier between them and the customers, or simply want to quit their jobs. Even if they do not do this and want to continue servicing customers well, they might be significantly challenged at the task because customer abuse is draining and hampers their cognitive and emotional abilities. Ultimately, all of this leads to lower service performance and lower customer satisfaction.

It is easy to see how these scenarios spell negative business impact, given that customer experience and satisfaction is one of the key elements that can make or break a company. There is, however, an even more negative scenario, which we have not touched upon so far. Sometimes, customer aggression leads to employees becoming aggressive themselves and mistreating both their customers and their coworkers. It is to this emotion regulation failure effect that we turn to next.

When Emotion Regulation Fails

His last words were "If everybody working for this organization is as incompetent as you, no wonder your airline loses money." He then stormed off. I wished him a good flight as if nothing happened.

The little old lady behind him in line had heard everything, of course, and she sweetly asked how I managed to stay so polite and cheerful in the face of his behavior. I told her the truth. "He's going to Kansas City," I explained, "and his bags are going to Tokyo."

(Tripp and Bies, 2009, 131)

We as customers and as business leaders might not like it, but from a psychological standpoint what we will discuss in this subchapter is a very natural response of employees when they encounter aggressive customers and experience negative emotions. Sometimes some of them strike back; in the literature on the topic, this is known more broadly as service sabotage, the "organizational member behaviors that are intentionally designed negatively to affect service" (Harris and Ogbonna, 2002, 166), or more narrowly – customer-directed sabotage or customer-directed deviant employee behavior.

The former term encompasses the wider repertoire of acts employees can resort to take revenge when feeling mistreated and includes company-directed sabotage. The latter, customer-directed sabotage, pinpoints behaviors that directly address the customer as the "recipient" of the revenge. We need to make it very clear from the onset – neither of these is in any shape or form a positive or functional behavior. The fact is though, that especially in its narrower form, customer-directed sabotage happens very often because of customer abuse and is a reaction to it (we will talk about how poor customer service causes customer abuse in the next chapter).

Critical to understanding why sometimes employees strike back is the concept of self-control, that is, "the ability to alter one's thoughts, emotions, and behaviors or to override impulses and habits, allows one to monitor and regulate oneself to meet expectations." (Maranges and Baumeister, 2016, 42). One of the most widely accepted models of self-control, the so-called strength model, views these abilities as akin to energy and as a limited resource. In essence, our self-control abilities can be depleted when used for a prolonged period of time, and on the positive side can be strengthened over time, similarly to using a muscle.

Of particular importance to our topic, Maranges and Baumeister note that

Self-control is used to override automatic impulses and behavior, and as such, depletion affects controlled processes in particular. This effect on controlled processes suggests that self-control depletion leads to a reduction of top-down control. Accordingly, people rely on habits, largely automatic responses, when their self-control is low...

(Maranges and Baumeister, 2016, 43)

When our self-control resources are depleted, in short, we have difficulties controlling our impulses, and as we just saw, one of the major consequences of customer abuse is that it diminishes employee's resources as it requires them to spent more time and energy in self-regulation of behavior and emotion.

Knowing this, one would expect that the exhaustion of our mental and emotional resources would make it more likely that employees would strike back and retaliate. Evidence for this, in fact, abounds.

In one of the first, if not the first, exploration on the topic, a team of three researchers interviewed more than 350 customer service representatives in a call center in Canada. They found out that a strong link "between customer interpersonal injustice and employee sabotage directed toward customers. Our research shows that employees retaliate in ways that are unauthorized by management in order to cope with customer mistreatment." (Skarlicki, van Jaarsveld, and Walker, 2008, 1342). In another study (also in Canada), a team or researchers investigated this relationship by analyzing more than 36 hours of real conversations between customer and employees of an insurance company's call center in Canada. What they found out is that customer incivility leads to employee incivility, and interestingly, this relationship is stronger when this aggression is targeted, i.e., when customers use more second-person pronouns. "Our results," the authors conclude, "support a resource-based explanation, suggesting that customer verbal aggression consumes employee resources potentially leading to self-regulation failure." (Walker, van Jaarsveld, and Skarlicki, 2017, 163).

This list can go on and on, and shows conclusively that there is a strong relationship between customer abuse and employee retaliation. As unproductive it might be, very often when customers act aggressively or mistreat employees, they strike back.

Unfortunately, that is not the only thing that happens. Studies have also shown that when they experience customer mistreatment, employees may start acting aggressively toward their own coworkers. One of the investigations we just discussed[29], for example, measured not only employee incivility toward customers but also toward other employees. The direct effect between customer incivility and employee incivility toward customers was stronger compared to toward employees – employees were more likely to strike back at customers for customers' mistreatment. But there is also an indirect effect that goes through burnout, and it affects mostly coworkers. This makes intuitive sense of course. Employees' reaction toward uncivil customers might very well be described as acting in the heat of the moment and under the influence of strong negative emotions like anger – coworkers have nothing to do with this situation. But customer abuse does more than this; as we saw, it creates the more long-lasting condition of emotional exhaustion and more generally speaking, burnout. Being emotionally drained and cynical, employees, as the study describes, may start ignoring or excluding coworkers while at work, raising their voice, or simply acting rudely toward them.

One of the key issues with customer aggression then, and in fact – with any form of aggression, is that it is a downward spiral in which mistreatment spreads like a flu. Rosen et al. (2016) asked 70 employees to answer one and the same survey three times a day for ten consecutive days measuring experienced incivility, self-control, and instigated incivility. What they discovered is that "experiencing incivility earlier in the day reduced one's levels of self-control (captured via a performance-based measure of self-control), which in turn resulted in increased instigated incivility later in the day." (Rosen et al., 2016, 1620). If someone acts rudely in the morning, you are yourself more likely to act rudely in the afternoon.

In another very interesting research, a team of researchers[30] asked 90 graduate students in a US university to meet regularly and participate in fictitious negotiation exercises. The outcome of the negotiations was not really what the researchers were interested in; they rather wanted to know how the behavior of one person affects their partner, and then the partner of the partner. What they discovered is that rudeness catches on quite easily. In fact,

> an interaction with a rude partner (i.e., Partner 1) in a previous negotiation affected the behavior of Partner 2 (carrier) towards his or her negotiation partner (third party) in the second negotiation. That is, if the carrier interacted with a rude partner in the first negotiation, his or her partner in the next negotiation perceived him or her to be more rude. ...
> (Foulk, Woolum, and Erez, 2016, 55)

In a "monkey see, monkey do" fashion, then, aggressive behavior spreads from person to person, and also from person to unrelated tasks and situations. Once we become exhausted, we become less able to control ourselves, which opens the doors to a negative spiral, which can go on and on, and on, thus potentially harming not only employees as the receivers of mistreatment but also other customers, coworkers, and as we saw in the previous chapter, their families.

With this, it is high time to chat about the reasons why customers might act aggressively toward employees, and from there, to see what companies and employees can do about it. But before that, it's worth doing a quick recap of everything we learned in this and the previous chapter about the consequences of customer abuse.

What Did We Discuss in this Chapter?

In what was probably a rather dark journey, in this and the previous chapter we had a look at the chain of events and psychological states that is set in motion when customers abuse employees. We spoke about the business-as-usual way we as human beings operate, and we discussed the process by which we regulate our behavior to achieve our goals.

Next to this, we outlined the framework known as Conservation of Resources, which postulates the primacy of resource management. Looking at customer abuse from this angle, it is seen as a stressor because it either diminishes or threats to diminish employees' resources, be they social, reputational, cognitive, emotional, or self-esteem related. Indeed, a host of research shows that customer aggression is one of the most stressful events that can happen to an employee. Not surprisingly, it is also related to a host of negative emotions like anger, frustration, anxiety, fear, and depersonalization, among others. Emotional dissonance felt by employees – the desire to get rid of these negative emotions in one way or another combined with the need to perform one's job to a certain standard – further aggravates things.

All of this is unpleasant in its own right, but there is also a more long-lasting effect related to it. The job of a service employee is a prime example of what researchers have called emotional labor. To perform one's role in a service economy, one does not only invest time and energy, but is also expected to display positive emotions. Emotional labor poses a significant challenge to employees' emotion regulation process, and this is exacerbated when customers abuse them – employees' job becomes even harder than it already was, and they need to invest even more resources to perform it.

These are not unlimited though. Combine the higher expenditure of resources with the lower ability to replenish them which negative emotions lead to, and soon you arrive at one of the modern-world's most prevalent diseases – burnout – which employees feel especially strongly in its emotional exhaustion dimension. Customer abuse, simply put, drains service employees. Burnout, and emotional exhaustion in particular, is related to a host of negative personal consequences, including but not limited to poor sleep quality, overeating, extensive mobile phone usage, more family conflict, lower marital satisfaction, and lower life satisfaction in general.

Naturally, the effects of customer abuse are also visible strongly in the workplace itself. When they are under stress, employees have a number of options to cope with it. There are, of course, productive ways to handle it, and that is what the second part of this book will be dedicated to. When it becomes too much though (and who would argue that a customer holding a knife to your throat or shoving a sausage in your mouth is not too much!), employees resort to other options. Have in mind that these are not things only service employees do – we all often turn to one or more of them.

One way to handle stress is simply to try to avoid it. In the workplace, this is manifested in lower motivation and job disengagement – creating a distance between ourselves and the stressful situation. We simply stop caring about what we do. A related way of handling stress is surface acting. Instead of running away from the situation, employees stay in it but put a barrier, a mask between themselves and customers (and not only abusive ones), and fake their emotions. This, unfortunately, is not a great strategy, as first, customers recognize it, and second, it is also not resource-free; in fact, studies show that surface acting in fact aggravates emotional exhaustion.

A stronger employee reaction in the same "escape" strategy is to outright quit their job. A study after study investigated customer abuse to turnover intentions and to actual turnover and showed unequivocally the strong relationship between the two.

Even if they do not resort to disengagement and quitting, but want to stay and try to do their job well, employees may have a very hard time doing this. In fact, burnout has been linked to outright physical changes in our brains, and a host of psychological studies show it extolls heavy cognitive and emotional costs, ultimately hampering employee performance. Unsurprisingly, the lower service quality delivered by employees ultimately results in lower customer satisfaction and worse customer experience.

All of these options, suboptimal as they might be, pale in comparison to the cases in which employees' emotion regulation strategies fail most utterly, and they strike back. I want to make it very clear here, that this is neither an unnatural reaction, nor one that I consider justified – my intention is to merely follow the whole chain of events. Indeed, a plethora of studies show that employee aggression toward customers is closely linked to them experiencing burnout and emotional exhaustion. They simply reach a point at which they cannot exert self-control and lash out.

Perhaps, most disturbingly, all of this does not stay confined to the specific customer–employee interaction. In fact, as Foulk, Woolum and Erez appropriately named one of their articles on the topic, catching rudeness is like catching a cold – it only takes one interaction and once you have it, you spread it around to customers, but also to your co-workers, and as we saw earlier, to your family as well.

In a nutshell, customer abuse unlocks a spiral of abuse, which just continues on and on if not interrupted along the way. It breaks the very tissue of our social world by damaging our perceptions of ourselves, and our abilities to navigate the world. There are things we can all do to break the chain, and it is my hope that this book will spark action. The consequences we discussed so far give us some hints as to how can we stand against customer abuse; before we have an in-depth look into this though, we need one final piece of the puzzle – why do customers act aggressively in the first place? On to discussion of what triggers customer abuse!

Notes

1 Prnewswire.com (2021).
2 Harter (2022).
3 Gallup (a)
4 Pendell (2022)
5 Pu, Ji, and Sang (2022).
6 Xiongtao et al. (2021).
7 Chen et al. (2021).

8 Hur, Moon, and Jun (2016).
9 Sliter, Sliter, and Jex (2012).
10 Chan and Wan (2012).
11 Riskin et al. (2015).
12 Wen, Li, and Hou (2016).
13 See for example Hur, Moon, and Han (2015).
14 Szczygiel DD and Bazińska (2021).
15 McFeely and Wigert (2019).
16 Society for Human Resource Management (2017).
17 McFeely and Wigert (2019).
18 Laurano (2015).
19 Karatepe, Yorganci, and Haktanir (2009).
20 van Jaarsveld et al. (2021).
21 Liu et al. (2022).
22 Savic (2015).
23 Rafaeli et al. (2012).
24 "a set of visual analogy problems, each comprising a 3 X 3 matrix of figural elements, such as geometric figures, lines, or background textures. One entry in each matrix is missing, and the participant is asked to fill in this entry from eight response alternatives presented below the matrix. The test instructs people to look across the rows and then look down the columns to determine the rules that guide the construction of the figures, and to follow these 20 rules in identifying the missing entry." (Rafaeli et al., 2012, 937)
25 See Porath and Erez (2007).
26 Lavelle et al. (2021).
27 Chan and Wan (2012).
28 Sliter et al. (2010)
29 Kim and Qu (2019).
30 Foulk, Woolum, and Erez (2016).

References

Al-Hawari, M. A., Bani-Melhem, S., & Quratulain, S. (2020). Do frontline employees cope effectively with abusive supervision and customer incivility? Testing the effect of employee resilience. *Journal of Business and Psychology*, 35, 223–240. https://doi.org/10.1007/s10869-019-09621-2

Altman, Daniel, Yom-Tov, Galit B., Olivares, Marcelo, Ashtar, Shelly, & Rafaeli, Anat. (2021). Do customer emotions affect agent speed? An empirical study of emotional load in online customer contact centers. *Manufacturing & Service Operations Management*, 23(4), 854–875. https://doi.org/10.1287/msom.2020.0897

Bamboohr.com, Hotel Receptionist Job Description Template. https://www.bamboohr.com/job-description/hotel-receptionist/, last accessed on January 11, 2023.

Careerswales.gov.wales, Hotel receptionist -> Job Role. https://careerswales.gov.wales/job-information/hotel-receptionist/job-role, last accessed on January 11, 2023.

Chan, K. W., & Wan, E. W. (2012). How can stressed employees deliver better customer service? The underlying self-regulation depletion mechanism. *Journal of Marketing*, 76(1), 119–137. https://doi.org/10.1509/jm.10.0202

Chen, J., Kang, H., Wang, Y., & Zhou, M. (2021). Thwarted psychological needs: the negative impact of customer mistreatment on service employees and the moderating role of empowerment HRM practices. *Personnel Review, 50*(7/8), 1566–1581. https://doi.org/10.1108/PR-06-2020-0489

Dailypay.com. (2022). What is the average employee retention rate by industry? [2022 Update]. https://www.dailypay.com/resource-center/blog/employee-retention-rate/, last accessed on January 11, 2023.

Dale Carnegie Research Institute. (2017). Employee engagement: It's Time to Go 'All-In': Making engagement a daily priority for leaders. https://studioassets.blob.core.windows.net/production/0-DCA/content/white-paper-and-ebook/english/Employee%20Engagement%20It's%20Time%20to%20Go%20All%20In.pdf, last accessed on January 11, 2023.

Fisk, G. M., & Neville, L. B. (2011). Effects of customer entitlement on service workers' physical and psychological well-being: A study of Waitstaff employees. *Journal of Occupational Health Psychology, 16*(4), 391–405. doi: 10.1037/a0023802. PMID: 21688917.

Foulk, T., Woolum, A., & Erez, A. (2016). Catching rudeness is like catching a cold: The contagion effects of low-intensity negative behaviors. *Journal of Applied Psychology, 101*(1), 50–67. doi: 10.1037/apl0000037

Gallup (a). State of the global workplace: 2022 Report. https://www.gallup.com/workplace/349484/state-of-the-global-workplace-2022-report.aspx, last accessed on January 11, 2023.

Gallup (b). Build an exit program that improves retention and creates positive exit experiences. https://www.gallup.com/workplace/246512/exit-perspective-paper.aspx, last accessed on January 11, 2023.

Gallup. (2020). The relationship between engagement at work and organizational outcomes. 2020 Q12® Meta-Analysis: 10th Edition. https://www.gallup.com/workplace/321725/gallup-q12-meta-analysis-report.aspx, last accessed on January 11, 2023.

Golkar, A., Johansson, E., Kasahara, M., Osika, W., Perski, A., & Savic, I. (2014). The influence of work-related chronic stress on the regulation of emotion and on functional connectivity in the brain. *PLoS One, 9*(9), e104550. doi: 10.1371/journal.pone.0104550.

Grandey, A. A. (2003). When "the show must go on": Surface acting and deep acting as determinants of emotional exhaustion and peer-rated service delivery. *Academy of Management Journal, 46*(1), 86–96. https://doi.org/10.2307/30040678

Grandey, A. A., Dickter, D. N., & Sin, H.-P. (2004). The customer is not always right: customer aggression and emotion regulation of service employees. *Journal of Organizational Behavior, 25*, 397–418. https://doi.org/10.1002/job.252

Greenbaum, R. L., Quade, M. J., Mawritz, M. B., Kim, J., & Crosby, D. (2014). When the customer is unethical: The explanatory role of employee emotional exhaustion onto work–family conflict, relationship conflict with coworkers, and job neglect. *Journal of Applied Psychology, 99*(6), 1188–1203. https://doi.org/10.1037/a0037221

Harris, Lloyd, & Ogbonna, Emmanuel. (2002). Exploring service sabotage: The antecedents, types and consequences of frontline, deviant, antiservice behaviors. *Journal of Service Research, 4*, 163–183. doi: 10.1177/1094670502004003001.

Harter, J. (2022). U.S. employee engagement slump continues. https://www.gallup.com/workplace/391922/employee-engagement-slump-continues.aspx, last accessed on January 11, 2023.

Hochschild, A. R. (2012). *The Managed Heart* (3rd ed.). California: University of California Press.

Huang, Y.-K., & Kwok, L. (2021). Customer mistreatment and employee customer-focused voice: the bright and dark sides of felt trust. *International Journal of Contemporary Hospitality Management*, 33(10), 3379–3399. https://doi.org/10.1108/IJCHM-12-2020-1497

Hur, W.-M., Moon, T., & Jun, J.-K. (2016). The effect of workplace incivility on service employee creativity: the mediating role of emotional exhaustion and intrinsic motivation. *Journal of Services Marketing*, 30(3), 302–315. https://doi.org/10.1108/JSM-10-2014-0342

Hur, W.-M., Moon, T. W., & Han, S.-J. (2015). The effect of customer incivility on service employees' customer orientation through double-mediation of surface acting and emotional exhaustion. *Journal of Service Theory and Practice*, 25(4), 394–413. https://doi.org/10.1108/JSTP-02-2014-0034

Karatepe, O. M., Yorganci, I., & Haktanir, M. (2009). Outcomes of customer verbal aggression among hotel employees. *International Journal of Contemporary Hospitality Management*, 21(6), 713–733. https://doi.org/10.1108/09596110910975972

Kim, H., & Qu, H. (2019). Employees' burnout and emotional intelligence as mediator and moderator in the negative spiral of incivility. *International Journal of Contemporary Hospitality Management*, 31(3), 1412–1431. https://doi.org/10.1108/IJCHM-12-2017-0794

Laurano, M. (2015). The true cost of a bad hire. https://b2b-assets.glassdoor.com/the-true-cost-of-a-bad-hire.pdf, last accessed on January 11, 2023.

Lavelle, J. J., Rupp, D. E., Herda, D. N., Pandey, A., & Lauck, J. R. (2021). Customer injustice and employee performance: Roles of emotional exhaustion, surface acting, and emotional demands–abilities fit. *Journal of Management*, 47(3), 654–682. https://doi.org/10.1177/0149206319869426

Liu, X., van Jaarsveld, D. D. & Yanadori, Y. (2022). Customer aggression, employee voice and quit rates: Evidence from the frontline service workforce. *British Journal of Industrial Relations*, 60, 348–370. https://doi.org/10.1111/bjir.12610.

Lynch, S. (2021). How I rebuilt my life after burnout: Stephen's story. https://happiful.com/how-i-rebuilt-my-life-after-burnout/, last accessed on January 11, 2023

Maranges, H., & Baumeister, R. (2016). Self-control and ego depletion. In: Kathleen D. Vohs & Roy F. Baumeister (Eds.), *The Handbook of Self-Regulation* (pp. 42–61). New York: Guilford Press.

McFeely, S., & Wigert, B. (2019). This fixable problem costs U.S. businesses $1 Trillion. https://www.gallup.com/workplace/247391/fixable-problem-costs-businesses-trillion.aspx, last accessed on January 11, 2023.

Michel, Alexandra. (2016). Burnout and the brain. https://www.psychologicalscience.org/observer/burnout-and-the-brain, last accessed on January 11, 2023.

Needham, I., Abderhalden, C., Halfens, R. J., Fischer, J. E., & Dassen, T. (2005). Non-somatic effects of patient aggression on nurses: A systematic review. *Journal of Advanced Nursing*, 49(3), 283–296. doi: 10.1111/j.1365-2648.2004.03286.x

Pendell, Ryan. (2022). The World's $7.8 Trillion Workplace Problem. https://www.gallup.com/workplace/393497/world-trillion-workplace-problem.aspx, last accessed on April 26, 2023

Porath, Christine, & Erez, Amir. (2007). Does rudeness really matter? The effects of rudeness on task performance and helpfulness. *Academy of Management Journal*, 50, 1181–1197. doi: 10.5465/amj.2007.20159919.

Prnewswire.com (2021). Global employee engagement software market size to reach around 370 USD Million by 2026 with CAGR of 13.5% Over 2020 to 2026 - Zion Market Research. https://www.prnewswire.com/news-releases/global-employee-engagement-software-market-size-to-reach-around-370-usd-million-by-2026-with-cagr-of-13-5-over-2020-to-2026--zion-market-research-301375185.html, last accessed on January 11, 2023.

Pu, Bo, Ji, Siyu, & Sang, Wenyuan. (2022). Effects of customer incivility on turnover intention in China's hotel employees: A chain mediating model. *Journal of Hospitality and Tourism Management*, 50, 327–336. doi: 10.1016/j.jhtm.2022.02.004.

Rafaeli, A., Altman, D., & Yom-Tov, G. (2019). Cognitive and emotional load influence response time of service agents: A large scale analysis of chat service conversations. In: *Proceedings of the 52nd Hawaii International Conference on System Sciences*.

Rafaeli, A., Erez, A., Ravid, S., Derfler-Rozin, R., Treister, D. E., & Scheyer, R. (2012). When customers exhibit verbal aggression, employees pay cognitive costs. *Journal of Applied Psychology*, 97(5), 931–950. doi: 10.1037/a0028559

Riskin, A., Erez, A., Foulk, T. A., Kugelman, A., Gover, A., Shoris, I., Riskin, K. S., & Bamberger, P. A. (2015). The impact of rudeness on medical team performance: A randomized trial. *Pediatrics*, 136(3), 487–495. doi: 10.1542/peds.2015-1385.

Rosen, C. C., Koopman, J., Gabriel, A. S., & Johnson, R. E. (2016). Who strikes back? A daily investigation of when and why incivility begets incivility. *Journal of Applied Psychology*, 101(11), 1620–1634. doi: 10.1037/apl0000140

Savic, I. (2015). Structural changes of the brain in relation to occupational stress. *Cereb Cortex*, 25(6), 1554–1564. doi: 10.1093/cercor/bht348

Setupmyhotel.com. Front Desk Services Audit Check list for Check-in process. https://setupmyhotel.com/formats/fo/392-service-stnd-checklist-check-in.html, last accessed on January 11, 2023.

Skarlicki, D. P., van Jaarsveld, D. D., & Walker, D. D. (2008). Getting even for customer mistreatment: The role of moral identity in the relationship between customer interpersonal injustice and employee sabotage. *Journal of Applied Psychology*, 93(6), 1335–1347. https://doi.org/10.1037/a0012704

Sliter, M., Jex, S., Wolford, K., & McInnerney, J. (2010). How rude! Emotional labor as a mediator between customer incivility and employee outcomes. *Journal of Occupational Health Psychology*, 15(4), 468–481. doi: 10.1037/a0020723. PMID: 21058859.

Sliter, M., Sliter, K., & Jex, S. (2012). The employee as a punching bag: The effect of multiple sources of incivility on employee withdrawal behavior and sales performance. *Journal of Organizational Behavior*, 33, 121–139. https://doi.org/10.1002/job.767

Society for Human Resource Management. (2017). 2017 Human Capital Benchmarking Report. https://www.shrm.org/hr-today/trends-and-forecasting/research-and-surveys/

Documents/2017-Human-Capital-Benchmarking.pdf, last accessed on January 11, 2023.

Szczygiel, D. D., & Bazińska, R. (2021). Emotional intelligence mitigates the effects of customer incivility on surface acting and exhaustion in service occupations: A moderated mediation model. *Frontiers in Psychology*, 11, 506085. doi: 10.3389/fpsyg.2020.506085

Tan, A. J. M., Loi, R., Lam, L. W., & Chow, C. C. (2020). Buffering negative impacts of jaycustomer behavior on service employees. *Journal of Services Marketing*, 34(5), 635–650. https://doi.org/10.1108/JSM-03-2019-0112

Tripp, T., & Bies, R. (2009). *Getting Even: The Truth about Workplace Revenge--And How to Stop It*. Hoboken, NJ: Jossey-Bass.

van Jaarsveld, D. D., Walker, D. D., Restubog, S. L. D., Skarlicki, D., Chen, Y., & Frické, P. H. (2021). Unpacking the relationship between customer (in)justice and employee turnover outcomes: Can fair supervisor treatment reduce employees' emotional turmoil? *Journal of Service Research*, 24(2), 301–319. https://doi.org/10.1177/1094670519883949

Walker, D. D., van Jaarsveld, D. D., Skarlicki, D. P. (2017). Sticks and stones can break my bones but words can also hurt me: The relationship between customer verbal aggression and employee incivility. *Journal of Applied Psychology*, 102(2), 163–179. doi: 10.1037/apl0000170.

Wang, C.-H., & Chen, H.-T. (2020). Relationships among workplace incivility, work engagement and job performance. *Journal of Hospitality and Tourism Insights*, 3(4), 415–429. https://doi.org/10.1108/JHTI-09-2019-0105

Wen, Ji, Li, Yina, & Hou, Pingping. (2016). Customer mistreatment behavior and hotel employee organizational citizenship behavior: The mediating role of perceived organizational support. *Nankai Business Review International*, 7, 322–344. doi: 10.1108/NBRI-02-2016-0009.

Workpulse, QSR industry operations vs employee satisfaction, https://www.workpulse.com/qsr-industry-operations-vs-employee-satisfaction/#:~:text=Compared%20to%20other%20industries%2C%20the,its%20new%20employees%20every%20year., 2020, last accessed on April 26, 2023

Xiongtao, H., Wenzhu, L., Haibin, L., & Shanshi, L. (2021). How gig worker responds to negative customer treatment: The effects of work meaningfulness and traits of psychological resilience. *Frontiers in Psychology*, 12, 783372. doi: 10.3389/fpsyg.2021.783372

Chapter 4

When and Why Customers Act Abusively?

I wish it was easier to write this chapter. I wish I could say "This is the one thing that triggers customer aggression." I wish it was as simple as that, but unfortunately it is not. In fact, going for an easy explanation would obscure a lot of important aspects of customer abuse, and would ultimately make it more difficult for us to fight it.

The short answer to what drives or triggers customer abuse is this: cultural factors, such as the "Customer is always right" philosophy, form the soil upon which aggression grows; whether this plant from hell will flourish or perish is further determined by customers' predispositions and idiosyncrasies; finally, situational factors, amongst which service dissatisfaction is the most prominent, create the conditions, which may support or suffocate abuse. As with any plants' growth, it is rarely enough to have just one of these factors in place to have a fully developed living being.

Seeking for a single-word explanation of customer abuse is futile. We can, for example, say that it is only when customers are unhappy that they lash out. This perspective makes aggressive behavior sound almost like a justified vengeance or a crusade on the customers' side to right a wrong. Perceived injustice by customers is indeed a major source of employee-directed aggression, there is no denying it. Consequently, it is also the biggest thing companies can improve on to fight customer abuse. But putting it all on customer satisfaction would be way too much. After all, we are all unhappy with some service interactions, or with some aspects of them. Yet, we don't all go around yelling at employees or threatening them or calling them stupid. Normalizing the reaction will clearly not help to eradicate it.

We can also say that abusive customers are a..holes, angry, ostracized individuals with whom we, the polite and law-abiding citizens, have nothing to do with. Hannah Arendt taught us an important lesson on this point close to 60 years ago. She followed the trial against Adolf Eichmann in Jerusalem for the New Yorker, and her reportages are brought together in her book, *Eichmann in Jerusalem*. She discusses a lot of aspects related

DOI: 10.4324/9781003402565-5

to the trial, including its legitimacy, Eichmann's behavior, the advent of Nazism in Germany, and plenty of others. The most critical insights though, at least in my humble view, is included as the subtitle of the book; its full title is in fact *Eichmann in Jerusalem: A Report on the Banality of Evil* (Arendt, 2006). It is the latter phrase that strikes me as something perhaps all of us would do well to keep in mind. It is not the most hideous, blood-thirsty, Jew-hating, or psychopathic individuals that organized the Holo-caust. It was people like Eichmann, a very ordinary, banal person who did it. Without any attempt of paying disrespect to anyone who has the doubt-ful pleasure of reading the book in your hands, it is people like me and you who often act aggressively toward employees. There are, of course, personality characteristics that make some people more likely to do it, but it's not the whole story.

We can also attribute customer abuse to an aspect of the modern-day consumption culture. By now, we are all taught that "the customer is always right," that the customer can demand the best possible service, that we are right in wanting more and more. Once again, I am not fundamen-tally opposed to this perspective, for it has brought some very welcome advancements in the way we live our lives. But if the customer is king, what does this make service employees, and what rights does it give him or her? This philosophy promotes a power-differential between customers and employees, which then leads to a much lower threshold for acting aggressively toward the latter. Yet, as we saw in the previous paragraphs, a single-item explanation is unlikely to bring us close to understanding the essence of customer abuse. After all, we all live in exactly the same con-sumption culture, we are exposed to the same messages, but not all of us act abusively toward employees, do we?

Research shows all three of these elements – personality, situational fac-tors, and societal factors – have their place in the cocktail of factors that ultimately triggers customer abuse. It is my humble view that even though it might complicate things, we need to have a look at all of them if we are to learn how to fight customer abuse. Only a holistic view would give us enough insights into what actions we can all take, what effect can we expect, and even which are the things we probably cannot change and need to learn to live with. With this in mind, it's time that we dive into the factors that under-pin customer aggression and more broadly – customer's deviant behavior.

Situational Factors

Poor Customer Service

So far, we spoke about customer abuse mostly from the perspective of employees; we discussed how it impacts their personal and professional lives, and we saw what costs companies pay when customers act aggressively toward their employees. Of course, this is far from the full picture. What we have deliberately left aside so far is the second party in this unfortunate transaction of rudeness – customers. To get a better understanding of why they sometimes act abusively toward employees, we need to also try walking in their shoes for a second. This is not intended to justify any of it; that aggression and abuse and mistreatment in any context are unacceptable remains my firm belief. Nevertheless, there is a lot we can learn about the process by which things escalate when we take the customers' perspective, and this is what we will try to do in this chapter.

To begin with, I think we need to ask ourselves a couple of very fundamental questions such as "Why customers buy things in the first place?," "Why do companies exist?," and "What do we want when we pay for products or services?" This might, as a first place, seem like just as a nice-to-have chat, but it is in fact essential if we are to understand things from customers' perspective.

The very basic premise of consumption is that we exchange one type of resource (typically money) for another (goods or services) if and when we value the latter higher than the former, and we cannot produce it ourselves. This holds true for both marketplace transactions such as buying apples or furniture, and for cases like paying our taxes. In the latter situation, it might be a bit more difficult to see it, but it's there; first, we always have options – when we pay our taxes, we are essentially saying that we are staying out of trouble with the authorities more than the money we will be paying; and second, we do pay to get services in return, of course, albeit in the rather long term.

If we exchange things when we value what we get more than what we give, the next question becomes what do we mean by "value" and who determines what value is. What I believe[1] is that value is always co-created between the customer and actors such as the company providing the product or the service, and how much value the customer receives from the transaction is always determined by the customer themselves. Value itself is not embedded in products or service; it is rather created in the consumption process, which in fact from this perspective is akin to a production process. Customers buy things to advance their stance in whichever way they have decided. There is no inherent value in pizzas, haircuts, smartphones, and apartments – it is only when customers use them and manage to do what they intended to that they create value.

Following this logic, a typical consumption process will unfold, broadly, like this[2]. A customer will realize they want to get something done, say, look better for a date tonight. We will come up with a solution, for example, getting new clothes, getting a haircut, etc. If we cannot get it or do it on our own, we as customers will find a supplier for the product or the service. We would buy the product or the service and use it to produce the intended result or see if it does the job.

Inherent at the end of this process is a question that looms large in our minds. It does not need to be a consciously asked question, but at the end of the day, we all ask ourselves "Did this product or service help me do what I wanted?," or in other words – "Was this purchase justified?" The reason for this is that we spent resources, and as we already saw, we are in fact all vigorous managers of various types of resources. What happens if we judge the purchase to be a satisfactory one? Well, we are basically saying, "I got more resources than I spent." In this case, all is well and everyone is happy and they lived happily ever after.

The more interesting question though is "What happens if we, for some reason, fail to create value?" What if we feel we are not getting enough bang for our buck?

You guessed it – we go straight back to what we discussed about stress in an earlier chapter: we, as customers, experience either a loss or a threat of loss of resources ("I spent money which didn't get the job done so now I need to spend more") or a failure to increase our resources when we invested some of them ("I wanted to improve my standing but nothing happened"). Yes, we experience dissatisfaction and stress, and the same process that we saw before from the employees' angle starts taking place in customers' minds.

When customers experience stress caused by a mismatch between the investment they have made and the outcome they get, they need to handle it. Translated to the consumption context, they are going to have the following options.

First, they might try to avoid situations that cause them stress. This translates to pure and simple churn. When the company causes us stress and if that is a pattern, we leave the company. Fair enough, we do not always have the option or don't want to cut our losses just yet. In these cases, we have a second option – we might try to change the situation.

In consumption context, changing the situation is very often done by engaging in an interaction with the supplier of the product or service. We call the contact center to get support, we return the item, etc. – in other words, we invest even more resources or vehemently try to protect ourselves against losses even more. Unsurprisingly, when we increase the bet, we start expecting even more, which opens a dangerous spiral for companies in which already stressed-out customers put in even more resources. We will return to that in a minute.

The third option is to simply distract ourselves from the case. This might be a viable option, but it is definitely not a sustainable one. I mean, if our TV breaks, we might try to manage our frustration by going for a walk, but no matter how nice our walk is, it is not going to fix our TV.

Similarly, we might try to change our thoughts about the dissatisfying experience. This is feasible indeed, and we might manage to calm ourselves down by seeing the situation in a different light. Again, though, this might help us control our anger, for example, but it is unlikely to fix the issue.

Lastly, if none of the things we went through so far works, we as customers are left with one final resort – we can try to manage our emotions. Customer dissatisfaction very often leads to feelings of anger, for example. If all else fails, we might try to manage the expression of our anger so as not to act aggressively toward employees.

In this process, there are two critical points at which customers might start becoming abusive toward employees. The first point is the initial dissatisfaction with the product or the service; the second one comes later in the process, when customers try to change the situation, or what in customer service language is called to initiate a service recovery process. True, some customers might lash out just because. You know, bad hair day, bad mood, etc. This does happen, yes. But a study after study shows convincingly, that the major source of customer abuse is fully within companies' control, and it is related to the initial delivery of a good product or service, or to taking appropriate mitigation efforts if anything goes wrong.

To being with, have a look at what one study participant shared with the researchers who asked customers to share their experiences with service failure management by companies.

> The lawyer was retained to represent me in court... After paying the retainer ($1000), he was never available... It was disappointing (Episode 1) ... When I tried to contact him again ..., he still would not return my calls. By this time, I was getting angry (Episode 2) ... I finally left one more message and I told him how incompetent he has been ... I would be filling a complaint of abandonment ... (I was) extremely angry with his representation. I felt like he deserved to be punished ... I ended up yelling, screaming and then crying, and told him I was going to try to have him disbarred (Episode 3). (Female, 36, U.S. legal service).
> (Surachartkumtonkun, McColl-Kennedy, and Patterson, 2015, 177)

This is a brilliant example of what the authors discovered. It is very rare that customer will become aggressive immediately after the initial service failure. More than half of the study participants reported negative emotions, but a low level of them in the beginning, and almost no one reported feeling rage. They felt mostly a threat to their economic resources and injustice, but almost no threat to their self-esteem or loss of control.

Things change dramatically if the customer is still unhappy after the first unsuccessful recovery episode (the "I was getting angry part in the quote above"). The threat to economic resources is much lower at this point but a quarter of customers feel a threat to their self-esteem and a fifth feel they don't have control. Hand in hand with this, emotions escalate and fully 70% of customers experience rage. If things keep going in the same direction, more and more customers start to experience loss of control, which further aggravates things.

A very similar pattern was discovered by researchers[3] when they investigated the progression of negative customer emotions throughout the interaction with companies related to fixing an issue. To use one excellent example,

> ...a Chinese middle-aged female customer arranged the purchase and installation of an air-conditioning unit in her apartment from a department store in Shanghai, China. Within 24 hours of installation, the unit began leaking water inside her apartment. Repeated attempts by phone to store personnel and a personal visit to the store manager failed to get the seller to acknowledge responsibility for the problem. It was not until two weeks later, following representations to the consumer affairs bureau, that the problem was acknowledged and action taken by the seller. Again at each episode, the interviewee's reported emotion progressed from an initial annoyance to frustration to extreme anger, as a sense of being cheated and then of desperation surfaced.... This interviewee felt so strongly about the incident that she became extremely emotional during the interview, even though the incident had occurred 6 months previously.
>
> (Patterson et al., 2009, 12)

In both of these studies, we can very clearly see the pattern we discussed before. First, there is the initial dissatisfaction or surprise – customers are not getting enough for their investment, which causes them negative emotions, albeit not particularly strong ones. In the beginning, the threat to loss of resources is related to a violated sense of justice and to economic losses. At this point, the situation is still manageable. It becomes much more difficult if companies don't address the issue appropriately. This is where economic considerations are left behind and feelings of threat start looming large. Customers feel that their very essence – their self-esteem – is put at risk. They feel they are not in control. Their sense of justice is violated. And this is when things are very likely to escalate and explode...

Now, saying the word "justice" in a book about consumption might seem odd at first; we are probably more likely to associate it with social issues like inequality, for example, rather than business challenges. Yet, years of research show convincingly that it is exactly the feeling of fairness or justice that is behind customers' satisfaction with customer service, especially in the context of service recovery – when companies try to mitigate the damage a failure to deliver is causing. Fairness, in this context, "…is perceived when the ratio of an individual's outputs (benefits) to inputs (financial and nonfinancial efforts) is balanced with the ratio of the other party … ." (Gelbrich and Roschk, 2011, 27). Inherent in this definition is that customers don't simply want to get something for themselves, especially in service recovery contexts; it is rather related to restoring justice – customers feel that companies are gaining more benefits than them, and consequently require a redress to equalize the relationship.

In the consumption context, justice is typically conceptualized as having three distinctive dimensions. First, there is the idea of procedural justice. It refers to "how the complainant perceives the means of decision-making and conflict resolution used by the organization" (Gelbrich and Roschk, 2011, 27). "Is the process easy?," "Is the process flexible?," "Does it allow for a timely resolution?" are all aspects of the process that fall squarely in the procedural justice bucket.

Next, you have interactional justice, which refers, perhaps quite obviously, to how the interaction with the company went. Customers perceive a high level of interactional justice when "information is exchanged and … outcomes are communicated in a polite and respectful manner" (Gelbrich and Roschk, 2011, 27).

Lastly, there is the idea of distributive justice. If procedural justice is about the process, and interactional justice is about the way things are communicated, distributive justice concerns the outcome of the complaint process. It captures, Gelbrich and Roschk explain, "the perceived allocation of organizational resources in response to a complaint, that is, the apparent subjective benefit customers receive to offset the inconvenience resulting from a company's failure" (Gelbrich and Roschk, 2011, 27).

Years of research show that all three dimensions play a vital part in the process of making customers happy with service recovery. They might have different impact depending on the situation and the industry, but all three of them matter. And more closely related to the topic of this book, justice perceptions have been shown to be a major driver of customer abuse. In one study,

> More than half of the customers reported a situation in which they had a problem with a product or a service provided by the organization, and their negative emotions over this organizational issue manifested as incivility. … For instance, one person wrote: '… When I called my cell phone company I called because I was frustrated with the organization as whole, not with the service person who happened to get stuck answering my call. I definitely took my frustration out on her because of this. However, I think it is because I saw her as the voice of the organization; I mean where else was I to put my frustration?'
>
> (Slitter and Jones, 2016, 211)

The evidence for this is not just anecdotal. For example, a survey among 68 companies in Korea, interested in whether perceptions of justice in any way trigger customers' dysfunctional behavior more broadly, including delayed payments, ignoring the supplier, and, of most relevance for us, acting rudely toward the supplier, discovered that all three dimensions of justice – procedural, distributive, and interactional – significantly impact customers' deviant behavior. The more injustice customers felt, the more negative emotions they experienced, and the more likely they were to mistreat suppliers in one way or another. Speaking of negative emotions, do you remember the study among call center workers we discussed previously that showed how longer messages and the ones that include more emotional words slow employees down (Altman et al., 2020)? The first time we went through the results we saw that negative affect has an especially deleterious effect on employee performance.

There was one very important aspect of this relationship that we didn't discuss back then though. The researchers not only discovered that negative emotions slow service representatives down but also that this slower response and the fact that more messages are needed to solve the customers' issues results in even more negative emotions on their side. A spiral of negativity takes shape – negative emotions lead to poor performance, which leads to negative emotions, and on and on it goes. As Yagil and Luria put it, "Customers frame their behavior as inseparable from script violations by the service provider. Deviance is viewed as a justified act of taking charge to substitute an unmotivated or incapable service provider." (Yagil and Luria, 2014, 921).

So far, we only discussed cases in which customers mistreated employees because of a company's fault. Things get even worse when customers perceive the employee him or herself to be acting in an uncivil or rude manner. In a seminal article by Kate Daunt and Lloyd Harris, they reported the results of a study with close to 400 customers who admitted they have deliberately acted in a dysfunctional manner in a hospitality setting in the last three months. In their words,

> ...perceptions of employee deviance are directly associated with the severity of customer misbehaviour ... . Thus, the data reveal that high levels of perceived employee deviance in a service outlet are linked with the perpetration of more severe forms of customer misbehaviour in the same service outlet (compared with low levels of perceived employee deviance).
>
> (Daunt and Harris, 2014, 234)

Once again, we see the role of perceived justice in the process – employee misbehavior is deemed unfair by customers and to restore justice, they strike back at them in a process very similar to the one we saw in the previous chapter when we discussed how employees often strike back when they experience customer abuse.

Relatedly, in another study in Korea,[4] researchers surveyed both employees and customers in a foreign language academy to understand if employee deviant behavior is related to customer one. When employees displayed a high level of what is called citizenship behavior (courtesy, sportsmanship, altruism) all was well – customers were more satisfied and displayed more citizenship behavior themselves, like providing feedback, helping other customers, and recommending the organization. Not so when employees acted in a deviant manner and purposely worked incorrectly or slowly, or when they ignored people at work, or when they were being nasty or rude to a customer. This kind of employee behavior lowered customer satisfaction and ultimately led to more deviant behavior on the customers' side as well.

Similarly, in another study of how when employees mistreat customers, they return the "favor," three researchers investigated this relationship in a restaurant setting in Taiwan. They interviewed more than 200 customers and discovered that "customers who perceive service sabotage on the part of frontline employees, would be more likely to participate in deviant behavior themselves. Employee service sabotage evidently has a directly positive effect on customer deviant behaviors" (Hu, Lai, and King, 2020, 1139).

Lastly, in 2016, Albrecht et al. (2017) reported the results of a study in which they had collaborators observe more than 200 employee–customer interactions and rate them according to the degree of friendliness the employee showed. In unison with the studies we discussed so far, they found out that the more unfriendly the employee was, the more unfriendly the customer acted. The relationship between the two was so strong that customer unfriendliness was fully 40% more likely to happen when employees were unfriendly.

So far, we spoke about two major causes of customer abuse – dissatisfaction with the product or service, and mistreatment of customers by employees; one especially dangerous situation is posed by the service recovery process during which employees try to fix service failures. There are, however, two more situations in which customers are very likely to be triggered to act aggressively.

The first one we already spoke about at some length before when we discussed how sometimes employees hide their real emotions and fake positive ones in front of customers. This is the so-called surface acting phenomenon. Previously, we saw that surface acting is often used by employees as a withdrawal strategy – to distance themselves from a potentially stressful situation. Ironically, surface acting has in fact been found to be more emotionally draining, and thus a dysfunctional form of emotion management. But surface acting does even more harm than this. A study among customer service representatives from a call center in China[5] discovered that when they employed the surface acting strategy, employees received more negative customer treatment and subsequently were even more exhausted at the end of the work day. So not only outright mistreatment by employees makes customers strike back, but even faked friendliness does so.

The second situation concerns what is known as the domino-effect. Remember when earlier we spoke about norms and we saw that there are two types of them: injunctive and descriptive ones. Injunctive norms are related to how we think one should behave and what is appropriate; others' approval of certain actions is a good indicator of injunctive norms. Descriptive norms, on the other hands, concern what one observes. For example, seeing that people greet each other politely tells us that this is an acceptable, if not encouraged, behavior. And when we see people running in the park, we might infer that this is what people do in this city. The domino effect is strongly connected with descriptive norms and refers to the fact that people tend to be influenced by how others are acting.

To investigate this, in a very interesting experiment, two researchers, Alastair Tombs and Janet McColl-Kennedy (2013), exposed participants to other customers dining in a restaurant and displaying either enjoyment, annoyance, or surprise. Importantly, the participants caught the emotion simply by observing customers. The ones who saw customers enjoying themselves felt more enjoyment, while those who observed annoyed customers experienced more annoyance. Emotions, like a flu, are contagious, and when customers act aggressively, they spread this behavior toward others as well.

So far, we saw four different situational drivers of customer aggression. It could be triggered by an uncivil or rude employee; it is very often triggered by poor service recovery; employees who surface act also experience more mistreatment by customers; and simply observing other people acting aggressively sends us a message that this is an acceptable behavior and we are more likely to go along.

Now, all of these are clearly related to other people's behavior. There is, however, one final situational driver that we need to have a look at, and one that is not in any way related to how others act. Research in the domain customer abuse shows clearly that a host of things related to the physical environment itself can increase the odds of aggressive behavior. Interestingly, these are all very subtle elements, which we as customers often don't recognize as having an impact on us, yet they profoundly affect our behaviors.

The Physical Environment

One of the leading researchers on how the sensory input we receive changes how we consume, Aradhna Krishna, explains that sensory marketing

> "engages the consumers' senses and affects their perception, judgment and behavior." From a managerial perspective, sensory marketing can be used to create subconscious triggers that characterize consumer perceptions of abstract notions of the product (e.g., its sophistication or quality). Given the gamut of explicit marketing appeals made to consumers every day, subconscious triggers which appeal to the basic senses may be a more efficient way to engage consumers.
>
> (Krishna, 2012, 332)

Examples abound.

Take touch for instance. It is the first sense to develop, it is a very personal sense, and we have a high level of control over it, but it has a limited reach (unlike vision or hearing). A plethora of often times outright amusing experiments show how subtly experiencing touch changes what we do. Here's a brief list: a tap on the shoulder increases our sense of security and makes us more likely to take risks (Levav and Argo, 2010); we are more likely to comply to requests when we are touched (literally) by the person asking us for it (Guéguen and Jacob, 2006); touching has been associated with better performance of… basketball teams! (Kraus, Huang, and Keltner, 2010); being touched (again, literally) by a waitress increases the tip we leave in restaurants (Hornik, 1992); and finally, touching a product makes us think we already own it so it increases the chance that we'll buy it – this is the so-called "endowment effect" (Mulcahy and Riedel, 2018).

Relatedly, temperature also has a profound impact on what we do. For example, studies shows that when we associate physical warmth and coldness with social one. Researchers explain:

> physical warmth positively influences social perceptions, social trust, and social proximity…, while feeling lonely (i.e., social exclusion) relates to perceptions of physical coldness or desire for warm remedies … . That is, experiencing physical warmth relates to interpersonal affection whereas experiencing physical coldness relates to exclusion and self-centeredness … .
>
> (Lee, Rotman, and Perkins, 2014, 234)

To give a final example, our attitudes and behaviors are also affected by our sense of audition. From sound symbolism to music tempo, research has discovered a host of ways in which our auditory environment changes how we feel. For instance, ice cream with the brand Frosh sounds creamier than one under the name of Frish. and the sound food make when eaten impacts our perception of its freshness. Going further, shoppers buy more French wine when French music is playing in the background and more German one if the music is German, classical music enhances pleasure while pop one increases arousal, and perhaps with a higher impact on our waistlines, high-pitch music promotes healthier food choices (Huang and Labroo, 2020), and so does low-volume one (Biswas, Lund, and Szocs, 2019)[6].

This list can go on and on, and shows unequivocally that our physical environment has a profound impact on how we act. Krishna's proposition that "subconscious triggers which appeal to the basic senses may be a more efficient way to engage consumers." (Krishna, 2012, 332) certainly appears to have a lot of merit.

The thing is, this very same logic holds, unfortunately, in the other direction as well – what can be used to engage consumers may also, inadvertently, make them dissatisfied with the service, and we already saw that this is one of the key triggers for customer abuse. Research investigating directly how factors from the physical environment increase the chance of customers acting aggressively is, unfortunately, scant, yet there is plenty of evidence to suggest the existence of this connection.

One such example comes from a study conducted as early as 1996 by two researchers, Wakefield and Blodgett (1996), who investigated which of the elements of the servicescape (the physical environment in which services are provided) impact customers' attitudes and behaviors the most. Following the seminal article by Mary Jo Bitner (1992), they defined the servicescape in leisure service settings as consisting of layout accessibility (the way furnishings, equipment, service areas, and other such elements are arranged), aesthetics of the facility (design, décor, etc.), seating comfort, electronic equipment and signs ("signs/symbols/artefacts that can be used to enhance the leisure experience" (Wakefield and Blodgett, 1996, 48)), and cleanliness, which is rather self-explanatory. In three different settings – major college football, minor league baseball, and casinos – they discovered that all of these factors[7] significantly impacted the perceived quality of service, which ultimately leads to lower customer satisfaction.

More directly related to the topic at hand, in 2012, Kate Daunt and Lloyd Harris reported the results from a survey with 380 customers who have acted in a dysfunctional manner in hospitality settings in the past three months. They found convincing evidence that servicescape characteristics significantly impact the severity of the dysfunctional behavior. These characteristics include, for example, level of crowdedness, temperature, air quality, music loudness, how appealing the exterior of the outlet was, and how well-maintained does the exterior look. Negative evaluations on those contribute considerably to customers' deviant behavior.

And finally, Sliter and Jones (2016) also included servicescape aspects in their investigation of what causes customer incivility. In a study among full-time customer service workers, they found out that a plethora of service environment aspects had a significant impact on the number of customer incivility incidents; these aspects include, for example, the layout of the facility (is it easy to find your way around), its aesthetics, its cleanliness, and busyness. Similarly, as in the Daunt and Harris' study, negative evaluations on these aspects contributed considerably to customer incivility.

As a brief recap, so far in this chapter we saw that the major triggers for customer abuse are dissatisfaction with either the product or the service the company provides, failure on the side of the company to successfully mitigate the consequences of the latter and do service recovery well, (perceived) mistreatment by employees, and various physical environment factors such as temperature, music, and crowdedness. While companies don't have full control over these factors, there most certainly are things they can do to lower the burden from employees. We'll talk more about this in the next chapter, but a clear message to all leaders who want to improve employee experience begins to emerge: if you want to improve employee experience, you need to eradicate customer abuse or at the very least – help – employees deal with it; and if you want to eradicate customer abuse or at the very least – minimize it – you need to improve customers' experience with your products or services, and with your recovery process. There is a hidden cost of bad customer experience and it is called customer abuse. When companies try to save money from CX efforts, their employees pay the price.

As correct as this is, it is of course not the only factor that triggers customer abuse. There is also the question of what personality factors make it more likely for customers to act aggressively, i.e., why do some people lash out while others don't? Relatedly, could there be personality traits that make some employees more likely to experience customer abuse? And are there employee characteristics that exacerbate the impact of customer abuse? These are the questions to which we will turn next.

Personality Factors

Personality Factors of the Customer

He spoke, and returned madly to the same reflection, and his tears stirred the water, and the image became obscured in the rippling pool. As he saw it vanishing, he cried out ' Where do you fly to? Stay, cruel one, do not abandon one who loves you! I am allowed to gaze at what

I cannot touch, and so provide food for my miserable passion!' While he weeps, he tears at the top of his clothes: then strikes his naked chest with hands of marble. His chest flushes red when they strike it, as apples are often pale in part, part red, or as grapes in their different bunches are stained with purple when they are not yet ripe.

As he sees all this reflected in the dissolving waves, he can bear it no longer, but as yellow wax melts in a light flame, as morning frost thaws in the sun, so he is weakened and melted by love, and worn away little by little by the hidden fire. He no longer retains his colour, the white mingled with red, no longer has life and strength, and that form so pleasing to look at, nor has he that body which Echo loved. Still, when she saw this, though angered and remembering, she pitied him, and as often as the poor boy said 'Alas!' she repeated with her echoing voice 'Alas!' and when his hands strike at his shoulders, she returns the same sounds of pain. His last words as he looked into the familiar pool were 'Alas, in vain, beloved boy!' and the place echoed every word, and when he said 'Goodbye!' Echo also said 'Goodbye!'

He laid down his weary head in the green grass, death closing those eyes that had marvelled at their lord's beauty.

(Metamorphoses Book III)

This was the story of Narcissus – the unfortunate mythological character who fell deeply in love with his own reflection and perished because of this affection; and also, the character who gave the name to a personality style which in some people is as pronounced as to be dubbed a personality disorder – narcissism. People who score high in narcissism are characterized by an exaggerated sense of self-importance, a strong sense of entitlement, being "preoccupied with fantasies about success, power, brilliance, beauty or the perfect mate" (Mayo Clinic), taking advantage of others, an insistence of having nothing but the best, manipulative behaviors, belief in their superiority, and expectation for this to be constantly recognized, among other things.

The Mayo clinic describes a host of behaviors that are signs of narcissism, and as you will notice, the majority of them are related to things we discussed previously, such as self-control, emotion regulation, dealing with stress, and anger:

- Become impatient or angry when they don't receive special treatment
- Have significant interpersonal problems and easily feel slighted
- React with rage or contempt and try to belittle the other person to make themselves appear superior
- Have difficulty regulating emotions and behavior
- Experience major problems dealing with stress and adapting to change

- Feel depressed and moody because they fall short of perfection
- Have secret feelings of insecurity, shame, vulnerability, and humiliation (Mayo Clinic)

Having been through these, it probably wouldn't come as a surprise that narcissism has been linked with aggressive behavior in general, and more closely pertaining with our topic, with customer abuse. In 2010, for instance, three researchers[8] published a paper in which they reported the results from a study showing that men with narcissistic tendencies are more likely to be unprovoked aggressors. They had about 140 participants fill in a narcissistic personality test, and then play a game in which they received and administrated electric shocks from/to an opponent who they thought is sitting in the adjacent room. During the "game," participants had the option to refrain from administering electric shocks at certain points. The question, then, is "Who aggresses?" and "How quickly?". The results support previously known findings that participants high in narcissism are more aggressive: they "displayed higher levels of (i) general aggression, (ii) initial aggression (i.e. narcissists' first acts of aggression were more extreme), and (iii) flashpoint aggression (i.e. narcissists were faster to aggress)." (Reidy, Foster, and Zeichner, 2010, 418). What Reidy and his colleagues also discovered, though, is perhaps even more worrying – people who scored higher in narcissism were also more likely to be unprovoked aggressors; for every one standard deviation on the narcissism scale, there was an about 50% higher chance that participants would needlessly administer electric shocks.

A personality trait very closely related to narcissism and part of the so-called "dark triad" (alongside with psychopathy) is Machiavellianism – the tendency to manipulate others to achieve one's goals and disregard of morality. People scoring high on this trait are more likely to agree, for example, with statements like "The best way to handle people is to tell them what they want to hear" and "There is no problem been dishonest if this help you to be more successful" (Oliveira and Veloso, 2015, 33). In 2015, a team of researchers published the results from a study[9] in which they measured Machiavellianism and other traits, alongside with participants' tendency toward dysfunctional consumer behavior. They wanted to see if it's possible to predict, based on personality traits and situational factors, whether a customer is more likely to act in a dysfunctional manner. Exhibiting the characteristics of Machiavellianism was one of the factors that contributed significantly toward this; those high in the trait were more likely to violate commonly accepted consumption norms, for instance disrespecting a company's sales representative and making a movie about it and posting it on the internet.

Another of the findings of this study is that people high in aggressive tendencies are also more likely to act in a dysfunctional manner in consumption contexts. These people are more likely, for example, to say that they "use the Internet to quarrel with people," to have "witnessed someone been beaten and I didn't do anything to stop it," and to say they have "argued energetically with an attendant that didn't do what I asked for." Like people higher in Machiavellianism, the ones who exhibited stronger aggressive tendencies were also more likely to violate consumption norms.

Perpetration of aggression, as we saw, is closely linked with pathologies like narcissism. Furthermore, studies show that it is also driven to a large extent by something much more common in our lives. The well-known Big 5 Personality Traits is a framework that is widely used to measure and study our, well, personalities. It includes extraversion, agreeableness, neuroticism, openness, and conscientiousness. At least three of these have been linked with aggressive behavior, albeit not necessarily in the same direction.

Studies have shown[10], for instance, that among men, trait aggression (a stable personality characteristic) is more common among people high in neuroticism, i.e., those among us (such as yours truly), who experience sudden and large shifts in mood, feel anxious, get upset easily, and struggle to recover from stressful events. In addition, people low in conscientiousness, the desire to perform one's tasks and duties diligently, are also more likely to exhibit aggressive behaviors. As the authors explain,

> The link between Conscientiousness and aggression is less clear than those of Neuroticism and Agreeableness, but one interpretation may be that individuals low on Conscientiousness are more impulsive and focus less on the potential consequences of their actions and thus are less deterred by the negative social consequences of aggressive and disruptive behaviors.
>
> (Dam et al., 2021)

And finally, people low in Agreeableness are also more likely to act aggressively. High Agreeableness is linked with behaviors like cooperativeness, kindness, and altruism, so it's not surprising that low scores on this dimension correlate well with aggressive tendencies. Very similar results were found by another group of researchers who studied anger and aggressive behavior among Serbian drivers; as in the research we just reviewed, they discovered that "neuroticism, agreeableness and conscientiousness predicted driving-related anger and aggression" (Jovanović et al., 2011, 43).

So far, we saw that personality traits like Narcissism, Machiavellianism, high neuroticism/negative affectivity, low agreeableness, and low conscientiousness are all linked with aggressive behaviors. But there is more. Continuing the investigation of which personality factors might make some people more likely to act aggressively with employees and other people, we turn to a paper bluntly titled, "More f#!%ing rudeness: reliable personality predictors of verbal rudeness and other ugly confrontational behaviors" (Park, Ickes, and Robinson, 2014).

The authors from the Department of Psychology at the University of Texas at Arlington discovered a host of traits that predict verbal aggression and other aggressive behaviors. First things first, people who score high on "affect intensity for anger and frustration" (AIAF) are more likely to talk aggressively to others. In case you are wondering, AIAF is the scientific term for how strongly do you and I experience anger and frustration, and is measured with items such as "I react to day-to-day frustrations in ways that other people consider extreme" and "My feelings of anger are more intense than those of most other people." (Park, Ickes, and Robinson, 2014, 31). In addition to verbal aggression, AIAF is also a reliable predictor of "ugly confrontational behaviors."

Likewise, people high in thin-skinned ego defensiveness (TSED) (my new favorite term!) are more likely to be verbally aggressive. TSED assesses the degree to which people have a hard time accepting criticism from others, i.e., how defensive they become. Think about people who are likely to agree that "People who want to blame me for their problems should just shut up and go away" and "I can't stand it when other people feel obliged to tell me what I'm doing wrong." That's TSED, and it predicts verbal aggression.

Before we close this part of the chapter, it's worth noting that further to everything we discussed so far, biases and prejudices held by the customer also impact how likely they are to abuse employees. A study of the antecedents of customer incivility by Sliter and Jones discovered an alarming list of these, including, for example, ageism, sexism, racism, classism ("wealthy people mistreating lower-class service employees" (Slitter and Jones, 2016, 211)), attractiveness bias, and even weight bias! And do have in mind that this study was conducted among customers themselves. Given that we are unlikely to openly report our biases and prejudices, the list is probably even longer than that.

A clear picture starts to emerge when we connect the dots, then. Clearly, people's behavior is triggered by certain situations and in certain environments. In addition, though, there are personality variables that make people more likely to abuse employees. A nonexhaustive list of these character traits includes, for example:

- Narcissism
- Machiavellianism
- High neuroticism/negative affectivity
- Low agreeableness
- Low conscientiousness

- ffect intensity for anger and frustration" (AIAF)
- Thin-skinned ego defensiveness (TSED)
- Reward responsiveness
- Biases and prejudices

The last bullet hints at a very important point. True, there are situational triggers and personality drivers of that unlock customer abuse. But the fact that biases and prejudices can spark customer aggression also means that there might be employee characteristics that make abuse more likely to happen. To be clear, this is not to say that customers are right to act like this; I'm merely pointing out the fact that there might be personality traits on employees' side that make them more likely to put them on the receiving end of customer abuse and/or to feel its effects more strongly. This is what we turn to next.

Personality Factors of the Employee

We already saw the significant role neuroticism plays in predicting customer aggression. Interestingly, employees who score high on these are also more likely to experience customer abuse and to feel its consequences more strongly. In a seminal article on customer abuse, Grandey, Dickter, and Sin (2004) reported the results from a study they did among call center employees investigating its impact on employees. They discovered that verbal aggression by customers leads to emotional exhaustion and time lost at work, which we already reviewed in the previous chapter. Pertaining more closely to our current topic, they also investigated the role of negative affectivity in this process; the latter is akin to neuroticism and is related to holding a negative outlook on the world and having the tendency to interpret ambiguous comments as negative ones. Their findings show that employees high in negative affectivity are more likely to report a higher frequency of customer aggression, and what is more, to find these episodes more stressful and to feel more emotionally exhausted from it.

In previous chapters, we discussed how emotional exhaustion, in turn, can have serious consequences for employees' performance. It might lead to withdrawal, inability to serve customers well, and in the worst-case scenario – to employees' sabotaging customers. The linkage between negative affectivity and customer-directed sabotage was investigated among call center employees in China. A team of researchers discovered that, sure enough, customer mistreatment increased customer sabotage among all employees. What is more important for us here is that this relationship was much more pronounced among those employees high in negative affectivity – the higher employees' score on neuroticism, the more likely they are to strike back at customers[11].

This is also corroborated by the study by Sliter and Jones (2016) we reviewed before; they interviewed a diverse group of service employees and confirmed the finding that higher levels of employee neuroticism/negative affectivity are related to higher levels of customer incivility. What is more though, is that they also investigated how likely is that low agreeableness among employees drives customer incivility. We already showed that customers who score low on this personality trait are more likely to act aggressively. What the study shows is that low agreeableness on the side of employees is also a reliable predictor of customer incivility – the lower the employee scored on agreeableness, the more likely they are to experience customer incivility.

Another consequence of customer mistreatment we discussed earlier is that it lowers employees' sense of self-verification, i.e., "the perception that one is viewed and treated in line with how they see themselves" (Amarnani et al., 2022) The latter is important for our well-being as it ensures that we have a coherent view of ourselves; when it's threatened, it puts our identity at risk and we try to restore it. When this happens, the researchers discovered, it prevents employees from going the extra mile for customers (or what is called in the academic literature customer-directed organizational citizenship behaviors). Now, this happens for all of the employees, but the effect, the researchers found out, is stronger among people high in self-esteem. In business-as-usual circumstances, the latter are more likely than those with lower self-esteem to go the extra mile. When they experience customer abuse though, their willingness to do something more for the customer diminishes, and they become as (un)likely as everyone else to go beyond what's expected of them.

And finally, before we conclude this part of the chapter, it's worth having a look at one final variable that might impact the amount of customer abuse employees experience and how strongly do they feel its effect – age, and related to it – job tenure. One might expect, following a perhaps old-school moral norms, that customers will treat more senior employees with more respect, but is this the case? Three researchers set off to examine this effect via a meta-analysis of existing studies. They pulled together 103 surveys covering close to 50.000 service employees in total. Their results support the notion that older employees are less exposed to customer abuse; the effect is not huge, but there is a clear decline of customer aggression directed at employees with an increase in the latter's age. As the authors note, "Aging workforce is not a threat but an advantage for service companies that aim healthy service relations and interactions. … Younger employees have less resources and need more support in handling customer mistreatment, compared to older employees" (Okan, Elmadag, and Elmadag, 2021, 107).

There's more good news for older employees (or, put differently, more negative news for younger ones...). Not only customer abuse decreases with employees' age – the latter's abilities to cope with it improve as well. Another study[12] investigated the impact of age on self-esteem and service performance. Interestingly, they found out that older employees feel higher self-esteem threat after customer abuse but are better positioned to cope with it. As a result, the threat to their self-esteem has a more limited impact on their service performance compared to their younger colleagues. It appears, then, that "older employees' stress management strategies of emotion control and active coping had a more positive effect on emotional exhaustion and cynicism compared to younger employees" (Johnson et al., 2013, 318).

So where does this leave us? In short, in addition to multiple customer personality traits potentially increasing the likelihood of customer abuse, there is a host of employee personality characteristics that can make the more likely to experience aggression from customers and to feel its effects more strongly. High neuroticism/high negative affectivity and low agreeableness are two dimensions that drive customer abuse when present either on customer or employees' end, for instance. We also saw that employees higher in self-esteem also feel the impact of customer abuse more acutely and their willingness to go the extra mile, which is under normal circumstances higher compared to low self-esteem employees, diminishes. Finally, younger employees and those with lower job tenure are also more likely to feel the impact of customer abuse more strongly and/or to have lower coping abilities.

Before we move on to seeing how we can apply all of these findings, we need to discuss one final root cause for customer abuse. In addition to situational and personality factors, there are drivers that stem from the very nature of our existing consumption culture. It is to a review of the societal factors for customer abuse that we turn now.

Societal Factors

Misbehavior by consumers is the great paradox of the modern culture of consumption— its positive characteristics evoke its negative ones. ... [I]t is unintentionally but powerfully fostered by the very marketing values and practices which shape and encourage legitimate consumption experiences.

(Fullerton and Punj, 1998, 393)

Before we delve into the societal or cultural factors that drive customers' aggressive behavior, it's worth making a perhaps lengthy, but I believe very important point. The contents of this subchapter might appear controversial at times. Following sound academic research, we will identify some of the otherwise perfectly logical and legitimate business practices as one of the key drivers of customer abuse. These practices, of course, are not intended toward making customers aggressive toward employees; I highly doubt that any business leader wants that.

The thing is, as Robert K. Merton showed in one of the most insightful conceptualizations of the phenomenon, every individual's actions have consequences, and sometimes some of them are not foreseen by that person or institution – our actions have unintended consequences. This can easily be seen in the case of traffic jams, for instance. No one intends to create it, yet the perfectly reasonable decision each of us makes – go by car because it's snowing, for example – ultimately lead to a traffic jam. Similarly, to give one of Merton's most dramatic examples, it might be perfectly reasonable for individuals to try to withdraw their money from a bank if it has been rumored to go bankrupt. The problem is, even if this is not true, the unintended consequence might very well be that it will go bust.

Similarly, the conditions for customer abuse to thrive might very well be created by perfectly reasonable business practices. In fact, it might well be argued that customers' abusive behavior is an unintended consequence of the key elements of the existing consumption culture and the customer-is-king philosophy. This chapter is not intended as a critique of either of those; as I mentioned in the introduction, I am myself in the business of creating better and better customer experiences every day. Nevertheless, it is important to know what our actions lead to. Even if for some reason we can't really stop doing them, we can in the very least put reasonable boundaries around them to limit their unintended consequences.

Consumption Culture Characteristics/Customer-Is-King Philosophy

Our age is the Age of the Consumer. It is, of course, many other things beyond that – the age of information, the age of extremes, the post-modern age, and so on. Yet, one of its clearest defining characteristics is the expansion of consumption and of consumption values to an unprecedented scale.

It all began to emerge in Britain by the mid-1700s and from there, spread to the rest of Western Europe and the United States in the 19th century[13]. At this point though, the signs of a rising consumer culture are still rather hard to detect, and the spread of consumer items such as better clothing and handy household items, albeit starting to increase among the average person, was still confined to a rather small portion of the population.

The signs of the rising consumer culture become much more visible when one looks at the late 19th and early 20th century, and especially after the Second World War, most prominently in the United States, where

...existing shops were rapidly extended through the 1890s, mail-order shopping surged, and the new century saw massive multistory department stores covering millions of acres of selling space. Retailing was already passing decisively from small shopkeepers to corporate giants who had access to investment bankers and drew on assembly-line production of commodities, powered by fossil fuels; the traditional objective of making products for their self-evident usefulness was displaced by the goal of profit and the need for a machinery of enticement.

(Higgs, 2021)

This trend, if anything, only sped up in the 20th century, only punctured by the two world wars and economic crises. Nowadays, consumption makes up a very large share of what we as people do, and the assortment of products and services we can and do buy expands daily. In a lot of ways, we don't have a choice but to consume. The alternative is possible only if we manage to live a self-sufficient life – not impossible of course, but related to a host of perks one would have to let go of.

Consequently, consumption became a central and defining part of what we do. Fullerton and Punj note the fundamental

shift of aspirations from the work sphere to the consumption sphere. ... The new-found importance of the consumption sphere has brought with it a lasting change in personal values. The impact of consumption values has helped foster among consumers a constantly expanding appetite for products.

(Fullerton and Punj, 1998, 396)

Our values change in such a way that hardship is neither a virtue nor an inevitable part of life. We can do it all, and we can get it all – there are no constraints to what we can buy if we make the effort to make the money to do so.

This is all supported by companies, in a self-perpetuating flow. Once it becomes possible to produce consumer goods at a large scale, there is also a need to be a demand for these. Marketing and advertising become a vital part of what a company does, simply because production is not an issue anymore – companies can relatively easily meet the demand, but they need to create it first. Demand generation becomes the word of the day, and it starts fueling a seemingly insatiable desire for more, newer, better goods and services.

With this, people, Fullerton and Punj continue,

come to see in consumption infinite opportunities for "new sensations and the spirit of adventure" ..., for self-transformation, and for self enhancement ... . Moreover, advertising and consumer promotions, particularly the creation of carnivalesque shopping atmospherics, have promoted "ordered disorder" … encouraging consumers towards trance-like states of personal excess and rebelliousness. What had once been disparaged as self-indulgence has come to be perceived as legitimate fulfillment of consumer needs. Conduct once denounced as frivolous, vain, extravagant or wasteful has come to be seen as exemplifying the good life.

(1998, 398)

In this process, products and services acquire much more than functional meaning – they start signifying who we are. Phones and cars, and travel destinations, and clothes, and sunglasses are not just items we use to get a job done, at least not if the job is to fulfill a purely practical, utilitarian goal. Products and services more and more become means to enhance our self-view and to define who we are; of course, advertising often makes deliberate efforts in this regard, as well as in assigning (new) meaning to otherwise mundane products.

These developments ultimately lead to customers expecting more and more from companies. Especially in our highly connected world, we constantly exchange views and opinions both face to face and crucially, via social media and other web-based platforms, such as ratings and reviews. Few things remain hidden in a marketplace like ours, and expectations quickly spread from one area to another. The lines of delineation between different market niches are becoming blurrier, and what a web-based retailer is offering we now expect from taxi services, and barbers, and hair dryer manufacturers. As early as 2015, PRNewsWire reported that fully 82% of the business leaders think that their customers have higher expectations than merely three years ago, and 60% say that it is difficult to please their customers.

In addition, while it is true that companies aim to create demand, which does increase our desire for more and more products, it also creates a very healthy competition between them which customers benefit from. A very logical development, then, is that the customer takes center stage in the efforts of companies to increase revenue and profit. Everything a company does orients toward satisfying (and creating) their needs; at the extreme view of this position, everything that makes the customer happy is worth doing as companies don't only need to meet customer expectations – to win, they need to exceed them. The customer, in a word, becomes the King.

I know it seems like I'm taking a critical stance toward all of the developments we reviewed so far, but that's not the full story. Yours truly, for instance, definitely prefers writing these words on his laptop instead of a typewriter, and having a refrigerator in the next room, and a washing machine to wash his clothes while writing this. Customers like me and you benefit hugely from the fact that we can now manufacture, distribute, and sell consumer products at such an unprecedented scale and cost. I for one most certainly welcome this outcome.

The issue, as we noted in passing before, lies in the unintended consequences, i.e., what else are these very reasonable actions each company undertakes creating when combined on a bigger scale. Of the highest prominence for us here is that it makes customers feel entitled and powerful, both of which create a soil for customer abuse to grow.

Entitlement and Power

In 2013, two researchers, Marek Korczynski and Claire Evans, published what in my humble view is one of the best analyses of the drivers of customer abuse on a societal/cultural level. Fair enough, they said, there most certainly are situational triggers of customer aggression, and there are psychological factors that make it more likely to happen. What they hypothesized is that there is also something in the very fabric of society that supports the spread of customer abuse. To understand if this is the case, they undertook an analysis of 30 book-length monographs related to the topic, i.e., a kind of meta-investigation combining what we know about customer abuse in a single source of truth.

Korczynski and Evans' conclusion is unequivocal:

> ...frequent customer abuse is associated with a configuration of the promotion of customer sovereignty (at organizational, sectoral and national levels), the weak position of labour, the higher social status of customers vis-à-vis workers and the structuring of service interactions as encounters.
>
> (Korczynski and Evans, 2013)

In fact, they discovered that in fully 96% of the cases in which these factors were in place, customer abuse was also high. On the flipside, the combination of these four items accounted for more than 40% of the occurrences of customer abuse. Make the customer King, give him power, weaken the position of labor, and increase that of the customer et voila, you've made yourself a cocktail of ingredients that with almost complete certainty makes one customer or another aggressive.

Korczynski and Evans' study is not the only one linking customer abuse with power. An important study[14] of the impact of sexual harassment by clients on women in occupations involving knowledge work discovered that being the victim of sexual harassment by clients led to higher stress, lower job, and health satisfaction, and ultimately to lower commitment, higher withdrawal, and higher turnover intentions – we spoke about these at length in the previous chapter. What is particularly interesting for our current discussion is that they also asked women to indicate how powerful the client was in the business relationship, e.g., does he have the power to take his business away from the company and would losing the client lead to career consequences for the women. The researchers found out that the more powerful the client was (according to women), the more likely they are to instigate sexual harassment; on an imaginary power scale of 0–100, an increase by 1pt in client power leads to 0.4 increase in the likelihood that they will make unwanted sexual advances toward women.

As for the customer-is-king philosophy and customer entitlement, there is even more evidence that it is on the rise and it's a major source of customer abuse. First things first, what does entitlement mean? The concept has its roots in the study of Narcissism, and entitlement is considered one of its dimensions, along with grandiosity, preoccupation, superiority, exhibitionism, exploitation, empathy, envy, and arrogance. In a word, a person who feels entitled "Expects special treatment and automatic compliance with his or her expectations." (Boyd III and Helms, 2005, 274). In the consumption context, these people feel that store's personnel should cater to their every whim, they should be able to ask a salesperson any question they have and get it answered instantly, they desire absolute empathy from store personnel when they have a problem, and absolutely believe in the saying "the customer is always right," among other things[15].

An entitled customer, then, is someone with extremely high expectations who holds firmly to them. That might seem as a recipe for being dissatisfied in life, and indeed, the results of a very interesting study hint exactly in this direction. After interviewing more than 220 Game of Thrones fans, a team of researchers[16] found out that the more they thought they invested in the show (time, money, and emotions), the more entitled they felt to get a great ending of the series and to be treated better. And the higher viewers' entitlement, the lower their satisfaction with the show was – those who invested a lot simply expect more and are much harder to please.

As we saw earlier, it is exactly situations like these that spark negative emotions on the customers' side and often lead to escalations of conflicts and aggressive behavior. For example, Zitek and Jordan (2019) conducted a total of six studies and found out that entitled people were less likely to follow instructions, as they felt these pose unfair demands on them. And this was about instructions on how are people to format their responses – imagine the difficulty of making such a customer to follow considerably more demanding instructions like queueing on a line or the ones on planes. Going further, a group of five psychologists investigated how entitlement is related with forgiveness. It turns out, as the researchers point out, that entitled people are just too proud to let go. "Narcissistic entitlement", they explain, predicts "less forgiveness and greater insistence on repayment for a past offense." (Exline et al., 2004, 894), and what is more, for entitled individuals, time is not the greatest healer – they simply don't experience the same increase in forgiveness in time as others.

As can be expected, entitlement ultimately leads to poor relationships and aggressive behavior. Studies by Moeller et al., for instance, show that "Entitled people adopt self-image goals (goals that aim to construct and defend a positive self-image), which then lead to interpersonal conflict and hostility." (Moeller, Crocker, and Bushman, 2009, 448), and Boyd III and Helms uncovered a 0.5 strong correlation between aggressiveness and entitlement – for every 1pt increase in entitlement, aggression increased by 0.5pts, which in the psychological realm is a very significant relationship.

The latter insight is also corroborated in the specific domain of customer abuse. Going back to a study by Sliter and Jones we discussed before, a number of customers shared with them situations

> in which they acted in an entitled fashion ... These scenarios typically described situations in which the customer acted superior to the service employee, had unmet, unrealistic expectations, or mistreated others to feel important/superior. One customer wrote: 'I expect excellent service wherever I go – it is what these people are paid for. When I don't receive this service, I make sure that that (service employee) knows I am displeased.'
>
> (Slitter and Jones, 2016, 211)

A similar conclusion was reached by Glenda Fisk and Lukas Neville, who were also interested in how customer entitlement affects service employees' well-being. They explain: "Findings from the current study corroborate past claims—the demands made by entitled customers of front-line wait-staff employees were commonly paired with acts of interpersonal aggression, behavior that left participants feeling dehumanized and subservient." (Fisk and Neville, 2011, 401)

What Did We Discuss in This Chapter?

In the first chapter of this book, we started our journey toward a better understanding of customer abuse. We defined it, and we had a look at how prevalent it is all around us, even though we often don't seem to notice it. Next, we investigated the impact it has on employees and organizations. We saw how it incites negative emotions like fear, frustration, and anger, and increases employees' stress, thus making them expend more precious resources to manage themselves and the show they put on. This is clearly not effort-free, and leads to emotional exhaustion and, more broadly speaking, to burnout, with all of its negative consequences for employees' lives. Ultimately, organizations pay a price as well.

Stressed and burned-out, employees face a number of options for coping with the consequences of customer abuse. Some disengage from their work tasks, thus lowering their service performance and increasing the time they (try to) spend off work. In the extreme end of this disengagement process, employees simply quit, leaving a whole for organizations to fill in. Even if they still want to do their job well, exhausted employees are much less capable of doing it; we saw in a plethora of studies that experiencing aggressive behavior against oneself decreases our performance on cognitive and emotional tasks alike. A particularly negative scenario plays out when employees fail to self-regulate their emotions and simply strike back at customers, thus further promoting this spiral of aggression.

In this chapter, we switched the perspective and had a look at the conditions and root causes of customer abuse. Broadly, we identified situational, personal, and societal (cultural) factors that increase the odds of customers lashing out. Among the situational factors, customer dissatisfaction with service performance or with service recovery is by far the strongest trigger of abusive behavior. Unmet expectations create frustration and anger, and when customers fail to self-regulate their emotional states or when they just can't take it anymore, they are much more likely to act aggressively. In addition, there are a host of factors in the environment in which the service takes place that can contribute to customer abuse, such as temperature, loudness, and crowdedness.

Furthermore, we had a look at a number of personality traits that increase the chance of a customer acting aggressively toward employees. These include, among others, characteristics like Narcissism, Machiavellianism, High neuroticism/negative affectivity, and low agreeableness. Some of these traits, like high neuroticism and low agreeableness, also make employees more likely the be a magnet for customer abuse. Last but not least, factors like age and job tenure also exacerbate the effect of customers' aggressive behavior on employees.

At the end of our journey toward understanding customer abuse, we had a look at the cultural factors that unintentionally contribute to the spread of customer abuse. As companies try to win in the market place by delivering better and better products/services and customer experiences, they also increase customers' expectation. Supported by the customer-is-king philosophy, this creates a feeling of entitlement and power in customers, both of which ultimately make customers more likely to act aggressively when their demands are not met.

Armed with all of this knowledge, it is time to move to the second part of our journey. In the next three chapters, we will explore the ways in which companies and employees can fight customer abuse. First, we will go through the avenues for preventing it from happening in the first place (Chapter 6). Next, in Chapter 7 we will have a look at how employees can better handle aggressive customers in the heat of the moment. Finally, in Chapter 8 we will review the opportunities for softening the blow – what can companies and employees do to lower the negative impact of customer abuse. On to a discussion on the best way to solve problems – avoiding them!

Notes

1 Following the Service-Dominant Logic paradigm – see for example Lusch and Vargo (2014).
2 This a super-simplistic view and it doesn't represent fully what happens in real life where people go back and forth, change their minds, decide things spontaneously, and so on. It is merely intended as a schematic representation that helps us go through the process.
3 Patterson et al. (2009).
4 Yi and Gong (2008).
5 Zhan, Wang, and Shi (2016).
6 For a review, see for example Krishna (2012).
7 Except electronics in baseball and seating in casinos
8 Reidy, Foster, and Zeichner (2010).
9 Oliveira and Veloso (2015).
10 See for example Dam et al. (2021).
11 See Wang et al. (2011).
12 Amarnani et al. (2019).
13 Fullerton and Punj (1998).
14 Gettman and Gelfand (2007).
15 See for example Boyd III and Helms (2005).
16 Melancon, Gardner, and Dalakas (2021).

References

Albrecht, A. K., Walsh, G., Brach, S., et al. (2017). The influence of service employees and other customers on customer unfriendliness: A social norms perspective. *Journal of the Academy of Marketing Science*, 45, 827–847. https://doi.org/10.1007/s11747-016-0505-6

Altman, Daniel, Yom-Tov, G. B., Olivares, M., Ashtar, S., & Rafaeli, A. (2020). Do customer emotions affect agent speed? An empirical study of emotional load in online customer contact centers. *Manufacturing & Service Operations Management,* 23(4), 854–875.

Amarnani, R. K., Restubog, S. L. D., Bordia, P., & Abbasi, A. A. (2019). Age as double-edged sword among victims of customer mistreatment: A self-esteem threat perspective. *Human Resource Management*, 58, 285–299. https://doi.org/10.1002/hrm.21949

Amarnani, R. K., Restubog, S. L. D., Shao, R., Cheng, D. C., & Bordia, P. (2022). A self-verification perspective on customer mistreatment and customer-directed organizational citizenship behaviors. *Journal of Organizational Behavior*, 43(5), 912–931. https://doi.org/10.1002/job.2610

Arendt, H. (2006). *Eichmann in Jerusalem: A Report on the Banality of Evil*. Penguin Classics.

Biswas, D., Lund, K., & Szocs, C. (2019). Sounds like a healthy retail atmospheric strategy: Effects of ambient music and background noise on food sales.

Journal of the Academy of Marketing Science, 47, 37–55. https://doi.org/10.1007/ s11747-018-0583-8

Bitner, M. J. (1992). Servicescapes: The impact of physical surroundings on customers and employees. *Journal of Marketing*, 56(2), 57–71. https://doi. org/10.1177/002224299205600205

Boyd III, H. C., & Helms, J. E. (2005). Consumer entitlement theory and measurement. *Psychology & Marketing*, 22, 271–286. https://doi.org/10.1002/mar.20058

Dam, V. H., Hjordt, L. V., da Cunha-Bang, S., Sestoft, D., Knudsen, G. M., & Stenbæk, D. S. (2021). Trait aggression is associated with five-factor personality traits in males. *Brain and Behavior*, 11, e02175. https://doi.org/10.1002/ brb3.2175

Daunt, Kate, & Harris, Lloyd. (2012). Exploring the forms of dysfunctional customer behaviour: A study of differences in servicescape and customer disaffection with service. *Journal of Marketing Management*, 28, 129–153. doi: 10.1080/0267257X.2011.619149.

Daunt, Kate, & Harris, Lloyd. (2014). Linking employee and customer misbehaviour: The moderating role of past misdemeanours. *Journal of Marketing Management*, 30. doi: 10.1080/0267257X.2013.812977.

Exline, J. J., Baumeister, R. F., Bushman, B. J., Campbell, W. K., & Finkel, E. J. (2004). Too proud to let go: Narcissistic entitlement as a barrier to forgiveness. *Journal of Personality and Social Psychology*, 87(6), 894–912. https://doi. org/10.1037/0022-3514.87.6.894

Fisk, G. M., & Neville, L. B. (2011). Effects of customer entitlement on service workers' physical and psychological well-being: A study of Waitstaff employees. *Journal of Occupational Health Psychology*, 16(4), 391–405. doi: 10.1037/ a0023802. PMID: 21688917.

Fullerton, Ronald A., & Punj, G. (1998). The unintended consequences of the culture of consumption: An historical-theoretical analysis of consumer misbehavior. *Consumption Markets & Culture*, 1(4), 393–423. doi: 10.1080/10-253866.1998.9670308

Gelbrich, K., & Roschk, H. (2011). A meta-analysis of organizational complaint handling and customer responses. *Journal of Service Research*, 14(1), 24–43. https://doi.org/10.1177/1094670510387914

Gettman, H. J., & Gelfand, M. J. (2007). When the customer shouldn't be king: Antecedents and consequences of sexual harassment by clients and customers. *Journal of Applied Psychology*, 92(3), 757–770. https://doi. org/10.1037/0021-9010.92.3.757

Grandey, A. A., Dickter, D. N., & Sin, H.-P. (2004). The customer is not always right: customer aggression and emotion regulation of service employees. *Journal of Organizational Behavior*, 25, 397–418. https://doi.org/10.1002/job.252

Guéguen, N., & Jacob, Céline. (2006). The effect of tactile stimulation on the purchasing behaviour of consumers: An experimental study in a natural setting. *International Journal of Management*, 23, 24–33.

Higgs, K. (2021). A brief history of consumer culture. https://thereader.mitpress. mit.edu/a-brief-history-of-consumer-culture/, last accessed on January 12, 2023.

Hornik, Jacob. (1992). Tactile stimulation and consumer response. *Journal of Consumer Research*, 19, 449–458. doi: 10.1086/209314.

Hu, H.-H. H. "Sunny," Lai, H.-S. "Herman," & King, B. (2020). Restaurant employee service sabotage and customer deviant behaviors: The moderating role of corporate reputation. *Journal of Hospitality & Tourism Research*, 44(7), 1126–1152. https://doi.org/10.1177/1096348020936331

Huang, X. (Irene), & Labroo, A. A. (2020). Cueing morality: The effect of high-pitched music on healthy choice. *Journal of Marketing*, 84(6), 130–143. https://doi.org/10.1177/0022242918813577

Johnson, S. J., Holdsworth, L., Hoel, H., & Zapf, D. (2013). Customer stressors in service organizations: The impact of age on stress management and burnout. *European Journal of Work and Organizational Psychology*, 22(3), 318–330. https://doi.org/10.1080/1359432X.2013.772581

Jovanović, Dragan, Lipovac, Krsto, Stanojević, Predrag, & Stanojević, Dragana. (2011). The effects of personality traits on driving-related anger and aggressive behaviour in traffic among Serbian drivers. *Transportation Research Part F: Traffic Psychology and Behaviour*, 14, 43–53. doi: 10.1016/j.trf.2010.09.005.

Korczynski, M., & Evans, C. (2013). Customer abuse to service workers: An analysis of its social creation within the service economy. *Work, Employment and Society*, 27(5), 768–784. https://doi.org/10.1177/0950017012468501

Kraus, M. W., Huang, C., & Keltner, D. (2010). Tactile communication, cooperation, and performance: an ethological study of the NBA. *Emotion*, 10(5), 745–749. doi: 10.1037/a0019382. PMID: 21038960.

Krishna, Aradhna. (2012). An integrative review of sensory marketing: Engaging the senses to affect perception, judgment and behavior. *Journal of Consumer Psychology*, 22, doi: 10.1016/j.jcps.2011.08.003.

Lee, S. H. (M.), Rotman, J. D., & Perkins, A. W. (2014). Embodied cognition and social consumption: Self-regulating temperature through social products and behaviors. *Journal of Consumer Psychology*, 24(2), 234–240. https://doi.org/10.1016/j.jcps.2013.09.006

Levav, J., & Argo, J. J. (2010). Physical contact and financial risk taking. *Psychological Science*, 21(6):804–810. doi: 10.1177/0956797610369493.

Lusch, R., & Vargo, S. (2014). *Service-Dominant Logic: Premises, Perspectives, Possibilities*. Cambridge: Cambridge University Press. doi: 10.1017/CBO9781139043120

Mayo Clinic, Narcissistic Personality Disorder. https://www.mayoclinic.org/diseases-conditions/narcissistic-personality-disorder/symptoms-causes/syc-20366662, last accessed on January 12, 2023.

Melancon, J. P., Gardner, M. J., & Dalakas, V. (2021). The era of consumer entitlement: investigating entitlement after a perceived brand failure. *Journal of Consumer Marketing*, 38(7), 780–790. https://doi.org/10.1108/JCM-09-2020-4138

Metamorphoses Book III. https://ovid.lib.virginia.edu/trans/Metamorph3.htm#476975716, last accessed on January 12, 2023.

Moeller, S. J., Crocker, J., & Bushman, B. J. (2009). Creating hostility and conflict: Effects of entitlement and self-image goals. *Journal of Experimental Social Psychology*, 45(2), 448. doi: 10.1016/j.jesp.2008.11.005.

Mulcahy, Rory, & Riedel, Aimee. (2018). 'Touch it, swipe it, shake it': Does the emergence of haptic touch in mobile retailing advertising improve its effectiveness? *Journal of Retailing and Consumer Services*, 54. doi: 10.1016/j.jretconser.2018.05.011.

Okan, M., Elmadag, A. B., & Elmadag, E. (2021). Frontline employee age and customer mistreatment: A meta-analysis. *Journal of Services Marketing*, 35(1), 98–115. https://doi.org/10.1108/JSM-06-2019-0246

Oliveira, Marília, & Veloso, Andres. (2015). Dysfunctional consumer behavior: Proposition of a measurement scale. *Brazilian Business Review*, 12(Special Ed), 24–49. doi: 10.15728/bbrconf.2015.2.

Park, A., Ickes, W., & Robinson, R. (2014). More f#!%ing rudeness: Reliable personality predictors of verbal rudeness and other ugly confrontational behaviors. *Journal of Aggression, Conflict and Peace Research*, 6(1), 26–43. https://doi.org/10.1108/JACPR-04-2013-0009

Patterson, P. G., McColl-Kennedy, J. R., Smith, A. K., & Lu, Z. (2009). Customer rage: Triggers, tipping points, and take-outs. *California Management Review*, 52(1), 6–28. https://doi.org/10.1525/cmr.2009.52.1.6

PRNewswire. (2015). Corporate America under pressure from consumers' rising expectations. https://www.prnewswire.com/news-releases/corporate-america-under-pressure-from-consumers-rising-expectations-300092468.html, last accessed on January 12, 2023.

Reidy, D. E., Foster, J. D., & Zeichner, A. (2010). Narcissism and unprovoked aggression. *Aggressive Behavior*, 36(6), 414–422. doi: 10.1002/ab.20356. PMID: 20623495.

Slitter, M., & Jones, M. (2016). A qualitative and quantitative examination of the antecedents of customer incivility. *Journal of Occupational Health Psychology*, 21(2), 208–219. doi: 10.1037/a0039897.

Surachartkumtonkun, J., McColl-Kennedy, J. R., & Patterson, P. G. (2015). Unpacking customer rage elicitation: A dynamic model. *Journal of Service Research*, 18(2), 177–192. https://doi.org/10.1177/1094670514556275

Tombs, A. G., & McColl-Kennedy, J. R. (2013). Third party customers infecting other customers for better or for worse. *Psychology & Marketing*, 30, 277–292. https://doi.org/10.1002/mar.20604

Wakefield, K. L., & Blodgett, J. G. (1996). The effect of the servicescape on customers' behavioral intentions in leisure service settings. *Journal of Services Marketing*, 10(6), 45–61. https://doi.org/10.1108/08876049610148594

Wang, M., Liao, H., Zhan, Y., & Shi, J. (2011). Daily customer mistreatment and employee sabotage against customers: Examining emotion and resource perspectives. *Academy of Management Journal*, 54(2), 312–334. https://doi.org/10.5465/AMJ.2011.60263093

Yagil, Dana, & Luria, Gil. (2014). Being difficult: Customers' sensemaking of their deviant behavior. *Deviant Behavior*, 35. doi: 10.1080/01639625.2014.901052.

Yi, Y., & Gong, T. (2008a). If employees "go the extra mile," do customers reciprocate with similar behavior? *Psychology & Marketing*, 25, 961–986. https://doi.org/10.1002/mar.20248

Zhan, Y., Wang, M., & Shi, J. (2016). Interpersonal process of emotional labor: The role of negative and positive customer treatment. *Personnel Psychology*, 69, 525–557. https://doi.org/10.1111/peps.12114

Zitek, E. M., & Jordan, A. H. (2019). Psychological entitlement predicts failure to follow instructions. *Social Psychological and Personality Science*, 10(2), 172–180. https://doi.org/10.1177/1948550617729885

Chapter 5

How to Prevent Customer Abuse?

By now, we have a very good overview of the phenomenon of customer abuse. We saw that's it's widely spread; we saw that it has very serious consequences for employees and companies alike; and we saw that it is driven by predictable, and most importantly – preventable! – reasons. In this second part of the book, we'll apply and add further elements to this knowledge with a singular purpose – fight customer abuse or in the very least, soften its blow to people and organizations.

This chapter is designed to help managers within companies implement practices that can prevent customer abuse from happening. There is no silver-bullet, of course, but there are certainly things leaders and managers can do to save their employees the burden of dealing with aggressive customers. Most of the practices we'll discuss here stem directly from the drivers and triggers of customer abuse we reviewed in the previous chapter. These range from better customer experience, through better service recovery, through implementing policies, systems, and processes, to creating an environment that is less conducive for customer abuse. Our first stop – better customer experience!

To Prevent Customer Abuse, Fix Customer Experience (CX) First

There is a lot of wisdom, and a tint of cliché maybe, in proverbs; one just got to love the insights distilled generation after generation and present in a succinct, aphorism style. I was a bit surprised to find that the one I had in mind in my mother tongue, also exists in English: Misfortunes never come singly. This is, unfortunately, very applicable to customer abuse. As we saw before, there is a whole chain of events that unfolds and a host of factors that are usually in place when customers act aggressively. We often tend to attribute it to "This customer is an a...hole.", and that might be a fair enough statement in some cases.

DOI: 10.4324/9781003402565-6

Yet, when saying or thinking that we should always have in mind that a much more prominent trigger of customer abuse is a service interaction gone rogue. The path from poor customer experience through poor service recovery to customer abuse is a much more common one compared to someone just walking in the office and starting to insult people. That is as much a bad thing, as it's more prevalent, as is it is a good one, as it is preventable.

The key message in the remainder of this subchapter, then, is this: the best way to prevent customer abuse is to never let it come to an angry customer to decide how to act. First, we need to deliver excellent customer experience; and if we fail at this, we need to build a strong second line of defense – excellent service recovery capabilities.

There are two reasons why I believe business leaders should care about these elements. First, a business trend I am personally super strongly in favor of is the advent of the CX philosophy of doing business. Dozens of books and hundreds of articles have already been written on the topic, and for a good reason: researchers and practitioners alike confirm that CX makes or breaks companies. Here is an excerpt from a list of reasons why that is put together by the CX thought-leader, Blake Morgan for Forbes:

- Companies with a customer experience mindset drive revenue 4–8% higher than the rest of their industries.
- Seventy three percent of companies with above-average customer experience perform better financially than their competitors.
- Customer-centric companies are 60% more profitable than companies that don't focus on customers.
- Loyal customers are five times more likely to purchase again and four times more likely to refer a friend to the company.
- American consumers will pay 17% more to purchase from a company with a reputation for great service.
- Sixty eight percent of customers say the service representative is key to a positive service experience.
- Customers tell an average of nine people about a positive experience with a brand, but they tell 16 people about a negative experience.

The list can go on and on, and it will keep sending the same unequivocal message: being customer-centric has tangible positive business impact. Deliver great CX, you win; deliver poor CX, and you are in trouble. Customers stick with companies that meet their CX expectations, pay more for their products and services, tell their peers about it, and, you guessed it!, are much less likely to abuse employees. Somewhat surprisingly, the latter has so far been somewhat overlooked as a benefit companies gain by delivering great CX. The fact that good CX means less customer abuse can in fact be seen as a hidden benefit of the former, or if we reverse the logic – customer abuse is the hidden cost of poor CX.

In a similar fashion, the recent years brought about a trend of paying significantly more attention than before on employee experience (EX). Albeit the nature of the relationship is not yet clear, there is evidence that suggests that EX and customer experience are intertwined. Consequently, a lot of the leaders in CX also turn their efforts toward improving EX. From mugs and t-shirts with positive messages, through improved office spaces, through more and more perks and benefits, to inspirational messages from leads designed to rally the organization behind a common purpose, companies invest massively in turning themselves into a place people passionately want to work for. This is excellent news, of course, yet I believe in a way we are missing the elephant in the room. A particularly strong driver of good EX, as we saw a couple of chapters ago, is staying abuse-free: if companies want to fix EX, they need to fix customer abuse; and if they want to fix customer abuse, they need to fix CX.

Of course, delivering great (or the expected) CX, this is not a simple thing to do. It is also quite difficult to describe what great CX is across the board – after all, banking is different than ship cruises, which is different than shoes. By now though, there is a ton of great advice on what good CX is and how to achieve it, and there are some common principles that underpin it.

One thing the majority of practitioners in the field agree on is that customer experience encompasses a lot more than we tend to intuitively think. We might be tempted to conflate it with customer service and thus narrow it down to what happens when the customer reaches out to our contact center to ask a question or file a complaint, for instance. The prevailing conceptualization of customer experience though is that it is much broader than this.

In a Harvard Business Review article in 2007, Andre Schwager and Chris Meyer put forward a definition that I still like to use today, as I think it best showcases the wide-ranging nature of CX. In their words, "Customer experience encompasses every aspect of a company's offering—the quality of customer care, of course, but also advertising, packaging, product and service features, ease of use, and reliability" (Schwager and Meyer, 2007). Everything, every interaction between a company and a customer, contributes to a customer forming an impression of the company and its products and services, thus creating a customer experience. As Schwager and Meyer suggest, this might be small things really, like how easy it is to open the packaging, or what is the music in the company's advertisement, or how well does this or the other button on the product work. Nothing is inconsequential.

Similarly, in their seminal book *The Experience Economy*, B. Joseph Pine II and James Gilmore note advance a theatrical concept of customer experience. They note that in the current business environment, the vast majority of products and services are commoditized, and the way for a company to differentiate from its competitors is by providing something more – a holistic experience. In this view, companies not so much sell products or services, but rather stage or orchestrate experiences, much like Disney does in DisneyWorld or how a band performs on a stage. And, similarly to Schwager and Meyer, they assert that "companies stage an experience whenever they engage customers, connecting with them in a personal, memorable way." (Pine II and Gilmore, 2019, 36). The word "whenever" is vital in the last sentence. Of course, some moments in the customer journey matter more than others. Yet, every interaction can be made or designed to matter and to contribute to the experience, and vice versa – every interaction can break it.

This last observation leads us to another key part of great customer experiences – they are extremely coherent. As Matt Watkinson notes in this book, *The Ten Principles Behind Great Customer Experiences*, "Great customer experiences leave nothing to chance. To create consistent, smooth customer journeys, every interaction needs to be considered, planned and designed." (Watkinson, 2012, 35). Because every interaction matters, every interaction needs to match others and contribute to the creation of a coherent experience. If we are in a posh restaurant, we need poshness all the way through; it just doesn't work if the restrooms are run down, for instance. And if we are to have a seamless purchase process, we need to ensure that all of the touchpoints and channels offer the same seamless experience; we can't afford for customers to bump into roadblocks along the way.

Which leads us to one of the factors that most consistently lead to great customer experiences – ease and effortlessness. Also in the words of Matt Watkinson,

> Interactions that put the onus on the customer, soaking up their time and energy, are quickly put off or replaced with those that are less demanding. Few things generate more goodwill and repeat business than being effortless to deal with.
>
> (Watkinson, 2012, 36)

Our brains crave ease. Our resources and energy are precious, as we saw earlier. We want to spend them only if it's necessary, and let's face it, waiting in the line to ask a question isn't something most of us would consider necessary.

In a similar fashion, great customer experiences create trust by being very reliable. We want to know what will happen next and we want to feel in control of events. Surprises, especially negative ones, are the enemy of this. An appliance breaking down is an enemy of this. Our computers starting to update when we need them is an enemy of this. Lack of taxis in the rain when we are in a hurry is an enemy of this. Reliability is a vital part of the customer journey simply because we are investing and we want to know what we will get out of our investment. Anything that falls short on helping us create value can break our experience.

Relatedly, we expect consistency in time. This is, in essence, the temporal equivalent of coherence – in the same way that the elements of a great experience all work together to create a memorable journey, we expect predictability. A company cannot afford to create a great experience one day only to fail to replicate it the next one. If I got a certain level of service at point A, I need to have the same at point B. Every interaction not only creates an experience but also sets the expectations for the next one. Companies cannot let their guard down and think that one bad experience will be compensated by two or three good ones. It's just not how our minds work – we crave consistency.

Furthermore, in the previous chapter, we discussed how environmental factors might contribute to customer aggression. For instance, crowdedness is one factor that agitates people and sparks negative emotions; companies would do well to avoid creating long queues on which emotions are likely to loom large, or in the very least to manage these better. Some simple tricks like having monitors so people can distract themselves and giving predictability over the expected waiting times help a lot with these, and so does splitting the queue in smaller portions, so that people get the feeling of making progress.

Temperature is another aggression-inducing factor, and one that is relatively easy to avoid. What exactly is comfortable temperature depending largely on the exact location, of course – Norwegians will likely suffer in Southern Italy and vice versa, so it's important to solve this on a location-by-location basis. What's important is that customers feel OK with how hot a place feels, and if you are to make a mistake, from a customer aggression perspective, it's better to do it in the colder direction.

The level of cleanliness of the facility is another factor that contributes to customer satisfaction, thus also to customer abuse. Ran down places, more broadly speaking, signal carelessness, which if not encouraging misbehavior, in the very least make people think it's more or less acceptable. This is not to say that the place needs to be posh or ultramodern, but keeping it well-maintained and functioning is a good advice if one wants to reduce customer abuse.

As a summary of what we discussed so far, given that customers are more likely to act aggressively when they consider their experience with the product or the service in question to be poor, a logical first step toward preventing customer abuse and improving employees' work experience is to provide better CX. In this subchapter, we discussed briefly the key elements of the customer experience and the environment in which it happens that companies can work to improve on. This isn't an exhaustive list, of course – there is a lot more that goes into an amazing customer experience and we merely scratched the surface. Still, I believe even covering the basics we outlined will have a host of benefits stemming from the fact that customers will be happier – from higher retention, through more positive word of mouth, all the way to less customer abuse and happier employees.

In what follows, we will turn our attention to another situation which if not handled properly, has the potential to lead to customer aggression – the cases in which something goes wrong in the consumer journey or the product/service usage process and the company needs to mitigate the damage, i.e., what is known as service recovery.

To Prevent Customer Abuse, Do Better Service Recovery

No matter how hard companies try and no matter how good their intentions are, infrastructure breaks, processes get disrupted, and people make mistakes, all of which potentially leading to poor customer experience. Now, when this happens, customers will have one of a few options in front of them. They might:

- Do nothing and keep going / Stay with the company
- Churn
- Voice their dissatisfaction. There are two considerably different options here:
  - Customers might stay with the company but voice their considerations with third-parties, i.e., with someone outside of the company
  - Or customers might voice their concern with the company (and depending on the outcome stay or leave).

At face value, the first outcome in which the customer just carries on and remains a customer of the company is the best one. There are inherent risks in it though, as it might be just delaying an inevitable customer exit of which the company has no clue (given that there has been no indication by the customer of the looming churn). Dissatisfaction might pile up or the customer might be forced to stay by a contractual obligation, or it might be too costly to leave immediately – the fact the customer stays doesn't mean that they are loyal.

Churn is clearly the worst possible outcome for the very obvious reasons that the company loses a client, that unhappy customers are likely to talk negatively of the organization, and that getting a new customer costs more than keeping an existing one, amongst others.

To safeguard against churn and to mitigate the potential risks inherent in relying on a customer just staying with the company and doing nothing, the vast majority of companies have long ago given customers the opportunity to contact them and ask a question or voice a complaint. This seems like an odd thing to say, but it's often better to have customers talk to you than to others. A low or decreasing number of complaints might mean that customers have nothing to complain about; yet, it could also mean that customers just don't complain and leave the company instead.

Studies show that customers who complain are twice less likely to spread negative word-of-mouth. Nyer and Gopinath (2005), for example, discovered that allowing customers to vent their dissatisfaction is enough to decrease their urge to tell others about it, thus doing much less harm to the business – only 16% of the complaining customers spread negative word-of-mouth. In comparison, 37% of the noncomplaining customers spoke negatively about the brand with others. In addition, it is only among the group of people who complained that satisfaction increased considerably in time. Satisfaction of customers who neither spread negative word-of-mouth nor complained increased marginally in the period they studied; satisfaction of customers who complained also increased, interestingly, albeit also marginally. Among those who complained, satisfaction increased by 0.7 points on a 7pt scale, which is about six times higher than the increase in the other two groups. By telling others about their experience, the latter group became committed to their view, cemented their dissatisfaction.

These insights show that good complaint management is a must for any company that wants to help its customers create value, and it benefits the company hugely. In the remainder of this subchapter, we will focus on the best practices for managing the interaction with customers, no matter if it was driven by the customer or the company. The key principle to have in mind here is that a poor experience is stressful for customers because, as explained by the Conservation of Resources theory, they either lose resources in the process or are threatened to do so. Naturally, then, what customers expect when they engage with a company about an issue is restoration of these resources, i.e., justice.

In a previous chapter, we briefly spoke about justice in the consumption context. We saw that it is typically conceptualized as having three distinctive dimensions: procedural, interactional, and distributive justice. As a reminder, procedural justice refers to how customers evaluate the process of arriving at a decision after making a claim – is it easy, flexible, timely, and so on; interactional justice describes how the communication with the company went and covers items such as politeness, respectfulness, etc.; finally, distributive justice captures the outcome of the complaint process and whether customers think it is large enough to offset the "inconvenience resulting from a company's failure" (Gelbrich & Roschk, 2011, 27)

Years of research show that all three of these are important during the complaint-resolution process. In a meta-analysis of more than 80 studies investigating how the different facets of justice affect post-complain satisfaction and ultimately – loyalty and word of mouth, Katja Gelbrich and Roschk (2011) discovered that distributive justice was critical for the so-called transactional satisfaction, i.e., of single interactions with the company, like a visit to an office, or a purchase. When it comes to cumulative satisfaction, though, or the broader, accumulated experience of customers, it is interactional justice that comes to the fore, followed closely by distributive justice. Interestingly, high transactional satisfaction is the leading factor behind customers spreading positive word of mouth, while of the two, high cumulative satisfaction is a much stronger driver of loyalty. It appears, then, that a very positive outcome would lead to high satisfaction with how a transaction went, thus making customers more likely to talk about it with others; it is the employees' behavior though, "characterized by listening carefully to the complainant, displaying regret for any inconvenience, and helping the complainant to understand why a failure occurred." (Gelbrich & Roschk, 2011, 26) that is more important in the longer term and which leads to loyalty.

Knowing this, the key question becomes "How can companies increase customers' perceptions of distributive, interactional, and procedural justice?" Perhaps, the latter is the easiest to describe and crack. The best practice for making customers happy with the process is to make it easy for customers to complain (within reasonable limits so as not to encourage false claims), solve the issue as quickly as possible, and give customers a feeling that you and they have control over it. Decreasing the amount of bureaucracy and showing ownership are the keys toward the first item. A good, efficient process from a customer perspective involves little to no documentation filing, a one-stop complaint-submission, and an omnichannel approach. A customer should be able to tell you, the company, how they feel easily and at their convenience. Furthermore, it is important to keep the customer updated at all times. An acknowledgement of the receipt is an obvious, although not necessarily widely followed element; so is following up a phone conversation with a summary over email for instance. Proposing steps for solving the case upfront and providing regular updates are also critical in the process and they give customers the feeling of control and the trust that the company is truly working to find a solution.

The interactional elements of a service recovery process are vital for customer satisfaction, and as we discussed at length before, for preventing customer abuse. Handling customers in a polite and respectful manner is absolutely a must in this respect, and I don't believe I should try to convince you that we all like to be treated well – this is, after all, the very basics of a good social interaction. Acknowledging that a problem has occurred and showing ownership over it are also excellent ways to increase the perception of interactional justice. The sooner we as customers start trusting the organization (again), the higher our satisfaction and the lower the chance that things will escalate. Employees' knowledge and competence also significantly contribute to a recovery process done well; the more people in the frontlines know about the products and services, the easier it is for them to solve the case, and once again, the more efficient and effective the interaction, the better we as customers feel after it. Providing an explanation is another good way to build trust. I'm not suggesting that we go into details like "It was my colleague John's fault because he was having a bad hair day," but employees can still provide a good idea of why something happened without thrashing the company in front of a customer. And finally, in the recent years, more and more researchers and practitioners have suggested that empathy is a critical element of delivering great customer experience in general and of a good service recovery in particular.

Looking at things from a customer perspective, trying to put ourselves in their shoes and understanding how important the issue might be for them are important parts of this process as they convey a message of care to customers. Making the customer feel like they are treated as individuals, instead of just another customer who's bitching about something is key. Once again, I wouldn't advise you to overdo it – after all, this is not a session with a therapist; it is critical, though, to show a human touch and appreciation of the customer's situation, and solving the issue from there. All of these bits and pieces – friendliness, acknowledging a problem has occurred, empathy, competence, providing an explanation – will contribute positively toward a fast and seamless recovery process, thus decreasing the odds that a customer might start acting aggressively.

And finally, a critical part of the service recovery mix is ensuring that a customer feels that the outcome of the whole process is fair, i.e., creating distributive justice. Complaints are, in a lot of ways, pleas from a customer to either get lost resources restored, or to stop the threat of losing resources. If the issue is a minor one and it can be solved quickly, the company might not need to do too much in this respect. As the loss of resources increases, though, organizations are going to have to resort to compensation mechanisms, which come in two basic shapes: economic and psychological. On the economic front, companies might, for instance, provide a discount for future purchases (e.g., from the next month's bill or from the next purchase of a product), a refund, or a product replacement. The question about the amount of economic compensation is a tricky one, as companies need to both make the customer satisfied and to make sure they are not providing incentives for customers to exploit these policies. The specifics of economic need to be explored on case-by-case basis, depending on the exact case and the specific industry a company works in, and this is relatively easy to do with A/B testing.

The second group of things a company can employ is to provide a compensation to try to restore employees' psychological resources. The latter is just a more scientific way to say that an apology will go a long way toward making customers happy with a service recovery. When it comes to apologies, it's not a matter of whether companies should do it – it's more a question of how to do it. Research shows[1], for instance, that in the case of process failures, the effect of an apology is comparable to that of economic compensation. Other studies suggest that there might be an even better way to restore psychological resources instead of apologizing – appreciating the customer and their efforts. In an investigation of this, a group of researchers discovered that "the shift of focus in the service provider–consumer interaction, from emphasizing service providers' fault and accountability (apology) to spotlighting consumers' merits and contributions (appreciation), can increase consumers' self-esteem and, in turn, postrecovery satisfaction." (You et al., 2020, 133).

All in all, a good, seamless process, combined with a friendly, competent, and empathetic interaction, and an appropriate compensation – economic and/or psychological – are all important elements of delivering a great service recovery and high customer satisfaction. Everything we discussed so far, though, is in the context of companies reacting to customer complaints, i.e., there needs to be a complaining customer for all of this to take place.

While allowing, and even encouraging, customers to complaint is indeed a great thing to do, this mode of supporting people during a poor customer experience contains an inherent weakness. Whatever a company does, far from everyone who is unhappy will complain. We might talk to others or secretly rant about it, but the majority of us will not call a company to talk to it about a poor experience. That is why when talking about customer complaints "No news is not necessarily good news"; "Companies are not aware of the number of customers who are dissatisfied because relatively few customers with problems complain. Instead of complaining, most people become less loyal and spread negative word-of-mouth." (Goodman, 2014, 21). This is known as the customer complaint iceberg, which is a fancy name for a simple phenomenon – not every unhappy customer will complain. Just how big is this iceberg? Some authors like Adrian Swinscoe (2010) estimate it to be about 4%, i.e., only 1 in 25 unhappy customers will log in a complaint. Going further, he suggests that for every customer complaint that you receive, unhappy customers will spread word-of-mouth, reaching 1,300 other people. He bases both of his estimates on a TARP study conducted in 1999. Other sources put the tip of the iceberg at about 6%[2]. Whatever the actual number is, the reality is that the number of unhappy customers who actually complain is likely quite low.

To Prevent Customer Abuse, Practice Proactive Personalized Post-Sales Service

A very good practice for mitigating the inherent weakness of relying on complaint management alone that more and more companies are adopting is to create the so-called close-the-loop programs. Their essence is that instead of an organization waiting for the customer to complain, they contact them on more or less regular basis and ask them to share their feedback. Then, the company acts to increase customer satisfaction, based on the insights they have gotten out of this research. These programs are indeed very effective in reducing churn, and it's no surprise they are taking hold in more and more companies.

Similarly to complaint management though, they also have an inherent weakness related to their scalability – close-the-loop programs suffer from a phenomenon akin to the customer complaint iceberg, which we might call the survey response iceberg. The thing is, even with the best of our efforts, far from all customers are going to reply to a survey asking about their opinion. There is no official data related to survey response rates, but the estimates of different companies provide a good start. In a limited meta-analytic exercise, Survey Anyplace (2021) puts the survey response rate at an average of 33%, with email and online surveys slightly lower (30% and 29%, respectively). PeoplePulse, based on their experience in the United States, puts the average response rate for online surveys at 41%. The Pew Research Center (2017) reported response rates for telephone surveys in the United States to be 9% in 2016. And last, CustomerThermometer claims that "Survey response rates in the 5% to 30% range are far more typical." (CustomerThermometer). In my experience, while broad, the latter estimation is quite accurate. It is indeed a rare occurrence to see response rates of over 30%, and they can go much lower, depending on the survey specifics, of course.

To further advance their ability to add value to their customers and retain them, the leading companies are now making the most of the different types of data they create to predict customer dissatisfaction and address it by doing what I have (Yorgov, 2022) called proactive personalized post-sales service. At its core lie two concepts:

Proactive Service is Better than Reactive Service

Evidence for this abounds. In one of the first explorations of how proactive post-sales service could benefit companies, Retana et al. researched the impact of doing proactive Customer Education on business results. In a field experiment in 2011, they examined the effects of proactively contacting customers of a public cloud infrastructure immediately after signing up on Key Performance Indicators (KPIs) such as churn, the number of questions asked, and service usage. During the two months' study, 2673 customers signed up for the service. Of them, 366 were randomly selected to receive "a short phone call followed up by a support ticket through which the provider offered initial guidance on how to use the basic features of the service." (Retana, Forman, and Wu, 2015, 3)

The experiment results provide conclusive evidence of the positive impact of proactively educating customers. On the one hand, those who received a company-initiated call to receive initial guidance were about 3% points less likely to churn in the first week, or a churn rate decrease of close to 50%. Second, these customers also asked approximately 20% fewer questions than the others. This is important, as it allows companies to decrease the costs for "labor-intensive reactive technology support." (Retana, Forman, and Wu, 2015, 4). Finally, showing how proactive education helps customers create more value increased the service usage by about 50%. In short, a simple company-initiated phone call after signing up to offer customers initial guidance significantly decreased churn and the number of questions asked and increased their use of the service.

Further evidence for the positive impact of proactive, personalized post-sales service comes from Shin et al., who compared proactive vs. reactive interaction for service failure prevention. They conducted several scenario-based experiments in a retail context (executed via surveys), varying whether the participants received proactive or reactive service. In the proactive case,

> respondents were asked to imagine that they visit a hypothetical electronics store called SAB Electronics to buy a new laptop computer and anti-virus software. At the checkout counter, an employee (referred to by the gender-neutral name "Jaime") tells them about the difficulty of installing the software and offers to install it in the store. Later that evening, the customer in the scenario reads a tech blog that says many consumers have found the anti-virus software installation difficult to perform on their own and should seek assistance from their retailer.
>
> (Shin et al. 2017, 172)

In the reactive scenario, customers were not told about the potential issues and had to call the store for support. The results show that proactive support increases customer satisfaction (6.32 vs. 5.33 for reactive) and repurchase intentions (6.27 vs. 5.18 for reactive).

Related to this, Becker et al. conducted a field experiment investigating the impact of proactive vs. reactive post-sales service on the number of inbound calls and, more importantly, on immediate churn. Working with a European telecommunications company, they contacted part of its newly acquired customers to offer post-sales service, while the rest (the control group) received no treatment. In the proactive scenario, "…the service agent asked customers for feedback, helped them with optional service features (e.g., setting up the mailbox), and provided information on common pitfalls (e.g., international roaming)—all based on a compulsory script." (Becker et al. 2020, 57). They reported fewer inbound service calls and immediate churn in the proactive condition than the reactive one. Interestingly, proactive post-sales service remained effective even when service agents tried to upsell the customer, albeit less effective than the plain service call with no up-selling.

Personalized Service is Better than Generic One

By now, personalization, unlike proactivity, is becoming commonplace for companies, and for a good reason. The importance of personalization is underscored by many sources, from leading consultancies to sound academic research. In fall 2021, McKinsey published the results of their Next in Personalization 2021 survey. Fully 71% of consumers expect personalization, and 76% get frustrated when a company "…shows or recommends [them] things that are not relevant…" (McKinsey & Company 2021). This is a huge share of customers – three out of four people demand personalization, and circling back to a point we made earlier – that post-sales service is not cross-selling—three out of four are annoyed when a company puts forward something irrelevant. Let's face it; it is just wasting people's limited time and attention. At the same time, there are significant benefits to be gained by personalization. McKinsey report that 76–78% of customers "are more likely to consider purchasing from brands that personalize" (McKinsey & Company 2021) to buy again from these companies, and to spread positive word-of-mouth. Very few other initiatives boost these KPIs as effectively as personalization.

In the academic world, the positive impact of service personalization is supported by several studies. For example, Ball et al. (2006) discovered that

> Personalization increases satisfaction and benevolence trust, which also have their effects on loyalty. A personalized relationship, built on communication, is more trusting and more satisfactory—in short, a "closer" relationship—and more likely to endure. Personalization adds psychological comfort to relationships and increases the psychological barriers to switching. Personalization increases benevolence trust, which is built up over time; therefore, switching service providers becomes a risk. Furthermore, personalization increases satisfaction, and switching providers may now involve an increased risk of lower satisfaction. So, for all these psychological dynamics, personalization of services is a substantial cause of loyalty.
>
> (Ball et al. 2006, 398)

Similarly, Mittal and Lassar (1996) investigated the impact of personalization in retail settings. Their findings further support the notion that "… for a business delivering service in interactive encounters with customers, 'personalization' emerges as the most important determinant of perceived service quality, and customer satisfaction and other patronage indicators." (Mittal and Lassar 1996, 95)

Going back to our topic of interest here, while there are no studies to explicitly test this, I would like to argue that customer abuse is most likely during a poorly executed complaint management, less so when service recovery goes well, even less likely during close-the-loop programs, and practically non-existent in proactive personalized post-sales service programs. The evidence for this comes from pretty much everything we spoke about so far.

Customer abuse becomes more likely when emotions loom large. This is indeed the case when a customer contacts the company proactively to complain about something. Given that we wouldn't make an effort if the issue was rather minor, we are, in most cases, talking about things the customer values greatly, and it's only natural for us to get more invested in such issues.

Close-the-loop programs take the sting out by giving customers the opportunity to voice their concerns, if there are any, before they escalate, and companies the chance to fix issues before they become too big. Because of their limited scale, though, these programs cannot reach every customer. To do this, companies can move to a proactive mode of service recovery, in which they reach out to customers with solutions to issues without the customer having to ask for them or to even flag a problem. Again, no study has tested this, but the logic of everything we spoke about so far points toward the fact that customer abuse will be minimal, if existent at all, when a company goes the extra mile to deliver superior value.

So far in this part of the chapter we covered two of the critical things a company can do to prevent customer abuse – fixing customer experience, i.e., doing it right and well the first time, and if that fails for some reason, handle poor customer satisfaction in a stellar manner. There are further actions organizations can take to prevent customer abuse from happening, and it is toward these items that we will turn next.

What Else Can You Do to Prevent Customer Abuse?

In a perfect world, all of our customers will be super happy with the work we are doing, employees will act in our customers' best interests and treat them well, and there will be no reasons for negative emotions to loom large. The reality is, we are not very likely to live in this perfect world, at least not any time soon. After all, great customer experience is not the only reason for customer aggression, and while CX is within a company's control, the host of other factors that might cause it are not. Fortunately, there are further actions you can undertake to make customer abuse less likely to happen.

The very first thing companies and employee organizations can do is raising the awareness of the issue, and especially of the acute negative effects it has on employees. This is, for instance, one of the goals I hope to be contributing toward with this book. While by now there are a number of books dedicated to workplace aggression (i.e., one occurring within the company's boundaries), and excellent ones at that, there are virtually none related to customer abuse, apart from the ones providing advice on handling difficult customers (also some excellent ones!).

Furthermore, campaigns targeted at a wider consumer audience will likely contribute toward preventing customer abuse as well. On the one hand, these will increase our awareness as customers of how our seemingly innocuous acts of incivility and outbursts impact employees. In a lot of ways such campaigns can be thought of as creating the type of norms we discussed previously – injunctive ones, i.e., what is considered acceptable and unacceptable. By showcasing the type of behaviors that are considered abusive, these campaigns have the potential to raise awareness of our own action, thus increasing the odds that in the heat of the moment we would pause and think before we lash out. At the very least, they increase the sensitivity toward the issue and make it more visible. This is also likely to help battle the domino effect we spoke about, because of which customer abuse tends to spread like flu.

Such campaigns have already been put in place in the recent years by trade unions such as the Union of Shop, Distributive and Allied Workers in the United Kingdom, which conducts an ongoing campaign against customer abuse under the "Freedom From Fear" banner. In the union's own words, there is already evidence that the campaign achieves excellent results: it

> has made huge strides in 2021. In August, as a result of our campaigning a new ground-breaking law to protect shopworkers from violence, threats and abuse was introduced in Scotland. We continue to fight for equivalent legislation in the UK Parliament and have been successful in progressing amendments to the Police, Crime Sentencing and Courts Bill to include protections for shopworkers. More can be done and the campaign continues; we won't rest until shopworkers have the protection they deserve.
>
> (USDAW)

In addition, more can be done to showcase a company's zero-tolerance toward customer abuse in both physical premises and online interactions.

I was initially going to name these "warning messages," but calling them "promotional" is a much better way to address the issue. These can be rather simple signs that showcase the company's commitment toward protecting its employees from customer abuse, asking customers to act politely, for instance. In a similar vein, employees might wear badges or pins asking customers to behave appropriately. These might seem like too small of actions, but they can have considerable impact.

Pearson and Porath quote the results from a study

conducted by Professor John Bargh and colleagues at New York University, participants were asked to unscramble words. Without their knowledge, their subsequent behaviors were evaluated. 2 In one group the scrambled words related to politeness; in the other, the words related to rudeness. Researchers found that the participants' behavior following the completion of the word test was predictably polite or rude depending on the priming that they had experienced by completing the word tests. People who unscrambled "polite" words were polite; people who unscrambled "rude" words were rude."

(Porath and Pearson, 2009, 145)

This phenomenon is known as priming, and its power lies exactly in the fact that it works on a subtle level, without pushing strong, sometimes even intrusive messages in people's faces.

Another good practice to prevent customer abuse is to ensure either dedicated staff or management is present or in the very least, has easy access to customers and employees. Both of these can help to tune down potentially explosive situations simply by signaling to customers that an authority figure is present. This is quite similar to the presence of police staff on streets – simply by virtue of the power embedded in them, policemen help to reduce dysfunctional behavior. Albeit expensive, as it requires the constant presence of one more person in the interaction, it might be worthwhile doing it, especially when customer is to be expected.

A more subtle variation of this approach is to develop an early warning system that notifies management or other personnel of either a high risk of customer abuse or of a situation that is escalating. One way to do this is "to profile and track customers who engage in dysfunctional customer behavior, which will enable firms to predict the future exhibition of dysfunctional customer behavior." (Yi, 2016, 138). Previous instances of customer abuse can be tracked down via companies' customer relationship management systems, and calls or emails from previous perpetrators of aggression can be directed toward specialized teams, for example. Creating such a database of offenses can also be used for more in-depth analyses of abusive behaviors' triggers, so that broader, more systematic improvements can be devised and implemented. And finally, it might seem far-fetched, but customer aggression can also be predicted on the basis of these data. No prediction is ever perfect, yet even knowing that there is a higher chance of customer abuse in certain situations or by certain customers is often enough, as it will allow the company to direct more of its resources toward these cases.

Relatedly, the study by Rafaeli, Altman, and Yom-Tov (2019) we discussed previously also hints toward another way to prevent customer abuse. Their aim was to understand how emotional and cognitive load created by customers, i.e., the use of emotional words and message length, impacts call center representatives' speed. To do this, they used a system that automatically detects and recognizes emotionally loaded words. This very same approach can also be put to good use in tracking conversations in real time and notifying supervisors and managers for situations that are about to escalate. This would help them to either provide the necessary support to their staff or to jump in and help manage the specific case at hand.

Finally, companies might also use coercive and/or reward power to prevent future instances of customer abuse. Unfortunately, by definition, these can only work after an initial act of aggression has taken place, but if nothing else, they send a strong signal to customers and employees alike that this behavior is not tolerated. Organizations can, for instance, sue customers who misbehave, especially when this involves acts of physical aggression toward employees. I realize all too well that this might seem a step too far and companies will have to also consider the potential reputational impact of such actions, but then again, having a reputation for being a workplace at which abusive behavior is tolerated isn't much better, is it? Flipping this suggestion on its head, business might also choose to reward customers who treat their staff well. It might seem far-fetched, but why not give a discount to customers who have a history of behaving well with employees, or ask aggressive ones to pay more? Car insurance policies work in a similar manner, after all – prior incident history is included as a factor when calculating the price of the policy, and given the personal and organizational costs of customer abuse, companies might tax aggressive customers for their dysfunctional behavior.

What Did We Discuss in This Chapter?

In the first half of the book, we embarked on an in-depth investigation of customer abuse. We defined it and saw that is, perhaps surprisingly, widely spread in practically all service sectors. Next, we went through the various consequences it has for both employees and organizations, and we had a look at the drivers and triggers of customer abuse – situational, individual, and societal ones.

The second half of this book is designed to apply all that we've learnt so far to try to prevent customer abuse, to see how employees and companies can best handle abusive customers, and how can they mitigate the damage caused by customer aggression.

In the first of the three chapters in this second part, we focused on the prevention mechanisms companies can apply. Given that one of the strongest situational triggers of customer abuse is poor customer experience, companies wanting to prevent it would do well do fix CX first. It might seem cliched, but it's worth emphasizing it – the best way to handle an issue is not having the issue in the first place. Managing customer expectations is vital in this process, as these form the benchmark against which customers will compare their actual experience. And while what great CX means is at least somewhat idiosyncratic, as a rule of thumb, companies that deliver satisfactory customer experiences leave little to chance and try to manage the customer journey from A to Z; they offer a coherent experience along the way; they build trust by being reliable; they provide seamless and stress-free interactions; and they are consistent in what they do in time.

No matter what they do though, sometimes the process is going to break leading to poor customer satisfaction. This leads us straight into the territory of the so-called service recovery – what do companies do when they fail to deliver what they are being paid for? These interactions have "strong negative emotions" written all over them, as customers are experiencing a loss of resources, which makes them stressed out and prone to escalate things. As a rule of thumb, a good service recovery makes customers satisfied with three aspects of the process: procedural justice (how well the process of recovery worked out), interactional justice (how well the employees handled the interaction), and distributive justice (how happy customers are with the outcome they got). Poor execution of the recovery process means a higher chance of customer abuse, so a very good practice for preventing it is to put in more efforts in a good, seamless, and satisfactory damage control.

Going a step further, I argued that the leading companies are less and less relying on customer complaints to manage customer satisfaction, and actively look for ways to get engaged with customers. In the more common shape of this process, they reach out to customers to seek their feedback, and then act on it accordingly. The ever-growing amount of customer data available to companies means they can start going a step further and proactively engage with customers – instead of waiting and doing it on a smaller scale, organizations, especially the data-rich ones, can predict customer needs and deliver proactive personalized post-sales service at scale. Such an approach has multiple tangible business benefits, one of which is that it makes it much less likely for dissatisfaction to escalate into aggression.

Finally, we discussed a plethora of other actions companies can take to prevent customer abuse. Running campaigns that increase the awareness of the issue and trying to communicate appropriate norms of behavior will help in increasing customers' sensitivity toward the issue. Companies might also consider adopting a zero-tolerance policy toward customer abuse (which we'll discuss in the next chapter), and communicating it clearly to customers both in physical premises and via digital channels. Furthermore, the presence or at least the easy access of management to potentially heated situations will also help in tuning emotions down. This can be supported by early warning systems applied on either customer level (knowing which customers are more likely to act aggressively) or interaction level (monitoring conversations for emotional words).

As no preventive mechanism is ever perfect, customer abuse is unlikely to be entirely eradicated by the above actions, but it can at least be reduced. Given this, it is critical that we review the actions employees and companies can take to manage customer abuse as it is happening, i.e., what can they do in the heat of the moment? This is the topic of the next chapter.

Notes

1 See for example Roschk and Kaiser (2013).
2 Knowledge@Wharton (2006).

References

Ball, D., Coelho, P. S., & Vilares, M. J. (2006). Service personalization and loyalty. *Journal of Services Marketing*, 20(6), 391–403. doi: 10.1108/08876040610691284

Becker, J. U., Spann, M., & Barrot, C. (2020). Impact of proactive postsales service and cross-selling activities on customer churn and service calls. *Journal of Service Research*, 23(1), 53–69. https://doi.org/10.1177/1094670519883347

CustomerThermometer, Average survey response rate—What you need to know. https://www.customerthermometer.com/customer-surveys/average-survey-response-rate/

Gelbrich, K., & Roschk, H. (2011). A meta-analysis of organizational complaint handling and customer responses. *Journal of Service Research*, 14(1), 24–43. https://doi.org/10.1177/1094670510387914

Goodman, J. (2014). *Customer Experience 3.0: High-Profit Strategies in the Age of Techno Service*. AMACOM.

Knowledge@Wharton. (2006). Beware of dissatisfied consumers: They like to blab. https://knowledge.wharton.upenn.edu/article/beware-of-dissatisfied-consumers-they-like-to-blab/

McKinsey & Company. (2021). The value of getting personalization right—Or wrong—Is multiplying. https://www.mckinsey.com/business-functions/marketing-and-sales/our-insights/the-value-of-getting-personalization-right-or-wrong-is-multiplying

Mittal, B., & Lassar, W. M. (1996). The role of personalization in service encounters. *Journal of Retailing*, 72(1), 95–109. doi:10.1016/S0022-4359(96)90007-X

Morgan, B. 50 Stats That Prove The Value Of Customer Experience. https://www.forbes.com/sites/blakemorgan/2019/09/24/50-stats-that-prove-the-value-of-customer-experience/?sh=2fa67e9d4ef2, last accessed on January 12, 2023.

Nyer, P. U., & Gopinath, M. (2005). Effects of complaining versus negative word of mouth on subsequent changes in satisfaction: The role of public commitment. *Psychology & Marketing*, 22(12), 937–953. https://doi.org/10.1002/mar.20092

PeoplePulse, Survey response rates. Tips on how to increase your survey response rates. https://peoplepulse.com/resources/useful-articles/survey-response-rates/

Pew Research Center. (2017). What low response rates mean for telephone surveys. https://www.pewresearch.org/methods/2017/05/15/what-low-response-rates-mean-for-telephone-surveys/

Pine II, B. Joseph, & Gilmore, James H. (2019). *The Experience Economy, With a New Preface by the Authors*. Harvard Business Review Press. Kindle Edition.

Porath, C. L., & Pearson, C. M. (2009). *The Cost of Bad Behavior: How Incivility Is Damaging Your Business and What to Do About It*. Portfolio Hardcover.

Rafaeli, A., Altman, D., & Yom-Tov, G. (2019). Cognitive and emotional load influence response time of service agents: A large scale analysis of chat service conversations. In: *Proceedings of the 52nd Hawaii International Conference on System Sciences*.

Retana, G. F., Forman, C., & Wu, D. J. (2015). Proactive customer education, customer retention, and demand for technology support: Evidence from a field experiment. Manufacturing and Service Operations Management. Available at SSRN. https://ssrn.com/abstract=2430012 or http://dx.doi.org/10.2139/ssrn.2430012

Roschk, H., & Kaiser, S. (2013). The nature of an apology: An experimental study on how to apologize after a service failure. *Marketing Letters*, 24, 293–309. https://doi.org/10.1007/s11002-012-9218-x

Schwager, A., & Meyer, C. (2007). Understanding Customer Experience. https://hbr.org/2007/02/understanding-customer-experience, last accessed on January 12, 2023.

Shin, H., Ellinger, A. E., Mothersbaugh, D. L., & Reynolds, K. E. (2017). Employing proactive interaction for service failure prevention to improve customer service experiences. *Journal of Service Theory and Practice*, 27(1), 164–186. https://doi.org/10.1108/JSTP-07-2015-0161

SurveyAnyplace. (2021). What's the average survey response rate, Benchmark. https://surveyanyplace.com/blog/average-survey-response-rate/

Swinscoe, A. (2010). Are you not getting many customer complaints but are still losing customers? https://www.adrianswinscoe.com/2010/05/not-many-complaints-but-still-losing-customers/

USDAW. (2022). Freedom From Fear. https://www.usdaw.org.uk/Campaigns/Freedom-From-Fear, last accessed on January 12, 2023.

Yi, Youjae. (2016). *Customer Value Creation Behavior*. Taylor and Francis. Kindle Edition.

Yorgov, I. (2022). *The New Customer Experience Management: Why and How the Companies of the Future Address Their Customers' Needs Proactively*. Routledge.

You, Y., Yang, X., Wang, L., & Deng, X. (2020). When and why saying "Thank You" is better than saying "Sorry" in redressing service failures: The role of self-esteem. *Journal of Marketing*, 84(2), 133–150. https://doi.org/10.1177/0022242919889894

Watkinson, M. (2012). *The Ten Principles Behind Great Customer Experiences* (Financial Times Series). Pearson Education Limited. Kindle Edition.

Chapter 6

How to Handle Abusive Customers?

In the previous chapter, we saw how companies can prevent customer abuse from happening. In short, delivering the expected experience is critical, and if that fails, having an efficient and effective service recovery process becomes another vital element in the mix. Furthermore, raising awareness for the issue, conducting campaigns to educate customers, and signaling the company's zero tolerance toward customer aggression are also major steps companies can take to eradicate customer abuse. Companies can also ensure management has easy access to potentially aggression-laden interactions, and might implement early warning systems to highlight the need for intervention in specific occasions. Finally, organizations can also use the powers of coercion and reward to punish or appreciate, respectively, mis- or well-behaving customers.

While these are excellent tools to try to prevent customer abuse from happening, it is very unlikely that all of it is going to be eradicated. Some customers are always going to lash out, no matter what we do. What we will turn to in this chapter is the best practices for handling aggressive or difficult customers while the interaction is unfolding, i.e., in the heat of the moment. We will talk about two groups of items: the things a company can do to support its employees, and what the latter can do to best deal with customer aggression. Earlier, we conceptualized one of the key difficulties caused by abusive customers as robbing employees of precious resources, like time, energy, positive mood, self-confidence, and so on. The main goal of both groups of interventions we will talk about is to tackle exactly this issue and provide employees with more resources to handle aggressive behavior. Our first stop – the policies and processes a company can put in place to help its employees handle abusive customers.

Policies and Processes

> While staff and the company have a duty of care for customers, this does not include accepting abusive behaviour.
>
> (Credit Services Association, 2021)

DOI: 10.4324/9781003402565-7

Those of you who have had the dubious pleasure to work with me have probably noticed that I have a rather unhealthy disregard and a distinct dislike for processes. The very thought of them makes me think of Ford-style organizations in which everything is scheduled and executed with limited deviations from the plan. For as long as I can remember having a view on this, it's always been that no process can substitute for people's knowledge and skills, and I've preferred to invest in people's learning and development rather than processes.

I have, as you can imagine, been rather wrong about this. My concern is still valid I think; every organization should take care so that its processes don't turn into a bureaucratic nightmare bogging people down in paperwork. But I have been missing a critical benefit of all companies' policies and processes – they are tools that either save employees' resources or allow them to replenish these. What a policy and a process do, after all, is specify a course of action in a fairly standardized situation. By their very nature, they serve the purpose of saving time and effort from having to figure things out from scratch. Furthermore, they have a strong signaling function. On the one hand, the very fact that the company has taken the effort to design it and has committed to following it, communicates to external audiences its engagement with the principles outlined in it. In addition, it also sends a strong signal to internal audiences, e.g., employees, that the company is fully with them and has their backs if something that violates these principles happens. For all of these reasons, adopting a process for handling abusive customers and a zero-tolerance policy that guides the company's efforts, I believe are two things every organization should do if it has committed itself to fighting customer abuse.

There are already some very good examples in this domain. For instance, in 2020, Thames Water put into effect its Customer Conduct Policy, which declares that "We won't tolerate aggressive or abusive behaviour directed towards our staff during any form of interaction, i.e. face to face, online, over the phone, or any other form of communication." They implemented a simple three-stage process for handling abusive customers. First, employees are to politely ask customers to change their conduct; should the behavior continue, Thames Water staff has the right to stop the conversation or otherwise remove themselves from the interaction; finally, specific cases might be referred to the authorities and "Any physical attack or violence will not be tolerated and will always be reported." (Thames Water, 2021). Furthermore, the company signals its commitment to the issue by opening three separate channels via which employees can get more information or report customer abuse, including the opportunity to write to the CEO of the company.

In 2021, UK's Credit Services Association (CSA), noting that "While the vast majority of customer interactions are calm and good tempered, from time to time our member firm staff do encounter unacceptable behaviour and aggression, including threats of violence and personal abuse." (Credit Services Association, 2021) issued an Unacceptable Behavior & Aggression Policy template, which its members can, should they decide to, adjust accordingly and apply within their organizations. Similarly to Thames Water, it includes a commitment to safeguarding staff from customer abuse, a process for dealing with it as it unfolds, and guidelines for actions to be taken after accidents have occurred. The process the CSA suggests attempts to deescalate the situation first by respectfully asking the customer to stop acting abusively, the involvement of management staff if things don't improve, and contacting the authorities in cases in which the behavior is extreme or unlawful. They also pay special attention to recording the occurrence of these accidents and the importance of management reviewing them to determine the best next steps.

As a final example, the UK's Health and Safety Executive (HSE) have a dedicated section on its website containing a host of useful resources on work-related violence, including review of the law related to it, excellent advice for handling verbal abuse, and a plethora of case studies. I strongly recommend that if you are serious about preventing and handling customer abuse you give it a look. One of the more helpful, in my view, documents they have prepared is an example policy on work-related violence, or "any incident in which an employee is abused, threatened or assaulted by a member of the public in circumstances arising out of the course of his/her employment" (Health and Safety Executive (a)). In it, the HSE outlines the responsibilities of both managers and employees in preventing work-related violence, covering, for example, the awareness of the company policy and process, treating reports of work-related aggression seriously and a zero-tolerance toward it ("Don't accept instances of work-related violence directed towards you or others" (Health and Safety Executive)), monitoring and recording details of incidents, being supportive to others, and a plethora of others. Furthermore, the example policy outlines the prevention and management measures a company might want to take, related policies, and actions following up the incident. Importantly, the HSE also suggests to include the training employees and management could (or should) undergo to help them prevent or manage customer abuse.

Based on what we've been discussing so far, then, a customer abuse policy would include in some share or form the following elements:

- **A definition of customer abuse.** At a minimum, I recommend that you specifically state that it includes both physical and verbal aggression, and covers threats and actual assaults against employees.

- **Purpose.**
  - What you might want to include here are at least three objectives.
    - That the company commits itself to protecting its employees against customer abuse and it has zero-tolerance toward it.
    - To make employees aware of what they can do if customer abuse happens
    - To make employees aware of all the actions the company is taking to prevent and help employees manage customer abuse.
  - Remember that the policy and the process are designed to be resources employees can use to handle aggressive customers. The objectives outlined above help exactly in this regard – they give employees the psychological comfort of knowing that they are not alone, they give them tools they can use, and they make them aware of the tools the organization is applying.
- **Scope**. My recommendation is to make it explicit that the policy covers all employees, no matter if they are client facing or not, and that it covers all communication channels. Companies offer a large (and increasing) range of opportunities for customers to reach them, and they should all be covered by the same policy.
- **Principles, i.e., what are the key values all the solutions outlined in this policy follow.** What I recommend is that you include at least two principles that cut across all decisions related to customer abuse that you might want to follow.
  - Commitment to customers and their rights. It is vital, I believe, that employees know that the unacceptable customer behavior policy does not mean that we are robbing customers of their right to complain or of their emotions.
  - Zero-tolerance toward customer abuse. This is to serve as a reminder that no situations and no customers are made exempt from this policy, no matter how much money they bring to the business.
- **Actions and processes to prevent and handle abusive customers.** My recommendation is that this section is made as detailed as possible so as to leave little room for misinterpretation. At the very minimum, you might want to outline what the company and its employees can do before, during, and after an accident
  - Before an accident. Include all steps taken to prevent customer abuse, such as the ones we discussed in the previous chapter. Don't limit yourself to them, though, and include all kinds of actions you've taken to stop customer abuse from happening, including measures for monitoring and recording such incidences

- During an accident. A good process and a range of steps includes:

  - Ask the customer politely to stop. The website Call Center Helper suggests adopting a three-strike policy – give the customer two warnings before taking the next steps in the process.
  - Involve a manager. If a customer's behavior doesn't change, the employee might ask a manager to join the interaction. Employees need to feel that they have the right and are even encouraged to seek management support.
  - Terminate a call. In a call center situation, terminating the call is the more common option compared to the previous one. Employees need to know they have a way out of a bad situation, and one that is considered absolutely legitimate from the perspective of the company.
  - Isolate the customer if the interaction is happening face-to-face. This is an important element in the mix, because an aggressive customer might a) ruin an otherwise good customer experience for others, and b) spark similar behaviors in others. It is a good idea to have a space in which employees, managers, or someone tasked specifically with dealing with abusive customers might take such clients so that others are not exposed to rude language or physical risk.
  - It might be a good idea to script at least part of the conversation with abusive customers. These situations are difficult for everyone, and knowing what works and what doesn't is vital. Companies will do well to test and refine a set of answers employees might use in such cases.
  - In some cases – call authorities. Make sure that employees know which cases are covered by this most extreme option.

- After an accident. The process doesn't stop once the situation is over. What I would recommend is to include

  - A management review of the situation (together with the employee). No matter if it's a phone call, an email exchange, or a face-to-face interaction, it's a good idea for a manager to sit down, listen to the situation (if there's a record), and discuss it with the employee.
  - The accident's details should be recorded in customers' files and used to decide how to proceed in future interactions with this customer.
  - It might be a good idea to send the customer a warning letter describing the situation, stating that it violates your company's policy and the steps the company might take in the future to prevent future accidents.
  - The database of recorded incidents should be analyzed periodically to derive opportunities for company-wide strategic actions for preventing customer abuse.

- **Support for employees.** It is a very good idea to make explicit all the resources employees can use to prevent or handle customer abuse. These include, for example:

  - A hotline for reporting customer abuse and/or for providing support for employees in handling the consequences of it.
  - Policies related to the unacceptable customer behavior.
  - What kind of training is available for employees to acquire the skills to handle abusive customers better?

- **Responsibilities of employees and management.** This is a summary section to help both groups orient better in what they need to do.

In short, developing a good process for handling customer abuse is important for a variety of reasons, ranging from its signaling function (showing that the company is fully committed to preventing it and to supporting its employees), through supplying employees with an important resource they can use while handling aggressive customers, to aligning the organization behind this goal. Unfortunately, no process or policy can fully take the burden from employees in the heat of the moment; they can serve as the skeleton, but it is the people who are in the frontlines that add the flesh and blood to a successful handling of customer abuse. It is vital, therefore, to arm employees with the skills that are needed to dealing with aggressive customers – this is what we'll do a couple of pages from now. Before we get to the skills, though, it's important to have a look at what are the best practices for having such difficult conversations. Knowing these will give us important hints into which are the skills employees need to have to handling abusive customers.

The Four Ingredients of Successfully Handling Abusive Customers

Calming an aggressive person is by all accounts a very difficult thing to do, to say the least. Just think about it. You are at work, trying to do your job well. You are going through the flight safety instruction protocol, when all of a sudden, a passenger at the back of the plane starts yelling. You go there to find out that the person is extremely unhappy with the fact that the flight is running 15 minutes late and the seats are rather uncomfortable, not to mention that you haven't brought them the glass of water they asked for five minutes ago. They are pounding their fists all over the place, red in the face, looking at you angrily and shouting like crazy. The situation appears to be going out of control and you already need to start doing the flight safety training. What do you do? Or what do you do when you need to inform a customer that for some reason or another, their payment cannot go through today but tomorrow? Or when the customer is visibly unhappy with the food that you are bringing them and starts calling you names, and curses, and threatens, and looks ready to jump into a fight. Again, all of that at the end of your 8-hour shift and while you are trying really hard to do your job well so you can get that promotion or a salary raise, for instance.

Now imagine a different scenario. You are standing in front of a building together with your colleagues. It's a sunny summer day, but you are not there to enjoy a cup of coffee and a bout of teambuilding activities – you are there to handle a hostage situation. A group of three people has just attacked a fitness center in the middle of town, and they are now demanding a couple of millions and a safe way out. This has been going on for hours now, and while the building, as can be expected, is surrounded by the police and a special squad, there has been absolutely zero positive development. The hostage-takers are now threatening that they will start killing one person every two hours lest their demands are met. You have been put in charge in handling this. What do you do?

While a cold meal and a hostage situation might look considerably different, they are actually quite similar in their building blocks. To help employees deal with aggressive customers, then, it makes sense to have a look at what those dealing with life-and-death situations know about handling them.

First things first, both customer abuse and hostage/barricade situations, kidnappings, personal crises, and other critical incidents that require the intervention of law enforcement agencies are all best defined as crises. Gregory Vecchi, ex-Chief of the FBI's Behavioral Science Unit and his collaborators explain: "A crisis is a situation that a person perceives as presenting insurmountable obstacles to achieving desired goals or outcomes... Further, there is the sense that these impediments cannot be managed through the usual problem-solving methods." (Vecchi, Van Haselt, and Romano, 2005, 537). By this definition, an angry customer is not so much different than a terrorist; they both feel that they are not getting what they want, be it a better dish, a payment done today, a wider plane seat, or millions of dollars. Also, by definition, they don't consider it possible to achieve their wish by more common, maybe even boring methods like, well, asking politely or paying more for a first-class seat.

In a very similar fashion, a crisis, Vecchi continues, "generally occurs in four predictable stages: pre-crisis, crisis, accommodation/ negotiation, and resolution" (Vecchi, Van Hasselt, and Romano, 2005, 537). In the first stage, everything is quite normal and people just go on with their lives in a mundane fashion. There are no emotions looming large and no signs of impeding danger. The crisis stage is of course the one we are much more interested in here. At this phase, emotions run free, and the person experiencing them is unable to reason rationally and to "cope with a problem that is perceived to be a serious threat. Here, frustration and tension increase as a result of conflict and the person being unable to deal with the challenge using previously effective coping skills" (Vecchi, Van Haselt, and Romano, 2005, 538). During the accommodation stage, the person instigating the crisis starts to calm down and to work through the situation, thus becoming more open to suggestions and potential solutions. Finally, at the resolution phase a solution is reached that is, in a perfect world, satisfactory for both parties.

Because a crisis represents a failure on the side of the perpetrator to handle a situation they find threatening, the goal of a crisis intervention, no matter the type of crisis, is to restore "the ability of a person to cope through the reestablishment of baseline functioning levels" (Vechi, Van Haselt, and Romano, 2005, 538). In other words, what everyone trying to deal with someone who is going through a crisis is aiming to achieve is to put them back into a "normal," calm state of mind in which they can reason about their own actions and look for more socially acceptable solutions. Easier said than done, right? Well, as difficult as this might be, there are certain common tactics that work for both negotiating with terrorists, dealing with abusive customers, and, one would guess, managing this quarrel with your spouse about where to order dinner from.

Rule number one: stay calm. It's a fortune-cookie type of advice, I know, but it's also one you cannot skip if you want to handle customer abuse well. Remember that a key issue with similar crisis situations is that emotions are running large and free. If you are not calm yourself, you are simply pouring more fuel into the fire. The abusive customer needs to feel that he or she is not touching you with their behavior, otherwise you are only reinforcing it. It is a bit like telling them "What you are doing has a profound impact on me," and at the end of the day, that's exactly what they want. Don't give it to them. Try to remain as calm as possible, keep your posture, control your tone of voice, and avoid abrupt bodily movements and nervous gestures like touching your hair; if you are typing on a computer, avoid pounding on the keys; remain polite during the whole interaction and show respect – this is what leading by example is. If you are in a physical space, maintain the appropriate social distance to avoid provoking the customer further. Show the customer what an appropriate behavior looks like and convey in all possible ways that they cannot intimidate you. This will also help you in the later stages of the process where you are going to need your cool mind to solve the issue at hand.

Rule number two is akin to the first one, but it adds something important to the interaction – you need to show self-confidence. These two – being calm and being confident – often go hand in hand, yet not necessarily, which warrants putting "Act with confidence" as a separate rule of thumb. There are cases in which people are confident, yet not necessarily calm.

Think for example of boxers before a match. They surely exude confidence, but probably the last think you would say about them is that they are calm; quite the contrary, they are full of emotions and aggression. This is not how you want to look like – it is not a boxing game but one of toning emotions down. It is certainly a good idea to show their level of confidence though. Talk in a way that shows the customer that you are in control and although you want to do your best to meet their needs, a deviation from the socially acceptable behavior wouldn't be tolerated. Don't interrupt them and don't patronize them. Maintain appropriate eye contact instead of averting your gaze – this shows that you are not scared (which I hope you are not!). Don't get defensive, don't start explaining yourself, and don't show the clear signs of withdrawal like crossed arms and shrugging your shoulders. Your goal is not to show that you can fight them, but it's also not to show you are a second away from fleeing the scene. It is your territory, it's your company, and it's your right to be treated well – show it.

So, you are calm and confident – what do you do next? Rule of thumb number 3 says that you need to try to establish a connection with the customer. Ideally, you would have done this even before the customer became abusive of course, but if not, it's absolutely critical to do it now. You've seen this done in negotiation situations in dozens of movies, and it's included there for a reason – people are significantly less likely to hurt people they know and feel somehow connected to. Your goal is to show the person that this is not a fight but a collaborative effort in finding a solution. You are one the same side; you are a team! Show it to them. Asking questions is absolutely the best advice there is for building a connection; it is vital that you couple this with listening carefully to what the customer is saying and trying to clarify things. Tyr to establish common ground by finding something you share. This is surprisingly simple to do, as studies show we feel closer to people who share absolutely accidental characteristics with us, like the first letter of our names or the same place of birth. A smile and some positive attitude can also do miracles of course.

And finally, rule of thumb number 4 is, as can be expected, to solve the issue at hand. There are two types of strategies for doing this, and only one of them works. Option one is what is known as an emotion-focused strategy. When we do this, we try to work with the other party's emotions and to calm them down; this approach involves "employees encouraging customers to alter their emotional expressions by, for example, asking a customer to 'calm down', 'relax' or trying to distract customers from their anger with humor." (van Jaarsveld et al., 2015, 276). Option two is to apply a problem-focused strategy and try to "alleviate customer stress and calming customers by, for example, presenting a solution to a problem such as replacing a defective product with a functional product" (van Jaarsveld et al., 2015, 276). Of the two, it is the problem-focused approach that brings better results, so unsurprisingly, as a rule of thumb employees need to be able to solve a customer's problem in a satisfactory way. This requires two elements to be in place. On the one hand, they need to have the skills and knowledge to do it, e.g., to be able to understand the issue at hand, and to be aware of the company's policies and processes for doing it. On the other, the company holds a significant responsibility on this end, as after all, an employee can only do as much as the company has empowered them to. Being flexible is critical in this regard. It is a good idea to embed a considerable amount of adaptability in this process, so as to give employees the space of maneuver during difficult interactions.

These four elements – remaining calm, being confident, developing a connection, and solving the problem – constitute the four basic building blocks of a successful handling of difficult or abusive customers in the heat of the moment. Of course, it's worth remembering that as mentioned in the previous subchapter, employees have one final tool in their toolbox – they could also involve other people in an interaction with aggressive customers, for instance their manager or if things become worse – law enforcing authorities. In my view, this option, which should always be available, shouldn't preclude employees from staying calm or acting with confidence, or trying to solve the problem – involving others is a last resort, which is to be used in really difficult cases.

With everything we discussed in this chapter so far, it is now time to turn to a critical question – what are the skills employees need to have in order to effectively deal with customer abuse? What should you, as an employee, know to be able to handle aggressive customers? What can you, as a business leader, help frontline facing people with? One of the best things about these skills and knowledge is that they are relevant in situations spanning so much more than customer abuse. We see them in play in business negotiations, in building lasting relationships, in making friends, in advancing your career, and a plethora of others. Let's check them out.

The Skills That Are Needed to Handle Abusive Customers

I like to think about the skills that we possess as tools. There is this view about the things that we can do which says that some of us have it while others don't; that some of us are innately good at something while others just don't have the talent; that no matter what they do, some people are just never going to be good at (fill in the blank). There is some merit to this, of course – I, for instance, being 182cm tall, am never going to be a great basketball player; and at the age of 40, I'm not going to win a marathon race, no matter how much I run. Physical limitations aside, though, I'm a strong believer in the idea that we can all become if not the best, then at least very

very good at things, for example in building connections and staying calm in threatening situations. These things are learnable, and we are limiting ourselves severely and unnecessarily when we consider them otherwise. True, some people might be better at them innately, but it doesn't mean that we cannot improve at them.

Secondly, I subscribe to the idea that our attitudes and thoughts about life is important, but what is more important is what we actually do, no matter what they think. There is a host of very good recommendations spread in the business world, which unfortunately often takes the form of fortune-cookie advice. Believe in yourself, stay calm, be confident, make friends, be more open, see the big picture – all of these are really good suggestions, yet for me they often fall short of making an impact because they are goals, not tools. I do want to stay calm and I do want to be better at making friends, but these things are goals, not actions that I can execute. What we need to do to start making progress in pretty much any area that we want to improve in is to figure out which are the discreet, easy to do behaviors that we can do that will lead us to our goals. Even these small acts can be surprisingly difficult to embed in our lives but difficult is not impossible. If we remember to do them and if we have the persistence to push through missteps, we can all become really really good at pretty much anything we wish.

What it important, then, is that we link everything we discussed so far with very specific things you as a customer facing person can apply and you as a business leader can train or nudge your employees to do in the heat of the moment when a customer is acting abusively, and that's exactly what I'll aim to do in the remainder of this chapter. Handling difficult situations is a skill and a learnable one at that (like any skill), especially if we make it easy for us or for other people turn them into small acts that can be executed repeatedly and without the great pressure of, say, climbing Everest in one single jump. We don't want to do that; what we want is to take a step, and then another one, and then another one. The remainder of this chapter is designed to do exactly that.

Employees: Know More

Arming employees with enough knowledge about customer abuse is a critical first step toward helping them deal effectively with it in the heat of the moment. There are three important elements when it comes to increasing employees' awareness. Starting from the widest view toward the issue, employees need to have a good awareness of the law that protects their health and safety at work.

Clearly, the legislation surrounding customer abuse differs by country. For instance, in the United Kingdom, it is governed by acts such as the

Health and Safety at Work etc. Act 1974, which postulates that "It shall be the duty of every employer to ensure, so far as is reasonably practicable, the health, safety and welfare at work of all his employees."

Similarly, the Joint guidance implementing a European social partner agreement for preventing workplace harassment and violence states that

> health and safety law applies to risks from violence (including verbal abuse), just as it does to other risks at work. Breach of contract may include the failure to protect an employee's health and safety at work. Employers have a 'duty of care' for all their workers. If the mutual trust and confidence between employer and employee is broken – for example, through harassment and violence at work – then an employee can resign and claim 'constructive dismissal' on the grounds of breach of contract.
>
> (Health and Safety Executive (b)

Furthermore, a plethora of other laws protect employees from harassment and discrimination on various grounds, like sex, religion, race, and others. And as a final example, the Public Order Act 1986 (S5) defines a person as guilty of an offence if he or she

> uses threatening [F1 or abusive] words or behaviour, or disorderly behaviour, or displays any writing, sign or other visible representation which is threatening [F1or abusive] within the hearing or sight of a person likely to be caused harassment, alarm or distress thereby.

All of these laws and regulations are designed to safeguard employees against harm against them, be it committed from employees higher in the ranks within the company, from fellow-workers, or from customers. Perhaps, the very first thing, then, any organization can do to help employees is to make sure that they know their lawful rights. This will have a triple benefit: it will show that the organization cares about them; it will help employees react appropriately and know what's OK and what's not; and it will give them confidence that they are protected by law.

The next piece of knowledge I'd advice employees to know very well and companies to make sure that this is indeed the case, is having an excellent understanding of the company's procedures and policies related to customer abuse. In the previous subchapter, we discussed at relative length how important it is for organizations to have a clear written way of handling, monitoring, and reporting customer abuse. While this is all great, I have, unfortunately, seen time and again the same mistake done by a host of organizations: treating the processes and policies as pieces of paper and not doing enough to put them into practice. These documents are worth absolutely nothing if they sit somewhere on the intranet of the company or if employees only see them when they sign their contracts. Making sure that a process and a policy are followed requires so much more than this, and first and foremost – communication.

People forget. This is perhaps such an obvious thing to say, that we, ironically, often forget about it. Swamped in the daily hustle and bustle, all of us need to make mental space to go through our days. Even with the best intention in place, we might simply forget to do something or what we are supposed to do when we encounter certain situations. The company policy and process of handling abusive customers, it follows, need to be constantly reminded to employees, and need to be easily available for all of them to consult whenever necessary; why not also consider simply printing it so people can refer to them without the hassle of searching for these on the intranet? Furthermore, you might consider involving employees in the development of these documents. We remember much better things that we have been involved in producing, thus employees will be more likely to follow the processes and procedures when they've taken part in their creation. Finally, nothing does a better job in making sure that the company's policies and processes for handling abusive customers are followed than trainings and role-playing exercises. To this last point we will return in just a second.

Before that, though, it's worth covering one final bit of knowledge that will help employees deal better with abusive customers, in addition to having a good awareness of the law and of the company policies – being able to tell the signs of conflict escalation. Clearly, this will do little to prevent it, but it will help employees prepare for it and mentally rehearse their actions. The provider of safety management and training solutions, HSI, for instance offers the following tips for recognizing conflict escalation:

- A person clenching his or her fists or tightening and untightening their jaw.
- A sudden change in body language or tone used during a conversation.
- The person starts pacing or fidgeting.
- A change in type of eye contact.
- The "Rooster Stance" – chest protruding out more and arms more away from the body.
- Disruptive behaviors – such as yelling, bullying, actively defying or refusing to comply with rules.

(HSI)

A good advice for employees is to also be well-aware of the situation they are in, in terms of who else is present and what is the spatial organization of the place (i.e., are there easily available exits, etc.). All of these things are potential resources they can use should the situation escalate.

With this, we conclude the "knowledge" part of what employees can do to handle abusive customers. So far, we discussed the five ingredients of successfully dealing with aggressive customers; these are remaining calm, being confident, developing a connection, shifting the mindset to a collaborative one, and solving the problem. Companies can support employees in this process by creating clear and easy to follow policies and procedures for handling abusive customers and giving them the tools to familiarize with these. On the employee side, the first thing employees can do to tackle such difficult situations is to make sure they are well aware of the law pertaining to customer abuse and of the aforementioned company policies, as well as of the signs that a conflict is about to escalate. The purpose of the latter is to give employees enough time to prepare for the difficult situation and attempt to prevent it.

Having a policy, a procedure, and a good amount of knowledge already puts employees and companies more broadly speaking on the path to handling abusive customers appropriately. The final, and arguably the most important, point that we need to discuss in relation to tackling situations in which a customer is acting abusively is what kind of skills are going to be helpful in such cases and how to most effectively and efficiently acquire these.

Training For the Critical Skills for Handling Abusive Customers

An Outline of a "Handling Customer Abuse" Training

Now that we have a good foundation for handling abusive customers in place and a good idea of the steps employees can take in such difficult situations, it is time to build on these and explore the development of which skills will help employees the most to deal with aggressive customers. Clearly, there is a lot every one of us can do and perhaps does to improve our skills both at and out of workhours. At the same time, companies are well-advised to organize dedicated training sessions for upskilling their personnel. The best practice for organizing such training sessions is to include at the very minimum three elements.

A knowledge session, during which employees get acquainted with the law, with the company policy and procedure, and with the theory behind handling abusive customers is one of the key ingredients. These sessions can take the form of in-person lectures or on-demand online ones, or reading materials. Sounds boring, I know. Nevertheless, this knowledge part helps in setting up the scene for the latter phases of the process and gives employees the broader context in which customer abuse emerges.

I'd recommend that the second part of the training plan for handling abusive customers is dedicated to showcasing best practices and success stories. Two elements are key here. First, employees need to see what good looks like, so it helps to either play a recording of an interaction with an aggressive customer that went well, or to play out such a scenario in front of them. It's very much worthwhile opening a discussion after such an exercise for employees to share their thoughts and personal experiences so they can better relate to the subject. Second, it's worthwhile giving employees guidelines for having a conversation with a difficult customer – almost a script if you like, although I'm against the concept of having these conversations scripted for it limits employees flexibility. These guidelines should ideally outline what-if scenarios: if the customer does A, then I will do B. Again, they don't need to be prescriptive – after all, they are designed to give employees additional resources in managing abusive customers and not to make them less empowered.

A huge benefit of these guidelines is that they help guide employees work at least in the beginning of the third vital element of a "handling customer abuse" training – the practice sessions. Once employees have sufficient knowledge, have seen what good looks like, and have had the chance to see it in practice, it is time for them to try their hand at it in a safe environment. Have someone play the role of an abusive customer and every employee try to deal with the situation; needless to say, make the customer script relevant by including the most frequently happening cases (one more reason to record and monitor customer abuse incidents). After the exercise, discuss as a group to come up with insights and conclusions.

In my view, it is very much worth having these three sessions in separate days or week, simply because that's a lot of content for employees to take in all at once. I'd recommend allowing them to go through the first (knowledge) session at their own pace, and they discuss as a group before continuing to the second session. And going back to the point that we, people, tend to forget things, I'd also advise you to hold refresher sessions once in a while. These also give you, the business leader, and employees the opportunity to reflect on what happened since the last time you had the training session, what worked, what didn't, and how can both of you improve.

What we discussed so far is an outline of a training module directly related to handling abusive customers. What we will talk about in the remainder of this chapter is how to train employees for skills that come in handy in this process. These skills are also helpful in dealing with aggressive customers and are helpful in a vast variety of different situations.

As we saw, there are four key elements of successfully handling customer abuse: remaining calm, appearing confident, establishing a connection, and solving the problem. These elements have their correlates in specific skills that are trainable and with enough effort everyone can master those. These are as follows:

- Remaining calm is related to the presence of high emotional intelligence and the skill to do emotional regulation well – how do we work with our emotions so that we make the most out of them instead of letting them govern our behavior

- Appearing confident is a lot about being assertive, i.e., staying in the healthy middle ground between passivity and aggressiveness
- Establishing a connection is all about listening and relationship building skills. Yes, these are skills. Some people seem to be naturally better at these and to avoid going into the nature–nurture debate I'll just say that no matter if this is true or not, we can all become better at listening and developing relationships.
- Finally, solving the problem is partially about being knowledgeable of the product or the service the company is delivering, partially about the processes and policies the company has in place to manage complaints (if that's what caused the aggression on the customer's side), and partially about the employee being adaptable, able to think on their feet, owning the issue, and being proactive.

In the remainder of this chapter, we will go through these one by one, describe what these skills involve, and how can employees learn them (and how can the company support them in learning them). On to the first skills: remaining calm!

How to Remain Calm in the Face of Abusive Customers

The first thing that any of us, be it at work or at home when we are facing difficult conversations, need to do is to try and remain calm. At a first glance this might sound like a fluffy, motivational advice – after all, we all know that we all want to be like that. The problem is how to do it, of course – how do we manage our emotions so that we don't strike back or become super nervous or agitated.

The problem with emotions is not so much that we do that or the other thing, though. The real issue is that emotions are like the proverbial hammer in the saying that to a man with a hammer everything looks like a nail – they are powerful drivers that push us toward acting in our most "natural" way, even when it is not the most productive response.

At this point, some of you might be of the opinion that our ability to remain calm when we are facing angry or aggressive people or customers is one that is entirely up to nature. There is, of course, merit to this. Some people seem inherently calmer than others, and some of us are much better in facing challenging situations. Yours truly, for instance and for his displeasure, is not part of this more balanced group of people; my "natural" tendency is to strike back – if some people freeze when facing distressing and frustrating situations and others prefer to flee the scene, I'd typically try to fight.

The good news is that while there is such an inherent predisposition for certain reactions, emotions need not be our rulers. We can all become much much better in managing (or as the more precise term goes – regulating) our emotions. It is by no means an easy process. There is a reason why emotions exist and it is to drive our behavior. To do the latter, they by necessity need to be powerful, which also makes them very difficult to manage or change. It is not impossible though, and there are behaviors and habits that can help us in this. The tips that we'll review in the remainder of this section mostly come from two strands of literature – emotional intelligence and emotion regulation.

The term emotional intelligence (EQ) became popular in the mid-1990s, mostly through the work of Daniel Goleman. In his paramount book, *Emotional Intelligence. Why It Can Matter More Than IQ*, he uses a quote from Aristotle to show the key challenge that we are facing when managing emotions. Unlike what a lot of people might be thinking, emotional intelligence is not about suppressing our feelings or impulses. It is not about not having these and it is not about keeping them to ourselves without letting them show. Emotional intelligence is much more about the appropriate display of emotions. As the aforementioned quote from Aristotle goes, "Anyone can become angry —that is easy. But to be angry with the right person, to the right degree, at the right time, for the right purpose, and in the right way —this is not easy." (Goleman, 2009, loc 50). As you can see, the literature around EQ is not only about remaining calm, which is our key point here. It concerns also emotions like being happy, sad, frightened, and many others. Still, it offers important insights into how can we remain calm.

Now, emotional intelligence is typically defined as consisting of five different elements: self-awareness, managing emotions, motivating oneself, empathy, and managing relationships. These are distinctive, yet interrelated aspects of EQ. For instance, one can barely do any management of their own emotions if they don't have a clear, honest view over how they react. By the same token, we can rarely build stable relationships if we don't manage our emotions well, and vice versa – functional relationships typically help us in managing our emotions. Knowing all this, what are the key insights that the EQ literature offers for employees facing abusive customers?

The very first thing is knowing how we react when we are dealing with aggressive customers. You need to know where you stand – what is the foundation you will be building on top of. For instance, some employees might be very good in knowing all the policies and processes of handling abusive customers but have a really hard time appearing confident – this requires one kind of intervention. Others might be very good in building relationships with customers thus neutralizing their aggressive inclinations, but really poor in actually solving customer issues – a completely different kind of training will be necessary in this case.

My best advice is for employees to rate themselves against the four elements of successfully dissolving potentially tense customer interactions, and to be as honest as possible in this. Do you remain calm? Do you appear confident? Do you build relationships well? Can you shift the customer's mindset? Can you solve their problem? Managers have a critical role to play in this, of course. Nothing helps in gaining self-awareness as an outside look and a receptive mind. You can help employees improve by first letting them know where they stand.

By the same token, do try to also understand what is each employee's strengths in terms of handling abusive customers. If they are good in building relationships, you might want to have them help others by coaching them or setting a good example. Or if some of them are good in getting to know and following the policies and processes, you might have these employees manage that part for the team. The opportunities abound, but none of them would be unlocked unless employees and managers have a clear view of where they stand.

The second tip for managing our emotions is very closely related to the first one, only this time instead of the more general (self-) awareness that we discussed so far, it concerns the specific emotions that we are feeling. Similarly to how this broader self-awareness is important for our self-regulation/management efforts, if we are to manage our emotions well, we first need to be able to pinpoint what these emotions actually are. At face value, this seems rather simple. We feel bad or good, or miserable, or happy. The thing is, as the emotional intelligence specialist Susan David says, "Many of us struggle to identify what exactly we are feeling, and oftentimes the most obvious label isn't actually the most accurate." (David, 2017, 35). She provides three tips for getting better at recognizing our emotions.

First, we need a wider emotional vocabulary. We are not just feeling good or bad, and neither are we simply feeling angry or happy. There is a plethora of words that might provide us with a better read of our exact emotional state in these situations. We might be grumpy, or frustrated, or impatient, or annoyed, for instance. Or in the case of happiness: why not thankful, trustful, relaxed, excited, or any other positive emotion? This is important because it does make a difference if we are frustrated or impatient – the way of dealing with those can be significantly different, and we wouldn't be doing ourselves a favor by simply subsuming them under the "angry" label.

Second, we need to consider the intensity of our emotions. "Angry" is not the same as "annoyed" – the former conveys a much stronger intensity, while the latter might, in comparison, seem like a minor irritation. Again, if we manage to pinpoint how strongly we are experiencing the specific emotion, we are better positioned to deal with it. A small annoyance we might be able to shrug under the carpet, but an intense anger requires a very active management effort. Hence, it is a good advice to rate the intensity of the emotion we have already labeled in the previous step.

Third, you might want to write things down. There are certain drawbacks to this, as we might begin to ruminate over our experiences, but as a rule of thumb, noting the situations that sparked the emotion and how we felt works. You might want to use phrases such as "'I have learned …'; 'It struck me that …'; 'The reason that …'; 'I now realize …'; and 'I understand …'" (David, 2017, 37) This helps with both identifying the specific emotion and reframing the situation in a more positive, productive light.

These things might seem super difficult to do in the heat of the moment, while there is an abusive customer in front of us. Yet, as with pretty much anything else in life, we become better at the things that we practice. Try to note how you feel when the customer starts yelling or using abusive language, and don't stop at "I am angry"; try also frustrated, scared, spiteful! Knowing this already opens the path to handling the rest of the interaction in a productive manner.

Another excellent tip for managing our emotions in the heat of the moment is to pay attention to our bodies. Leah Weiss explains:

> [I]f we focus our attention on our bodies, they can be our anchor in what's happening right now, even if the sensations are unpleasant. This is how anchoring works: We bring our attention into our bodies, noticing—rather than avoiding—the tension, circulation, pain, pleasure, or just neutral physical experience of, say, our right shoulder or the arch of our left foot. This practice helps us snap back to reality.
>
> (Weiss, 2017, 53)

There are a number of things we can do to effectively anchor ourselves to our bodies. One of the most brilliantly simple ways of doing that is to take a single breath. When we are in a stressful situation, all kinds of stressful thoughts are running through our minds; this chatter is very very often much worse than the actual situation itself. What taking a single breath does, then, is that it interrupts this flow of negative thoughts that we are having and brings us back to reality. A second good advice for anchoring ourselves in the moment is to pay attention to our emotions. Again, name them! Doing so means that they become somewhat detached from you, thus also easier to manage. These negative emotions are not you – they are something that is happening to you, and that you can handle.

Once you do these things, even for a brief period of time, you will start noticing how you handle stressful situations much better. There will be small improvements at first. Maybe you managed to not yell back at the customer for a second; or you remained calm for brief 30 seconds before you became anxious again. Whatever these wins are, celebrate them. We will get to building confidence in the next part of this chapter, but it's also very much worth noting it here – it is important that we give ourselves credit for the things we do well. True, we might not have handled the whole interaction with the abusive customer the way we wanted, but we managed for a minute. That's great! Now we are starting to feel the right path. Help your brain build that habit by releasing some dopamine by celebrating success!

Summing up what we discussed so far, awareness is absolutely critical for managing our emotions well. If we want to improve or to use our strengths most effectively, it is vital that we know where we stand in the first place. Know how you react when something stressful happens, how you would feel when someone starts being abusive, or when you have an annoyed customer in front of you. What emotions do these situations spark? Name them and be as specific as you can. "Good" and "bad" are too generic of terms; go with distressed, frustrated, annoyed, irritated, and so on instead. Do consider if you are experiencing these strongly or not. Embrace these emotions! Don't try to hide from them – they are there anyway and it's not about suppressing them, but working with them. Stay engaged in the moment by, for instance, taking a single breath to stop the negative chatter in your head. And finally, celebrate the small wins; teach yourself that you are doing something well! Perfection is not important, especially while you are only beginning to learn how to handle emotions well – progress is. Acknowledge the things that you are doing well and reinforce your own path to success by giving yourself credit.

More insights on how to manage our emotions well come from what in the psychological literature is known as "emotion regulation," which we briefly spoke about in a previous chapter. There are a number of insights that guide researchers working in this domain.

In the first place, "emotions arise when an individual attends to and evaluates (appraises) a situation as being relevant to a particular type of currently active goal ...)" (Gross, 2014, 3). The goal could be anything really. From small, short-term ones like getting a snack or a cappuccino, to overarching goals like getting a Master's degree or being a good father. What is important is that the goal we have should give meaning to the situation we are in, and emotions are borne in these situations.

The second important feature of emotions is that they are multifaceted and "involve loosely coupled changes in the domains of subjective experience, behavior, and central and peripheral physiology..." (Gross, 2014, 4). We tend to focus on how we feel in the moment, but a central aspect of emotions is also that they prepare or compel us to act in certain ways. These behavioral impulses are, as one might suppose, coupled with physiological responses like increased (or decreased) heart rate or changes in posture, for instance.

These two primary features of emotions are part of what is known as the modal model of emotion, according to which "emotions involve person–situation transactions that compel attention, have meaning to an individual in light of currently active goals, and give rise to coordinated yet flexible multisystem responses that modify the ongoing person–situation transaction in crucial ways." (Gross, 2014, 5)

In brief, a situation in which we are involved in some way happens. We might have just spilled our coffee, or a biker might have startled us, or we might have realized that we didn't send this important email. This situation, in turn, grabs our attention and we are compelled to attend to it. Once we've done that, the next thing that we do is to evaluate (i.e., appraise) what does this mean to us in light of our goals. We want to drink coffee or to keep our attire clean? Well, if we spilled our coffee, then our appraisal of the event will be highly negative and is likely to annoy us. On the other hand, if we don't want to advance in our career or if we are disengaged from work, then not sending this email might not be such a big deal after all. Depending on the specific appraisal that we reach, we then act in certain ways. In both of the examples, we just saw the deed had been done, but in the case of wanting to keep our clothes clean we might start looking for ways to clean them, for instance, while if we are not bothered too much by this email we didn't send we might decide that we can just send it tomorrow. Note that this process appears very rational and slow when written down on paper, but in reality, it is, of course, much faster and more often than not goes unnoticed by us – this doesn't mean that it is not happening though.

Even though this process is mostly unconscious, the fact that when we experience emotions we go through these stages gives us ample opportunities to intervene and manage them. As we briefly discussed in a previous chapter, we have at least five points at which we can regulate our emotions. The first two concern the situation, which gives rise to emotions.

First, we might aim to select situations that promote or hinder certain emotions; for instance, if we want to avoid feeling annoyed, we might try to avoid meeting this annoying colleague or neighbor of ours (I'm not saying that we should, but merely that we can do that). And vice versa, we might (and we do) seek situations that we generally know are going to make us feel better, such as having a drink with friends, or going for a walk in the park.

Next, we can try to manage the situation so that it is not as [fill in the blank] as it typically would, i.e., to make an unpleasant situation a less unpleasant one. A classic example is buying a gift for someone we suspect might be less than happy with us or not having too much coffee before a presentation that makes us nervous. Getting a shot of anesthetic before a painful dental procedure falls under the same rubric, just like promising ourselves that if we do X, we will treat ourselves with Y.

A third point at which we might intervene to manage our emotions is at the "attention-grabbing" stage: "Attentional deployment is one of the first emotion regulatory processes to appear during development ..., and it is used from cradle to grave, particularly when it is not possible to modify one's situation." (Gross, 2014, 10). The two most widely used strategies here involve distracting ourselves from something negative, such as turning our gaze away from something we find disgusting or looking at our phones when we are bored, and turning our attention toward something that sustains a certain emotion, such as thinking about the time that we gave an excellent presentation to remind ourselves that we are good presenters.

A fourth, and vital!, element of emotion regulation is the so-called cognitive change. We might not avoid the situation and we might not be able to modify it and we might not be able to distract ourselves from it, but we can try to think about it differently. That is, for instance, the strategy that underlies the business cliché stating that problems are opportunities – it is an attempt at emotion regulation, and except for the fact that it has become somewhat empty from content, it is a very good way of managing our emotions. A problem is by its nature something that makes us scared, annoyed, frustrated; it puts us in a defensive state of mind. An opportunity, on the other hand, is a chance to grow, to do something more; it puts us in a promotion state of mind. Similarly, we might consider things as learning opportunities, or as chances to prove we are really good at something. And lastly, this process might also involve rethinking what kind of emotion are we experiencing at all – Am I nervous or excited? Sad or nostalgic or grateful? Bored or content?

And finally, a fifth group of strategies for emotion regulation emerges very late in the process – when we initiate a certain behavior. We might have been unsuccessful in regulating our emotions thus far, but we have one last chance: we have the opportunity to suppress the action that the process has lead us to, like yelling at someone, or crying, or snapping at people; by the same token, we might have not managed to evoke a positive emotion in ourselves, but we can still do the deed, such as buying a present for our loved one or giving a great presentation. A lot of the tactics that we discussed when we spoke about emotional intelligence come to play at this stage. Think, for example, of physical exercise or breathing exercises. These are both ways for decreasing the "experiential and physiological aspects of negative emotions" (Gross, 2014, 10), and the reason they work is that they make us less reactive, thus less likely to give ourselves to the impulse.

Knowing all of this, it's a good time to ask ourselves which of these strategies really work and which are rather dysfunctional, especially in cases in which we are facing an abusive customer.

Starting with the first option – situation selection - broadly speaking, while it's sometimes a good idea to avoid certain situations, there is at least one major drawback to this approach – we close ourselves for opportunities to explore the world. After all, if we only chose to be involved in situations in which we are certain about the outcome and we know it is likely to be a positive one, we would become tremendously preoccupied with what we know works well for us. While unpleasant, a host of opportunities and learnings and ideas and positive emotions often come from chance encounters, which we would have otherwise avoided. Again, this is not to say that we need to necessarily always seek situations that might make us uncomfortable, but it's a good idea to keep some of the options open.

More closely related to the topic of the book, more often than not employees simply don't have the option to avoid an abusive customer, and even if they do, at the end of the day it would come with the price of not ever learning how to deal with them. At the end of the day, it's a rather dysfunctional approach to call a manager every time a customer begins to act rather aggressively, not to mention that most companies (rightfully) will object to such an approach. And then again, even if they do, it robs employees of the opportunity to be exposed to difficult customers and to strengthen their skills.

Modifying the situation is by all means something that both companies and employees would do well to do when it comes to abusive customers. In the case of customer abuse situation, modification done well would do two things. First, it would minimize the chances of aggressive customers holding the reign; the ways of doing that we already discussed in a previous chapter. Secondly, another point we reviewed earlier is that key to managing such difficult situations lies in having enough resources, be they strict processes, zero-tolerance policies, skills, knowledge, or others. In short, anything that increases employees' resources helps them in dealing with abusive customers. Situation modification is, then, one of the best things a company and its employees can do to help the latter remain calm in the face of customer aggression.

The third thing that people do to manage their emotions – attention deployment (or distraction) - isn't really handful in customer abuse situations. It wouldn't be very beneficial if we, employees, start thinking about something entirely else like this holiday in Spain last year in the midst of talking to an aggressive customer, would it? As we saw earlier, one of the tips for remaining calm is to in fact to do something akin to exactly the opposite of this – grounding ourselves in the moment (by taking a deep breath or otherwise). So, choosing to avoid such situations isn't very productive, trying to modify them is absolutely a good course of action, and distracting ourselves is also a no-go.

This leaves us with two final options – reappraising or reevaluating the situation, and modulating our behaviors; we might either find a different meaning in what's happening or try to alter the direction of our actions, for instance by suppressing them. One of the best researched contrasts in the domain of emotion regulation concerns the effectiveness of these two tactics – reappraisal (reevaluation) and suppression of responses.

The results are unequivocal – of the two, it is the reappraisal of the situation and/or our emotions that works in our favor, and we will do well to avoid suppression. One of the leading researchers in the domain, James Gross, notes that

> Affectively, experimental studies have shown that suppression leads to decreased positive but not negative emotion experience…, increased sympathetic nervous system responses…, and greater activation in emotion-generative brain regions such as the amygdala…. . Correlational studies are largely congruent with these experimental findings and, if anything, suggest a more negative profile of affective consequences for suppression, in that compared to people who do not report using suppression, people who report using suppression experience less positive emotion and more negative emotion, including painful feelings of inauthenticity as well as depressive symptoms.
>
> (Gross, 2014, 10–11)

In addition, suppression leads to worse memory and less liking from our social interaction partners, while reappraisal can improve performance on standardized exams and people who use this tactic say they have better relationships with their friends.

In short, in our efforts to regulate our emotions we are well-advised to try to see the situation we are in and our feelings in a different light, rather than to suppress our emotions. There are caveats to this, of course – no solution, especially in the field of psychology, is unequivocally good or bad – but in most cases if we can, we'd better reevaluate our emotions.

What we discussed so far in this part of the chapter was ideas on how to remain calm in the face of customer aggression. We reviewed tips coming from two different, yet interrelated, streams of literature – emotional intelligence and emotion regulation, and, hopefully, got some very practical tips on managing our emotions. In the next section, we will turn to the second piece of the "dealing with abusive customers" puzzle – acting with confidence.

How to Be Confident?

Now this might seem like an odd question to ask. At least that's what I would have thought a couple of years ago. Yours truly is in fact a not really confident person, to say the least. I would do all the things that this kind of people do. I'd do excessive bodily movements when I'm stressed. I'd overreact when I feel threatened (which happens often). I'd become super nervous when put in new, different situations that I'm not experienced in handling. I'd be ashamed to talk to strangers. The list can go on and on.

Being confident, like emotion regulation, seems at first like one of those qualities that people either have or don't have. It's a bit counter-intuitive to think that we can purposefully develop confidence in ourselves. And while it is true, of course, this is more of a product or a result from many other things we have done, it is exactly this that also unlocks the opportunity to influence our confidence levels. As with emotion regulation, it's a matter of following the adage that "It's easier to act your way into a new way of thinking than to think your way into a new way of acting"[1]. Confidence, then, is in a lot of ways a skill, rather than something people just possess.

And just so we are clear, there is a fine line between self-confidence and self-esteem. The latter refers to holding oneself in high regard and having a sense of our own importance for and in the world. The former, which concerns us here, is all about knowing that we can handle whatever comes our way, and projecting this to others. It is not about thinking you are perfect, and it is not about being selfish, and it is not about holding oneself to impossibly high standards. Self-confidence is merely about the belief you have in yourself that you can manage things. As one can expect, self-confidence is a valuable asset to have, as it "helps people gain credibility, make a strong first impression, deal with pressure, and tackle personal and professional challenges. It's also an attractive trait, as confidence helps put others at ease." (PsychologyToday.com)

So, the key question in front of us now is how do we project self-confidence in the face of abusive customers? How to show them that we know who we are and we know the red lines that shouldn't be crossed, and we are in charge and capable of handling the situation. To help with this, we will introduce the concept of assertiveness – on we go.

The idea of assertiveness in my view is absolutely critical for being able to handle customer abuse properly. Broadly speaking, you are likely to meet three distinctive types of people. There are those among us who would go really really far to defend their point of view or goal. They would argue in such a way that it makes you feel like they are not listening to your point at all. They would attack your perspective and would try to make it look ridiculous. Basically, they wouldn't stop for nothing to get what they want.

You might also meet the exact opposite type of people – the very quiet, agreeable ones, who would do anything to avoid conflict. You ask these people something and they say Yes, even if they don't really mean it, simply because saying No seems almost rude to them. If they want something, they would either keep it to themselves before summoning the courage to spit it out, or would ask for it in a very subtle fashion.

So those are the aggressive and the passive among us. The former pushing and requesting and being blunt, and the latter keeping their wants to themselves and being compliant so as to avoid conflict. Neither of these approaches seems very productive, does it? The aggressive one might get us what we want, but certainly doesn't leave the other person wanting to meet us again; the passive one is much more likeable, but it's also much more difficult to achieve things this way, plus often people might be absolutely fine doing something (for us) but we'd never know it because we never asked.

In between these two approaches lies the assertive way of expressing ourselves and handling any kind of situations. When we act assertively, we do defend our standpoint and we do ask people to do things for us, and we do express our wishes, unlike in the passive approach. But unlike using the aggressive one, we do it in a respectful, confident manner; we listen to other people's point of view, and critically, we accept the possibility of them saying No to what we ask for as something completely normal, which the other person has the right to.

To give one example, imagine that you are at work, your car doesn't start, and you are running late for picking up your kid after school. You know that a colleague of yours lives really close to the school and they are going home by car and they are leaving in 5 minutes.

Now, a passive approach to this would be to wait, and wait, and at the end of the day not ask your colleague to give you a ride. You are worried that you'd be intruding yourself in their private space, plus, they know your car is out of order because you discussed it over lunch – if they want to help you, they'd ask themselves. If we handle this aggressively, we would ask them to give us a ride, and would sometimes even assume they'd do it! If they say No, we'd go like Oh, come on, it's super close to your house, why wouldn't you do it?! And if at the end of the day they don't help us, we might hold a grudge and even tell others that our colleague refused to help us.

The assertive way of managing this kind of situation is to ask politely if the person wants to help us. We would explain calmly the circumstances and why this is important for us, and would say that we'd appreciate it if the person lands us a hand. Critically, if the person says they prefer to not do it (for whatever reason), we would be fine and respect their decision; the rationale is not even important in this case – our colleague might have all kinds of reasons to refuse, ranging from feeling insecure in their driving skills, through their car not being clean enough, to wanting to have me-time on the ride home. It really doesn't matter – what is important is that we ask and we respect the other person's right to refuse.

This also works in the other direction, of course. We get asked to do dozens of things every day, some of which we are happy to oblige to and others which we prefer not to do. If we are aggressive, we might react with too much force to even small requests. Simply put, we snap at people. If we are passive, we tend to say Yes to whatever it is people ask from us, even if we don't have the time or don't want to do it.

An assertive approach would again fall somewhere in the middle between these two approaches. The critical thing is to remember that we do have the right to say No, but we don't necessarily need to do it aggressively. Think firm instead – assertive people are firm, but not rude. They would express their wishes and would be open to negotiations if the situation allows them – if not, they are happy to walk away from the discussion. If you don't want to give your colleague a ride, you have the right to not do it; but you also don't need to go crazy over such a request and laughing in the person's face or telling others that they had asked you to do this preposterous thing. It's all about the respect to the other person and to yourself. You have rights, and others have them too; your emotions are not more important than theirs, but then neither does what they feel matter more than what you do. Equality and respect.

By this point, I believe you would be fairly convinced that acting assertively is productive in life; let's now see how does this play out in the cases that matter the most for us here – when facing abusive customers. To begin with, it's useful to consider two aspects of assertiveness in such a situation: verbal and physical, i.e., do we talk like and do we look assertive. As we saw, "An assertive person is emotionally honest, direct, self-enhancing, and expressive. He/she feels confident, self-respecting at the time of his/her actions as well as later." (HealthyPlace.com). The only way we can convey this is by the way we talk and by the way we work with our bodies, so it's useful to review the best practices in this domain.

Let's start with some tips on speaking assertively. First things first, "Speak in a clear, steady voice – loud enough for the people to whom you are speaking to hear you." (HealthyPlace.com). We are not talking about yelling here, but merely about a strong, confident voice – not too loud so as to appear to be angry but also not too soft so that you seem intimidated. Also, speak slowly – slower than you might usually do even. This has two benefits. One, it helps you to keep your speech fluent. When we rush things, we say things that we wouldn't typically do, so slow down. And two, it signals that you are calm.

When responding to the customer, be clear and to the point. This is mostly in order to avoid creating confusion in the conversation, which if anything might make things worse. On that note, I think it's important that you don't immediately start demanding that the customer changes their behavior. Some people would be rude from the onset of the conversation. As we will see later, trying to manage their emotions does not work. I'll repeat that – do not try to manage customers' emotions by telling them to calm down or to behave themselves, at least not in the beginning of the interaction. Emotion-focused problem-solving is not nearly as effective as problem-focused strategies (which we'll discuss in a minute). Just focus on your job.

Another good advice is to "Assert your right to ask for more information and for clarification before you answer." (HealthyPlace.com). Do ask questions to understand better what the situation is and keep an open mind about it. In the next section, we'll talk about building a relationship with the customer, and active listening is perhaps the very best thing that you can do to do that. You have the right to ask questions, and if a customer disagrees with that, you have the right to tell them that you do.

At one point, after you've given the customer ample time to change their behavior to a more socially acceptable one, you might want to cut it. In these cases, a good advice is to make your position very clear; you might, for instance, say something along the lines of "Sir/Madame, you did/said [this and that], and I believe it is [rude/unacceptable, etc.]. May I ask you to forebear from such behavior/words in the remainder of our conversation?" On that note, do not say "I'm sorry but", especially when framing this latter ask – "I'm sorry but I'm going to have to ask you to behave properly" is not a good way of doing this. After all, you are not sorry! You have the right to be treated well, no matter how frustrated the customer is.

As a final suggestion, if appropriate, agree with the customer on at least some points. You might, for instance:

- Agree with the truth - Find a statement in the criticism that is truthful and agree with that statement.
- Agree with the odds - Agree with any possible truth in the critical statement.
- Agree in principle - Agree with the general truth in a logical statement such as, "That makes sense." (HealthyPlace.com)

The power of agreement lies in shifting the mindset to a collaborative one. You are not against the customer – you are with them. The crux of the matter is very often in finding the common ground and having a definition of the issue at hand that you share. Surprisingly many arguments and challenging situations can be resolved by taking the time to define them well at the onset. You can be the leader in this interaction: the person who steps back, see the full picture, and guides the customer to a place where you both want to be.

Moving on, the principles that apply to our verbal behavior can be fairly easily translated into our body language. To appear assertive, "Stand straight, steady, and directly face the people to whom you are speaking while maintaining eye contact." (HealthyPlace.com). Don't shrug your shoulders, as this is a clear marker of submissive behavior, and don't lean on one side. What you are looking to do is to make the other person aware that you have the same rights as them and you will stand your ground.

It is critical that you maintain appropriate eye contact and you look the person directly in the eyes. Remember, assertiveness is about being open and direct, and that's what you want your body to convey. Eyes fixated on the tip of your shoes don't do that, and neither does looking away (averting the gaze is a clear sign that you feel uncomfortable in the situation – even if you do, try not to show it). By a similar token though, don't lean forward toward the person – this might be interpreted as a threat, as it looks like you are about to attack them.

If you are standing up, keep your body weight evenly balanced on both feet. Again, you are trying to communicate that you have not been kicked out of your confidence zone and that you are managing to keep your balance – show this with your body. Relatedly, "Feet are firmly planted, flat on the floor (including when sitting), typically slightly apart to provide a firm base." (Changingminds.org). In a similar vein,

When standing, keep your feet planted firmly on the ground, shoulder width apart from each other and distribute your weight equally on both legs. Keep in mind that you should angle your feet outward and in the direction of the person you are speaking with, to signal that you are receptive to hearing that person's ideas and opinions.

(AmericanExpress.com)

The latter will also come in handy in the next section, when we try to establish a rapport with the customer.

It is also important to maintain the right social distance. You don't want to be too far from the person, as this will only increase the psychological distance between you too, and might seem as if you are trying to run away, not to mention that you and them will have to raise their voices to talk, which is dangerously close to yelling. Then again, you don't want to be too close to the customer. There is a safety reason for that, as you don't know if they wouldn't snap and become physically aggressive, but in addition if you are the one who closes the distance it might make them feel threatened and we don't want that either. Clearly, what is appropriate social distance differs by culture, but a good rule of thumb would be 1.2–2.0 meters.

If you have to walk, make sure that you do it in a purposeful, focused fashion;

Walk at an even pace with medium strides. If you take tiny, tiny steps you will come across as a scurrying mouse, and barging ahead as if you are about to invade a small republic not only looks aggressive, but suggests you are stressed and out of control.

(Hartley)

The speed of walking conveys a lot, and while you don't want to appear disinterested and walk super slowly, you also don't want to convey that you are in panic by walking around like crazy.

Your head movements are also a good way to convey assertiveness: "Gestures are used to emphasize truths" (Changingminds.org). Nodding is especially effective in this regard, but clearly you don't want to do this excessively. Nevertheless, a nod or two would show both that there is some truth in the other person's words (there always is), and that you are listening actively.

And finally, a word of advice about probably the most expressive parts of our bodies – our hands and arms. Mary Hartley gives a succinct and easy to remember but very hard to enact answer to what do we need to with our hands: nothing. Have you noticed all the small movements that we do with our hands, especially when we are nervous? Playing with our hair or rings or beards, constantly moving our hands around, crossing them in front of our bodies, making jerky, flappy hand movements, and all the rest. Well, these are a no go if you want to appear assertive. If you are to do something with your hands make your gestures big ones, i.e., avoid movements from the wrists or the elbows and do only ones from the shoulder. If you feel like you don't know what to do with your hands, you might either hold something with both of them (but in a nonthreatening manner!), like a pen or a folder (but avoid hiding yourself behind it). Your hands should convey openness, thus your palms would be up, instead of clinched in a fist. And I don't know if I need to say this explicitly, but I will for the sake of completeness – there should be no finger-pointing and absolutely no touching.

I hope that by now you are fairly confident that there are very specific, practical things you and/or your employees can do to help them a) remain calm and b) act with confidence when facing an abusive customer. These two are absolutely necessary ingredients in the process of dealing with aggressive customers, as nothing good is likely to come out of such an interaction lest we stay calm and assertive. In the next chapter of the book, we will talk more about the ways we can develop our self-confidence in the long-run, but before that it's time to talk about the third element of a successful customer abuse handling process – establishing rapport.

How to Establish Rapport?

The most straightforward definition of what rapport is describes it as "a relationship characterized by agreement, mutual understanding, or empathy that makes communication possible or easy" (Merriam-Webster). It's all about this feeling of being heard and understood, of a smooth flow of the conversation, and openness and why not even warmth toward the other. Clearly, this a situation that we would all like to be in with all of our clients, as there is a plethora of benefits of having such a close relationship with them, like, well, the higher likelihood that they'll do more business with us. Importantly, establishing rapport is also an almost surefire way to both prevent and to handle customer abuse, and in the next couple of pages we'll see how this works in practice.

There are two important notes that we need to make before we start. First, while establishing rapport is generally a very good idea in most situations, there are some cases in which you are better off following the more strict, formal policies and processes of the company. Think, for instance, about sexual harassment, e.g., when a waitress received unwanted sexual comments from customers. Trying to establish rapport in these cases is only going to put more fuel into the fire, so do not do that – my best advice is to follow your company's policy for handling such situations. You (no one!) should play nice with others to avoid being abused by them – again, assertiveness is the skill we are hinting at here. Being kind and open and warm is all good up to the red lines that you cannot and do not want others to cross.

The second note we need to start with is that a loss of what we'll discuss here can and in fact should happen before the customer snaps. Sometimes, customers are abusive from the very first second of the interaction; other times situations escalate on the go. Whichever the case, establishing rapport from the onset of the conversation can only bring benefits, so, if possible, start building it from the very beginning and carry on until the end of the interaction.

So how do we do that? How do we build rapport? How do we develop "a relationship characterized by agreement, mutual understanding, or empathy that makes communication possible or easy" (Merriam-Webster). And most importantly, how do we do that while the customer is acting abusively with us? Let's see some of the best techniques that exist.

If you are wondering where to begin, a simple mutual introduction is an excellent starting point. There is a reason, after all, why in movies we see negotiators in hostage or other crime-related situations asking for the perpetrator's name. By the same token, there is a reason why victims of crimes are well-advised to say their names to the perpetrator. In both cases, it serves the very same function – it draws us out of anonymity. It is much easier to behave inappropriately or to hurt others, and it is much easier for others to inflict damage on us if we are nameless; it's almost like we are objects, and objects don't have feelings.

In their beautiful book, *The Mind Club*, Daniel Wegner and Kurt Gray explore the nature of our perception of the mind in ourselves and in others. After all, how can you and I be certain that other people have minds? We could be the only one in the whole world! How do we know that the person or the other entity, more broadly speaking, we are facing has a mind? In their studies, they have discovered that there are two dimensions people use to distinguish things that have a mind from those that don't: "people see minds in terms of two fundamentally different factors, sets of mental abilities we labeled experience and agency." (Wegner and Kurt, 2016, 10).

The experience dimension covers whether the entity we are facing is capable of feeling things, be they happiness, pain, etc. The agency factor is all about, as Wegner and Gray put it, thinking and doing – can the entity in front of us enact certain behaviors? Can it have control over its actions or is it driven by primal impulses alone? Along these dimensions, they have discovered that people perceive God, for instance, to have a whole lot of agency, but no experience, while a toddler sits in the exact opposite end and has a whole lot of experience, but no agency. In the sweet sport, from a mind-attribution perspective, you have yourself and other men and women, who have a lot of both agency and experience; they can feel and they can act according to their will. Reversing this, the more human we are perceived to be, the more experience and agency people consider that we have, and one of the most fundamental things that signal our humanness is our names.

A simple introduction, then, increases the amount of experience that gets attributed to you – you are no longer an object, but a creature with a mind that can feel! And in other direction, when someone introduces themselves, it reminds them of their own mind. They are no longer a name-less entity that acts on pure impulse; they have agency and they can at least to a certain extend control their actions. Introduce yourself, and if the situation permits, ask the customer to share their name. As Hubspot advises, "Icebreakers aren't just for summer camp and first days of class; they can also benefit your interaction with a customer. The best way to do so is by telling them who you are beyond your role as their support rep." (Amaresan, 2022). This way you are both no longer two faces from the crowd but two equal, full-blown human beings with feelings and with self-control who experience pain and pleasure – it is as simple as that.

A second very powerful thing you can do to establish rapport is to find a point of similarity between yourself and the customer. Note that this does not in any way need to be a very deep similarity, like "You and I have both been through a difficult divorce." Not at all. Studies show that even very small and somewhat artificial similarities are enough for people to start feeling closer to each other. The psychologist Sam Maglio points out that "Merely traveling in the same direction creates interpersonal attraction and relationship satisfaction just as readily as merely eating the same food or eating from the same plate fosters trust, cooperation, and acceptance of advice." (Maglio, 2020, 117).

What is perhaps even more amusing is that we consider things and people who share the first letter of our name as being more similar to us. Because of this so-called name-letter effect, we are more likely to be attracted to people whose names share our first name initials, to choose a place to live that features that, or to "make donations when approached by someone with a similar name to make a contribution, or when their first names resembled the name of the university" (Psychologistsworld.com). We need just a bit to feel similar to someone, and similarity breeds liking, i.e., rapport. We like what is like us. We know it, it's easy for us to process, it's non-threatening. And having in mind that our brains are lazy by design (or to put it more in their favor – they prioritize survival and reproduction needs, and energy efficiency), pretty much anything that slightly hints toward similarity to ourselves is good and well-liked. Again, there is no need to go very deep. Simple things like same names or even same name letters will suffice; same place of birth; both wearing blue today; same phone brand; both wearing a beard – all of these things can help, so use them to your advantage. Needless to say, don't overdo it as first, you don't need to become friends for life and second, some customers might see this as an intrusion into their personal space. Still, try it gently and see what happens; you can always backtrack but you can't always advance.

Further to the points we discussed so far, it is a very good idea to try to shape messages in a positive light. This is somewhat of a cliché in the business world, and you never hear top managers talk about problems but only about opportunities, and they don't say "layoffs" but "restructuring," etc. Be mindful of that, as people might take this as bulls…ing instead, so don't overdo it. Nevertheless, there is nothing wrong in saying "I'm not sure of the answer, but I will find out now and get right back to you" instead of "I'm not sure" or "I'm sorry, I'm new." (Amaresan, 2022). This creates an atmosphere of positivity, or in the very least avoids the customer panicking about the issue, and is a nice subtle way of showing that you've got things under control. You see, you being new is not anything anyone can do something about. The fact that you will check, though, already shows that you are making the first steps toward solving the case.

A next tip that you would be well advised to follow to handle the situation is to avoid using technical jargon as much as possible. Clearly, this one is all the more valid in case the customer has become agitated because of a complaint they have to make, but it's a good tip for customer service in general as well. The point is, do not try to appear more knowledgeable by using long sophisticated words – do your best to talk at the level of the customer instead. Again, the goal is to remove any barrier there is between you and them, and one of the surefire ways of doing that is to speak as they do. Similarity breeds liking – try to sound like them.

On a related note, do not try to speed things up! Talk slowly. You need the customer to understand what you are saying, and it has the added benefit of showing confidence. No one wins in situations in which the customer is not able to follow the conversation, so make sure to pace yourself.

The crux of the matter very often lies in the so-called curse of knowledge: we somehow seem to think that if we know something, then everyone knows it. I'd rather risk a lengthy unnecessary explanation than rushing things. It's a marathon that you are running, not a sprint. Make sure that you use the appropriate tempo lest things become extremely difficult in the second part of the race.

A lot of what we discussed so far has to do with how you talk to the customer, but there is an even more powerful thing you can do than talking. Perhaps, the best advice one can give about building rapport with customer (and with other people in our daily lives) is called active listening. While talking is still involved as that's the primary way for us to communicate to others, the emphasis when it comes to active listening is completely different. You know how very often we talk to someone and we notice how they avert their gaze from time to time, or reply to what you are saying in a way that shows they are not completely there, or they look at their phone, or do something else in that regard? Do you feel listened to? Do you think your conversation partner is paying full attention to your words and emotions and thoughts? Of course not. And how does that make you feel? Dejected? Ignored? Unimportant? Of course it does, and that's super normal. We don't feel particularly well connected to the other person when they don't listen to us.

Active listening, then, is all about two things. First, it's a lot about truly understanding what the other person is trying to communicate – both the explicit meaning and the emotion that's behind it[2]. We are not talking about understanding the specific words here – we all do that if we are fluent speakers of the language. Active listeners attempt to capture the subtle clues that the conversation partner is sending to derive a fuller and deeper understanding of the message. Is the person talking slowly and fluently or hurriedly and stumbling mid-sentence? Do they look composed when talking? What's the intonation of their sentences? The list can go on and on, but the crux of the matter is this:

> Listen for total meaning: When someone is conveying a message, there are two meanings to gather: the content and the feeling or attitude underlying the message. An active listener is not only tuned in to the information conveyed, but also how it is conveyed and any nonverbal cues present.
>
> (O'Bryan, 2022)

The second goal of active listening is to express interest and involvement in what the other person is saying, and a care for it[3]. While the first objective was to receive information and to understand, this second point relates to how do you act in the conversation and how well are you managing it. It's all about conveying interest, and as with the first point we spoke about, we can do this both verbally and nonverbally, and we'll do well to be mindful of both aspects. Active listening is a lot about showing that you are engaged in the conversation and that you actually care about what the other person is saying. You don't necessarily need to get deeply involved – that's not the point. What we all need to do to become better listeners, though, is give our undivided attention to the conversation we are having.

In case you are wondering if active listening can help manage a difficult conversation such as the one with an abusive customer, studies convincingly show that it does. In 2020, Guy Itzchakov of the University of Haifa published the results of two studies which aim to clarify that very question. The results show that there is a ton of value in improving our listening skills, as "listening training had lasting effects on employees' listening abilities, anxiety reduction, and perspective-taking during difficult conversations." (Itzchakov, 2020, 938).

That is all very good, but what are the specific things we can do to improve our active listening skills? What are the techniques that can help us become better listeners? Fortunately, these are rather simple things that you can start doing immediately, as long as you have them in mind. Asking more questions is the first thing that is worth doing, and not just during challenging situations. If I may share a very personal view, this is one of the most widely underused, if not undervalued, skills that we might have. In fact, we are even discouraged to develop it; one needn't think beyond our early childhood or school experiences, in which asking questions is not exactly held in high regard.

There is, of course, a plethora or reasons why asking questions is a good thing to do, starting with the most obvious one – any new knowledge we acquire is a result of the existence of a question, be it an implicit or an explicit one. In the context of active listening and handling customer abuse it has a perhaps even more important function – asking questions shows that we are interested in what is going on. Maybe the worst thing that might happen during a business presentation or a first date or a school reunion is not to have too many questions, but to have none. We all know what this means: "I don't care enough about [whatever] to engage in a conversation with you." That is the same message we are sending customers if we are not asking questions, and that's not how a rapport is built, is it? We want the other party to talk; we want them to share things; we want to know what's going on in their world. That's what questions help us achieve.

And then there's more. In a beautiful book best described as a manifesto for asking more and better questions, Hal Gregersen memorably said

Questions are reframed in ways that prove catalytic. They dissolve barriers to thinking, like limiting prior assumptions, and they channel creative energy down more productive pathways. People who have been feeling stuck suddenly see new possibilities and are motivated to pursue them.

(Gregersen, 2018, 19)

Imagine being able to do that! To open new worlds! To channel customers' positive, productive energy instead of their destructive flows. What follows is a number of tips and tricks for doing that.

- Send physical cues that you are listening. Face the person who is talking and keep your gaze (appropriately) fixated on them; clearly, don't stare at them, but show them that they have your full and undivided attention. If you can match their body language, do it. That's a very powerful way to show that you are on their side. And I hope it's needless to point this out, but don't do anything else. There is a frustrated person in front of you who is super close to lashing out – this is where your attention needs to be, not on your phone or the cars passing by. Active listeners first and foremost listen.
- Rephrase, i.e., restate the issue the customer has in your own words, but only do it sparingly. Of course, there are benefits to saying out loud what the customer had said, but as Robin Abrahams and Boris Groysberg note in an especially insightful HBR magazine article, "Rephrasing what your interlocutor has said, however, can increase both emotional friction and the mental load on both parties. Use this tool only when you need to check your own comprehension — and say, explicitly, 'I'm going to put this in my own words to make sure I understand.'" (Abrahams and Groysberg, 2021).
- Clarify. There is absolutely nothing wrong in asking clarifying questions. No, we will not sound stupid and yes, we have the right, even the responsibility, to do it. So many times, the key reason for communication breakdowns lies in assuming that we have understood something. Well, there is no need to assume as you have a much simpler and more effective solution in your hands (well, mouth) – ask a clarifying question. Here's an example from Zendesk: "Start by saying the last few words of your customer's statement back to them. Imagine a customer calls in to complain about receiving a dress in the wrong size. You could say, 'To clarify, the dress is a size 10 and not a size 8?'" (Inabo, 2022).
- Mirror. The power of this technique lies in the fact that it creates similarity (or in the very least the illusion of it). Its essence lies in doing or saying what the other person is doing or saying. When it comes to body language, it's about assuming the same pose as your interaction partner or doing the gestures they are doing. Clearly, don't go too far, especially if the person has assumed an attacking pose, but do try to at least partially convey this similarity. It works the same way with verbal

communication, only instead of copying gestures, you take the last few words the customer said and repeat them back, making them sound like a question. The beauty of this is that it can easily go unnoticed, but at the same time it nudges people to keep talking, which is what you want to achieve. On that note, a slightly alternative version of this technique is to remember a couple of key phrases the customer uses and use them while you are talking. This shows that you have things in common, which, as we saw, is an excellent foundation of rapport.

- Summarize. The core of this technique is to make a brief pause from the flow of the conversation to wrap up where you (together) stand before continuing. This has the huge benefit of chunking the ideas and thoughts into smaller bits, meaning that there is a much higher chance that you and the customer agree on some of them – it is difficult to completely agree with a whole book, for instance, but you can agree with certain chapters or paragraphs. Start from there. Summarize what had been said to make sure you understand and you've established common ground, and continue building from there.

- Encourage. That's the art of the seemingly minor verbal cues such as "okay," "yes," and "uh-huh," and non-verbal ones like nodding. The idea is that while the customer is talking, you show interest in what you are saying without actually interrupting the. Phrases like "Can you tell me more about that?," "Really?" and "Is that so?" are also handy in such situations. Saying things like that conveys that you are listening, and what is more – that you would like to learn more. Remember, you being able to understand the other person in-depth is critical for building rapport, and for that you need them to talk.

- Use concrete language. As you might have noticed, language gives us the opportunity to refer to one and the same object in a very abstract ("that"), somewhat concrete ("item," "clothing"), or very concrete way ("shirt"). The difference seems rather trivial, yet in an article published in 2021 in the *Journal of Consumer Research*, two of the leading researchers in the field of marketing – Grant Packard and Jonah Berger – show that this is not the case. They conducted a total of five studies and the results unequivocally point to the fact that "customers are more satisfied, willing to purchase, and purchase more when employees speak to them concretely. This occurs because when sales reps do that, 'customers infer that employees … are listening (i.e., attending to and understanding their needs)'" (Packard and Berger, 2020, 787). In a word, try to be as specific as possible when talking to clients. Instead of saying "Let me bring you that," go with "Let me bring you the size 8 black shoes," and instead of "You will receive your refund shortly" say "You will receive your money back shortly." (money is more specific than a refund)

- Do not rehearse while the interaction partner is talking. One of the key issues that makes listening so difficult is that we can think faster than we can listen; by the most common estimates, we can process three times more words in a certain period of time compared to words we have heard. That's all very good, but it leaves a lot of brain power unused, and quite naturally perhaps, we end up talking to ourselves while we are listening to our partner – exactly what we need to avoid doing to listen actively. Abrahams and Groysberg (2021) advise us to "Take a brief pause after they finish speaking to compose your thoughts." Clearly, this will slow the rate of the overall conversation down and might seem a bit unnatural, as we are better used to people interrupting each other than to having a, say, five second pause between exchanges. The benefits, though, outweigh this. One, you will show that you are actively listening to what your interaction partner is saying. And two, slow and calm is exactly what we are looking for in a customer abuse situation, as this also helps the other person compose their thoughts instead of going with their emotion and urge. This is going to be a difficult thing to do, I know, but give it a try. Make a rule for yourself –"I won't reply before I count to three," for instance. Both you and the customer need that time.

And finally, we cannot talk about building rapport with the customer without talking about empathy. Being empathetic has taken strong prominence in the customer service domain in the last couple of years, and with a good reason. Remember when we spoke about emotional intelligence earlier in this chapter? Back then, we focused mostly on self-awareness and management of emotions, and only briefly said that another key component of it is empathy.

Daniel Goleman distinguishes between three interrelated yet distinct facets of empathy. Cognitive empathy refers to "the ability to understand another person's perspective." (Goleman, 2017, 119), emotional empathy is about feeling what the other person is feeling, and emotional concern is being able to understand what the other person needs from you. All three of these are important in any customer interaction, especially if we are looking to establish rapport with the customer.

Customers want to know that the person sitting in front of them really cares about them and their needs. Businesses these days seem to be quickly becoming somewhat roboticized, and so does customer service. Pushed by the need for efficiency, our customer service interactions have lost the sense of humanness to them, the feeling that the other party is capable of truly understanding you (the customer). A good advice, then, for establishing rapport with a customer, is to show empathy and compassion. Show the customer that you know what it's like to walk in their shoes and that you appreciate what they are going through. This will go a long way into building a meaningful interaction, albeit probably short-lived, given the nature of the interaction, relationship, thus helping you manage any situation that might arise better. Having said that, do not forget about the assertiveness principle. The fact that you understand the feeling and appreciate it does not mean that the customer has the right to tell you to shove things down your throat, to use an earlier example. No one has the right to do that. Empathy is about stepping in the person's shoes, not about allowing them to be abusive. Ask them questions to understand where the frustration is coming from, imagine yourselves in their situation, and try to offer an appropriate solution. That's all there is to a successful customer interaction.

We've been through a lot in this subchapter, and it's time to wrap it up before closing the loop by talking about the skill that will complete our toolbox of skills for handling abusive customers – problem-solving. What we saw here is that establishing rapport with a customer is critical for being able to better dissolve a situation ripe with tension, and we offered quite a bit of tips (I hope) for doing that. From asking customers about their names, through finding similarities between the two of you, through shaping messages in a positive light, to active listening and empathy – all of these are good and relatively simple ways in which you can close the distance and build rapport. That is all very good, but this kind of relationship is only part of the story. After all, there is an underlying issue that is still lurking beneath the surface and that needs to be solved. It is to review the best practices when solving a customers' problem that we turn to now.

How to Help the Customer?

In an earlier chapter, we reviewed in detail the key factors that drive and trigger customer abuse, and we saw the major reason why it happens is poor customer service, often combined with other situational, personality, and societal/cultural factors. While we might be tempted to attribute customers' aberrant behavior to them being a..holes, this is in fact rather rarely the case. The thing is, given the right (or in this case – wrong) circumstances, there is a good chance that all of us will behave inappropriately or even aggressively. One of the best things we as business leaders and customer service reps can do, then, is to avoid sparking negative emotions in customers, i.e., deliver excellent experience that meets their expectations.

Nevertheless, even with the best intentions in mind, some things inevitably are going to break, and some customers will be triggered to act aggressively or in the very least, impolitely. For some reason, the company hadn't delivered what it promised, and for some reason, personality or societal, the customer's negative emotions have surfaced. The result of this process is stress, and we already observed at length what happens when employees are under strain; the effects are not in any way different for customers, as we are all human beings. The question, then, becomes: "How can we alleviate the stress the customer is experiencing?"; "How can we take the sting out?"

Going back to our earlier discussion, stress is in essence caused by the decrease in one's resources or the threat of decreasing them. This is very easy to see in the case of poor customer service. A car had broken down? Well, the customer just lost some money plus the opportunity to travel from one place to another, which spells further loss of resources, such as having fun with the kids or visiting their parents. A laptop not working? The customer is losing resources again – no Netflix, i.e., no fun on Friday night, or no opportunity to do their work, i.e., loss of financial resources. The haircut didn't exactly turn out as the customer expected it to be? Loss of popularity, which is a social resource. What the employee experiences when a customer acts abusively, the customer experiences when the company doesn't deliver – as simple as that.

Now, the question then becomes, how can you, the employee, manage this situation? How can you remove the stress from the interaction? You have managed to remain calm and confident, and you have done our best to establish rapport. The final piece of the puzzle is to actually solve the issue they have, and that's the bit that should also put an end to their negative emotions, hence also aberrant behavior. How can we do that and what skills do we need?

The very short answer to this is: "Give the customer more resources." (and I don't necessarily mean throw money at them) and/or make sure they feel they aren't going to incur further loss of resources. First things first though, if the client is talking angrily to you, it's a good idea to not interrupt them and wait until they have released their frustration. This is not ideal, obviously, as you would have to endure a nasty tirade, but then again, there's also very little choice that you have. The alternative – to interrupt the customer mid-sentence – might seem very tempting but it is unlikely that you will achieve anything positive. Option 1: the customer becomes even more angry because you are interrupting them. Option 2: they do shut up, but then you lose the opportunity to understand what's bothering them. As we saw earlier, it might be a better idea to actually ask more questions about what the customer is saying. It might appear that you'll be putting fuel in the fire, but in fact you are also showing interest and concern, not to mention that you are gathering valuable information. With this in mind, your best call is to let them vent for a while and then take it from there. None of us is particularly reasonable when we are driven by emotions, are they?

Next, it's time for you to show that you are a resource for the customer and not someone they have to fight with. You are the one who knows how to deal with the issue and you are the one who can solve it for them.

Show it to the customer. They need to know they can take the vase, put it in your hands, and then receive it back fixed. No arguments, no heavy bureaucracy – just efficient and effective problem-solving.

Part of all that we already discussed in the previous section when we spoke about the importance of active listening and empathy. Try to make the customer feel you are on their side by asking questions, encouraging them, mirroring them, and reflecting on what they said. Another critical element to add to the mix is the sense of ownership. Being there to listen to them is all good, but at the end of the day results are important for customers, too. Show them that you won the process, that their issue is your issue now, and you will fight to the last drop of blood to get it solved. OK, I admit that that's crossing the line a bit, but you get the idea.

A very good approach for doing that is to use "I" instead of "we" or "you" while talking. In 2018, Grant Packard and his collaborators published the results from five studies which

> reveal that firm agents who refer to themselves using "I" rather than "we" pronouns increase customers' perceptions that the agent feels and acts on their behalf. In turn, these positive perceptions of empathy and agency lead to increased customer satisfaction, purchase intentions, and purchase behavior.
>
> (Packard, Moore, and McFerran, 2018, 541)

This insight also ties well with the concept of assertiveness we discussed earlier, so don't be afraid to say "I" when talking to clients – if anything, it will make them feel you have things covered.

Another good suggestion is to outline the next steps for them. I am clueless as to why people don't do that. My dentist doesn't do it; my hairstyle doesn't do it; they don't do it when I call the support of whichever company you chose. Our brains are prediction making machines. They live slightly ahead in time than "us" and try to prepare our bodies for their next actions. Predictability is, thus, vital. Give the customer a sense of what will happen behind the scenes; explain the process to them. This will not in any way give them control over it, but it will do something better – it will give them a sense of control. They now know what to expect, when, and from whom. It could be a really simple thing like "Thank you. I will now check with … and will get back to you in a minute."

By the same token, if you don't have a solution right away, feel free to share it with the customer. There is nothing wrong in that – after all, the issue could very well be a complicated one. What is important, though, is that you are open and honest with them. Speed of resolution is critical in these situations. So if you can, solve the case as quickly as possible. Yet, speed and openness of communication is no less vital, and while the solution might not be entirely in your hands, the messages you convey are. Similarly, if you need to transfer them to a different department or need to get someone else involved, do so of course, but make sure that you explain this to the customer.

Another good practice is to show that you feel for the customer. Tetiana Shataieva of HelpCrunch offers the following suggestions for doing this – you might, for instance, chose to say things like

- Thank you for reaching out! I totally "feel" for you. Here is what I'm going to do to turn things around.
- Wow, I am so sorry to hear that. No wonder, you feel this way. Let's get things right asap.
- I appreciate you letting me know about the issue! I definitely will make sure that it gets sorted.
- Ohh, it sounds like a serious issue. I am so sorry you have to go through this. But you've come to the right place to get this resolved.

(Shataieva, 2021).

These phrases might sound a bit off, especially compared to what we are used to, but even if you don't go that far on that route, it's a good idea to show some compassion. Note that you don't necessarily need to apologize, especially in the early stages of the conversation. After all, you don't know what caused the issue, and it might not be the company's fault. What you can do, though, is to show that you understand the feelings and you are there to help. Again, it's about the customer relying on you and your expertise to recover or prevent further loss of their precious resources.

And finally, arriving at the crux of the matter, you need to have an extensive knowledge of your company's products and services, and what you are allowed and not allowed to do if a customer complains. Knowing your boundaries will ensure that you don't overpromise and underdeliver later on. For example, if your company doesn't offer replacing vehicles while a customers' car is being repaired, well, don't say that to the customer. At the end of the day, arriving at a good solution will be a matter of you navigating the murky waters between internal policies and customer demands.

Being flexible is also key here. Know what you can and cannot employ as an ammo in these conversations. In a similar vein, you need to sound professional and knowledgeable. Earlier we said that it's a good idea to avoid technical jargon, and that is indeed the case, but you do need to ensure that the customer feels you know what you are talking about. Confident, steady voice helps tremendously, as well as asking insightful questions. This extensive knowledge of what the company offers and the potential issues also helps in being flexible. Typically, as the British saying goes, "There is more than one way to skin a cat.", but you need to know everything there is to know about the aforementioned "cat-skinning" to be able to select the best option.

Even with the best intentions in mind and after you have shown the customer that you care deeply and you want to help, it might not be possible to solve their case in a manner that is satisfactory for them. For example, it might be that the company doesn't offer 100% refunds for certain items, or that you can't book them on that flight that leaves in 30 minutes. The best advice in these cases is to be assertive about it. After all, you are working within the limits of what is possible and acceptable from the company's point of view. You might report the situation upward in the hierarchy so the company takes measures to improve in the future, and that's an advisable thing to do, but in the specific case you might be left without further options. Well, if there's nothing else you can do, bite the bullet and rely on all the other suggestions we discussed earlier. The customer might not be way too happy, but you've got to be assertive about it and explain things very clearly to them. Again, you are the one who's in charge and owns the issue – show that leadership.

What Did We Discuss in This Chapter?

This chapter has been quite a journey. After discussing what we can do to prevent customer abuse from happening in the first place in the previous one, here we focused on the cases in which the customer does become aggressive and rude despite our best efforts to avoid it. We saw that there are two key elements to handling such situations. The first one is in the company's hands, and includes the development of zero-tolerance customer abuse policies and processes that guide employees on how to go through these interactions. Ideally, these would cover the company's intention (the policy's goal), roles and responsibilities, and the specific process that employees can follow to notice, handle, report, and monitor customer abuse. The policy and the process of handling aberrant customer behavior serves as one piece of additional resource for employees in their toolbox, and ensures that they know the company's got their backs, and that they don't invent the wheel every time.

The second key element is more in employee's hands, and concerns the amount of knowledge and skills employees have for dealing with customer abuse. There are four key ingredients to successfully diffusing a situation of tension between a customer and an employee, and all of these can be trained and practiced upfront so that when a situation happens, the latter knows how to react. These are: remaining calm, acting with confidence, establishing rapport, and solving the customer issue. We discussed at length what each of these means and offered (hopefully) practical advice and tips on becoming proficient in these areas.

Even with the best of our intentions though, customer abuse is still likely to continue happening, albeit in smaller proportions. We might try to prevent it, and we might be well-equipped to handle it well, but some customers will still lash out and yell and act disrespectfully, and we saw earlier that the consequences of experiencing customer abuse can be very significant for both the employee and the company. With this in mind, our next and final stop will be an overview of what the company and the employees can do to mitigate the damage customer abuse causes. With this, we would have created and covered a holistic approach to customer abuse issues, starting with its prevention, going through handling it well when it happens, and helping everyone go through its consequences more productively. On to the final chapter!

Notes

1 To the best of my knowledge, the author of this saying is unknown with certainty
2 See Abrahams and Groysberg (2021).
3 See Abrahams and Groysberg (2021).

References

Abrahams, R., & Groysberg, B. (2021). How to become a better listener. https://hbr.org/2021/12/how-to-become-a-better-listener, last accessed on January 13, 2023.

Amaresan, S. (2022). 12 Tips for building rapport with customers. https://blog.hubspot.com/service/building-rapport-with-customers, last accessed on January 12, 2023.

AmericanExpress.com. How to look confident: Body language and posture. https://www.americanexpress.com/en-us/business/trends-and-insights/articles/4-ways-your-body-language-can-project-confidence/, last accessed on January 12, 2023.

Callcentrehelper.com. A policy for dealing with abusive customers, last accessed on January 12, 2023. https://www.callcentrehelper.com/policy-angry-abusive-customers-123183.htm

Changingminds.org. Assertive Body Language. http://changingminds.org/techniques/body/assertive_body.htm, last accessed on January 12, 2023.

Credit Services Association. (2021). Template unacceptable behaviour & aggression policy. https://cdn.ymaws.com/www.csa-uk.com/resource/resmgr/docs/general/unacceptablebehaviourpolicy-.pdf

David, S. (2017). A Vocabulary for your emotions. In: HBR Guide to Emotional Intelligence (HBR Guide Series) (pp. 35–44). Boston, MA: Harvard Business Review Press. Kindle edition.

Goleman, D. (2009). Emotional Intelligence. Why It Can Matter More Than IQ. Bloomsbury. Kindle Edition.

Goleman, D. (2017). What is Empathy? In: HBR Guide to Emotional Intelligence (HBR Guide Series) (pp. 119–123). Boston, MA: Harvard Business Review Press. Kindle edition.

Gregersen, H. (2018). Questions Are the Answer: A Breakthrough Approach to Your Most Vexing Problems at Work and in Life. Harper Business.

Gross, J. J. (2014). Emotion regulation: Conceptual and empirical foundations. In J. J. Gross (Ed.), *Handbook of Emotion Regulation* (pp. 3–20). The Guilford Press.

Hartley, M. How to develop assertive body language. https://maryhartley.com/how-to-develop-assertive-body-language/, last accessed on January 12, 2023.

Health and Safety at Work etc. Act 1974. https://www.legislation.gov.uk/ukpga/1974/37/section/2, last accessed on January 12, 2023.

Health and Safety Executive (a). Example policy on work-related violence. https://www.hse.gov.uk/violence/toolkit/examplepolicy.pdf, last accessed on January 12, 2023.

Health and Safety Executive (b). Preventing workplace harassment and violence. Joint guidance implementing a European social partner agreement. https://www.hse.gov.uk/violence/preventing-workplace-harassment.pdf, last accessed on January 12, 2023.

HealthyPlace.com. Assertiveness, non-assertiveness, and assertive techniques. https://www.healthyplace.com/depression/articles/assertiveness-non-assertiveness-and-assertive-techniques, last accessed on January 12, 2023.

HIS. Conflict De-Escalation Techniques. https://hsi.com/resources/conflict-de-escalation-techniques, last accessed on January 12, 2023.

Inabo, S. (2022). What is customer rapport? (+8 ways to build it). https://www.zendesk.nl/blog/customer-rapport/, last accessed on January 13, 2023.

Itzchakov, G. (2020). Can listening training empower service employees? The mediating roles of anxiety and perspective-taking. *European Journal of Work and Organizational Psychology*, 29(6), 938–952. https://doi.org/10.1080/13594 32X.2020.1776701

Maglio, S. J. (2020). Psychological distance in consumer psychology: Consequences and antecedents. *Consumer Psychology Review*, 108–125. https://doi.org/10.1002/arcp.1057

Merriam-Webster. Rapport. https://www.merriam-webster.com/dictionary/rapport, last accessed on January 12, 2023.

O'Bryan, A. (2022). How to practice active listening: 16 examples & techniques. https://positivepsychology.com/active-listening-techniques/#principles, last accessed on January 13, 2023.

Packard, G., & Berger, J. (2020). How concrete language shapes customer satisfaction. *Journal of Consumer Research*, 47. doi:10.1093/jcr/ucaa038.

Packard, G., Moore, S. G., & McFerran, B. (2018). (I'm) Happy to Help (You): The impact of personal pronoun use in customer–firm interactions. *Journal of Marketing Research*, 55(4), 541–555. https://doi.org/10.1509/jmr.16.0118

Psychologistworld.com. The name-letter effect: Why people prefer partners with similar names. https://www.psychologistworld.com/emotion/name-letter-effect-attraction#references, last accessed on January 13, 2023.

PsychologyToday.com. Confidence. https://www.psychologytoday.com/us/basics/confidence#building-confidence, last accessed on January 12, 2023.

Public Order Act 1986 (S5). https://www.legislation.gov.uk/ukpga/1986/64/section/5, last accessed on January 12, 2023.

Shataieva, T. (2021). 7 customer service problem-solving techniques with examples. https://helpcrunch.com/blog/customer-service-problem-solving/, last accessed on January 13, 2023.

Thames Water. (2020). Customer conduct policy. https://www.thameswater.co.uk/media-library/home/about-us/governance/our-policies/customers/customer-conduct-policy.pdf, last accessed on January 12, 2023.

van Jaarsveld, D. D., Restubog, S. L. D., Walker, D. D., & Amarnani, R. K. (2015). Misbehaving customers: Understanding and managing customer injustice in service organizations. *Organizational Dynamics*, 44(4), 273–280. https://doi.org/10.1016/j.orgdyn.2015.09.004

Vecchi, G. M., Van Hasselt, V. B., & Romano, S. J. (2005). Crisis (hostage) negotiation: Current strategies and issues in high-risk conflict resolution. *Aggression and Violent Behavior*, 10(5), 533–551. https://doi.org/10.1016/j.avb.2004.10.001

Wegner, D., & Kurt, G. (2016). *The Mind Club*. Penguin Publishing Group. Kindle Edition.

Weiss, L. (2017). Stay grounded in stressful moments. In: *HBR Guide to Emotional Intelligence* (HBR Guide Series). pp. 53–56. Boston, MA: Harvard Business Review Press. Kindle Edition.

Chapter 7

How to Mitigate the Damage from Customer Abuse?

The sad reality is that whatever we do and no matter how hard we work to prevent it, customer abuse is going to happen. As we saw, it is driven by a variety of factors, ranging from situational, through personal, to societal ones, of which a company or an employee can only control a few. Some people are just going to continue to give us a hard time.

Clearly, further to trying to prevent it, then, we also need mechanisms and skills to handle it as appropriately as possible. This is what we discussed in the previous chapter. Having a zero-tolerance policy, a clear and efficient process, and training employees on the essential skills for dealing with aggressive customers thus become vital.

But handling something unpleasant well does not mean that it wouldn't hurt us in any way. On the one hand, all of the elements we spoke about so far are only going to help, but given that we are talking about a social phenomenon, none of them is going to be 100% effective. On the other, going through bad things, even if successful, still touches us deeply. It's like running a marathon – you might be able to do it and you might even achieve a very good result, but it doesn't mean that you won't feel the pain after that.

This then is the focus of this chapter: what can companies and employees do to limit the negative blow from experiencing customer abuse. In the unfortunate case that it happens, there will be repercussions in the short and in the long run. The question is, "How can we mitigate them?" What can you as a manager do and what can you as an employee do about it?

All the answers and tips we will see in this chapter stem directly from the proposition we outlined earlier – that encounters that are considered stressful indicate that the person is experiencing a loss or a threat of loss of resources. In a word, when we are under stress, we feel like we are attacked and something precious for us will be taken away. To mitigate that, then, we can work to restore the resources and to remove the threat. When dealing with the consequences of customer abuse, the best advice

DOI: 10.4324/9781003402565-8

for managers and employees alike is, in a nutshell, to simply restore the drained resources, be they reputational, energetic, or otherwise.

What Can Managers Do to Mitigate the Damage Customer Abuse Causes?

There are two sides to the what-can-managers-do-to-alleviate-customer-abuse-damage question. The first one is related to answering how can managers do it; to this question we will return in a couple of pages. The second one requires us to ask who, i.e., knowing which employees are actually going through difficult times because of customer abuse, and it is to a brief overview of this question that we will turn now.

Knowing Which Employees Experience the Effects of Customer Abuse

The very short answer to this second question is that the customer abuse monitoring system that you've put in place should be able to give you an answer after a relatively simple analysis – just have a look at who reported the accidents and when, and you will know where you, as a manager, might need to intervene. Clearly, the managers would also know this if they are involved in the day-to-day operations of the team – simply being on the floor with the employees would provide insights into this. Still, given that after all, not all interactions involving rudeness will be reported as abuse, and rightfully so, and that a manager cannot potentially listen to all interactions, a more scalable solution is needed in the mix.

The boom in artificial intelligence in recent years provides such an opportunity. Albeit applicable in call or chat settings only, it can serve as a great addition to the reporting system you have in place. In 2021, Stefano Bromuri and his collaborators published the results of a project, aimed to contribute to decreasing employee's stress caused by negative customer interactions. They first developed a deep learning model to identify emotion patterns in call center interactions and then further enhanced the model in a real-life environment in more than 4,500 service interactions. Based on this model, it was possible, the researchers report, to "predict service agent stress with a balanced accuracy of 80%" (Bromuri et al., 2021, 581). This means that by using an automated speech analysis to recognize emotions during conversations, managers can now know which employees face high stress as a result of negative customer interactions, thus being able to intervene to mitigate the damage and offer additional timely and relevant training.

Related to the topic of "'Who?," knowing which employees are more likely to react negatively to customer aggression and retaliate is another thing managers can do to mitigate the consequences of customer abuse. This can be done by following the insights we shared earlier on when we spoke about the personality factors influencing this, like high neuroticism and low agreeableness. I personally believe that it would be a bad advice to screen out potential employees during the hiring process based on these characteristics, and I would not go as far as that. What is important, though, is that the management has these employee characteristics in mind so they can monitor more closely how these employees react and offer appropriate training.

Furthermore, it is a good idea to offer potential employees a good idea of what the job they are about to take on entails. The researcher Danielle Dorice Van Jaarsveld and her collaborators propose, and I believe right-fully so, to "integrate a realistic job preview into the hiring process to help reduce high voluntary turnover rates in service organizations" (van Jaarsveld et al., 2015, 277). Prospective employees might, for instance, go through a handful of situations that are likely to happen to them during a regular workday or they might simply be presented with such. While it is clear that some candidates might be put off by what they see, it is better to have it this way, rather than hire an employee with the wrong expectations only to have to replace them shortly after.

Moving on from knowing which employees are facing the effects of neg-ative customer abuse the most to how can managers support their teams in dealing with aggressive customers, perhaps the two most important and well-researched things they can do is to provide, on the one hand, empow-erment, and on the other – social and organizational support. Let's have a look at how these two would work in a customer abuse context.

Empowerment Helps Mitigate the Consequences of Customer Abuse

In psychological and managerial research, empowerment is typically con-sidered from different angles. The structural perspective toward empower-ment focuses on "organizational and managerial conditions which relate to sharing informal power and information, access and control over resources and rewards, and on the leaders who design them" (Coun et al., 2021, 2831). Researchers who investigate empowerment from this point of view focus predominantly on the organizational and managerial practices that foster it. The psychological perspective toward empowerment, on the other hand, shifts the focus toward the employee, and looks at empowerment as something that employees' experience, i.e., are they feeling empowered or not?

This latter, much broader perspective of psychological empowerment, which is conceptualized as including four elements: meaning, competence, self-determination, and impact. Empowerment means, psychologists suggest, that employees experience these four things in their work. First, they consider the work as fitting what they strive for and their beliefs and values. Meaning is about the "feelings of sense and enjoyment in their work" (Coun et al., 2021, 2834) that stems from doing what we believe makes sense and is worth doing in this world. Second, empowered employees have a high sense of competence or self-efficacy. They feel they can do their job well. It's not about self-esteem, which rather refers to how highly we regard ourselves, but about whether we can cope with whatever the world throws at us or whatever we want to push forward. Third, self-determination "reflects autonomy in the initiation and continuation of work behaviors and processes; examples are making decisions about work methods, pace, and effort" (Spreitzer, 1995, 1443). This is perhaps the most commonly known element of empowerment – being able to select the goals and the means by which to pursue them. Lastly, the concept of impact reflects employees' feelings and perceptions that they can influence the outcomes of their work, i.e., if they do something, is anything going to happen at all?

A plethora of studies have found out that empowering employees is a very sound managerial advice. For instance, psychological empowerment has been shown to lead to higher job satisfaction, more organizational commitment, innovative behavior, workplace proactivity, and customer satisfaction. Pertaining closely to our topic of discussion here, empowering employees is a really good way of decreasing the negative effects of customer abuse. While on its own empowerment cannot stop it from happening, it can significantly improve an employee's situation and alleviate the damage. Evidence for this abounds.

In 2021, a group of researchers published the results from a study they conducted in South Korea, investigating the relationship between customer aggression and employee stress and job satisfaction. By collecting and analyzing data from about 300 restaurant employees, they discovered, sure enough, that customer abuse causes them stress and leads to lower job satisfaction. More importantly for us here, Bi and collaborators also explored whether empowerment helps to mitigate this relationship. They asked employees a series of questions to understand how empowered they felt; things like "I have the authority to correct jay-customer-related problems when they occur," "I am encouraged to handle jay-customer-related problems by myself," "I am allowed to do almost anything to solve jay-customer-related problems," and "I have control over how I solve jay-customer-related problems" (Bi et al., 2021). Encouragingly, they discovered that among those employees who felt empowered, "a customer's verbal abuse did not have a significant effect on employees' job stress …, whereas, in the group of less empowered frontline employees, customer verbal abuse significantly affected employees' job stress" (Bi et al., 2021).

In another study conducted in Korea, a group of researchers investigated how customer mistreatment leads to negative affect, which then leads to poor sleep and not feeling recovered in the next morning. To do that, they interviewed about 70 call center employees over a period of approximately a week, and as can be expected based on what we've seen earlier on, that was indeed the case. More importantly for us here, "for employees who had low job control, customer mistreatment was significantly positively related with end-of work negative affect, but not for employees who had high job control..." (Park and Kim, 2019, 262). Put differently, those employees who feel they are in control felt the negative effect of customer mistreatment significantly less than those who don't.

Further evidence for the power of empowerment to mitigate the damage done by customer abuse comes from China. A group of researchers led by Jiuming Chen, conducted a study among property agents and their supervisors and discovered that customer mistreatment makes employees feel less competent and autonomous, which in turn decreases their job performance and job satisfaction. This effect was mitigated successfully, though, in cases when the organization had high-empowerment human resource management practices in place. These include, for instance, "participation, involvement, training and development, information and work time control, that provide employees with the critical ingredients of empowerment—the ability, opportunity and authority to make things happen" (Chen et al., 2021, 1570–1571).

Results from a study conducted with hotel frontline employees in the United Arab Emirates lend further credence to this view. Achilleas Boukis and his collaborators interviewed more than 350 such employees, and investigated whether an empowering (providing high guidance to employees and high autonomy) or laissez-faire leadership (high autonomy but low guidance) styles help mitigate the damage done by customer incivility. Of these two, empowerment works considerably better and lowers employees' perceptions of stress, rumination, desire for retaliation, and job withdrawal. In a word, supervisors who "actively display trust to FLEs with regards to their ability to handle such episodes" and "...act as a psychological shield for FLEs" (Boukis et al., 2020) manage to help their employees tackle the consequences of customer incivility and abuse, and go through them more easily.

All of these studies, and many more, unequivocally point toward the conclusion that feeling empowered helps employees deal with customer abuse more easily and mitigates the damage it does to their psychological well-being. Before we continue with our review of the actions managers can take to support employees in the handling the consequences of difficult conversations with customers, it's worth saying a couple of final words about empowerment, inspired by the study by Boukis et al. we just went through.

Empowerment is not equal to absolute freedom, and it would be wrong to think that letting employees take decisions will lead to chaos and lack of coherence in the way the company approaches customers. Going back to the definition we saw earlier, it most certainly is about employees being able to call certain shots, but it's also a lot about self-efficacy, and connectedness, and impact. Simply letting people cope with whatever comes their way is not empowerment – it's leaving them on their own. An approach that prioritizes empowerment does just what the root of the word suggests: it gives people the resources to make certain decisions themselves and to use their own discretion in their daily work. It's about trust grounded in a good cooperation between the supervisor and the employee, and about giving the latter a voice and an opportunity to make an impact. And speaking of voice and trust, we now move to the second very important thing managers can ensure is in place or can in the very least facilitate – social and organizational support for employees.

Social and Organizational Support Helps Mitigate the Consequences of Customer Abuse

The advice for managers and organizations as a whole to ensure sufficient support is available for employees, stems directly from our conceptualization of customer abuse and its consequences, and more specifically with the resource depletion theory of stress. According to the latter, there are multiple classes of resources that each of us possesses and strives for, and we experience some situations as stressful because something either diminish or threatens to diminish them. A useful distinction is to think of these as personal or contextual resources. The former includes things like personal qualities, energy, time, etc. The latter points toward things that can only be acquired in social contexts, and it is to these that we turn our attention now, as they are a vital source of resources. In fact, dozens of studies conducted in the domain of customer abuse show that social and organizational support is one of the most effective ways to buffer its impact on employees.

It's useful to first try to define "social and organizational support." Others, in our case – coworkers, be they peers, managers, or why not subordinates – can provide support in a large variety of ways. For instance,

By providing instrumental assistance or advice about how to successfully manage a stressful situation, social support helps to promote employees' ability to exert situational control. Social support also helps employees divert their attention away from a present difficult situation and reinterpret stressors in a more constructive way. Moreover, through the provision of feedback that contains caring, encouragement and understanding, social support can mitigate the stress of employees in threatening situations.

(Wang and Wang, 2017, 468)

Furthermore, Schat and Kelloway propose that informational support is also part of the organizational support mix, in that it covers training that the organization has initiated or prepared to "to provide them [employees] with information and other resources that they could then use to help themselves deal with various aggressive and violent acts they may confront while carrying out their work responsibilities" (Schat and Kelloway, 2003, 114).

In a word, then, social and organizational support boils down to employees' perception about the degree to which the organization, including peers and managers, pays attention and cares about their well-being[1]. This can manifest itself in a large variety of ways, ranging from landing a sympathetic ear, through the provision of policies and processes for handling customer abuse, to providing encouragement in the face of adversity. Whatever it is, we can expect that this transfer of resources from the outside world to employees will help them deal with the consequences of customer abuse. And this indeed has been proven in numerous studies in a variety of contexts.

For instance, in 2012, Chan and Wan (2012) discovered that work stress made employees spend less time answering customer complaints, and consequently the perceived quality of their work and customer satisfaction was lower, and this effect went partially through the feelings of fatigue that handling stress causes. Importantly, though, participants who were put in a high social support condition in this experiment showed no such decrease even under high stress – they spend the same amount of time answering customer complaints.

Relatedly, Gong et al. conducted a study among close to 350 sales service people to explore the relationship between customer verbal abuse and turnover intention. As we discussed before, these two are closely related, and that's what the authors confirmed as well – experiencing verbal abuse makes employees want to quit their jobs. Pertaining more closely to the current discussion, the researchers also measured what they call organizational atmosphere, i.e., things like whether "the company will try its best to provide me with the training or relevant support for the work" and "the company cares about my personal development" (Gong, Sun, and Zhang, 2018). As hypothesized, the more employees perceived that the company does these things, the less likely they were to quit, even in the face of abusive customers.

Furthermore, Wang and Wang (2017) did a study among frontline healthcare workers in China to investigate the linkage between mistreatment by customers, emotional exhaustion, and employee withdrawal (i.e., putting less efforts to work or taking longer breaks). This relationship was indeed in place, but what is more important for us here is that when employees experienced more social support, customer mistreatment left them considerably less exhausted, compared to when there was limited social support. In other words, social support helps safeguard against one of the key reasons for burnout and the negative behavioral consequences it leads to – emotional exhaustion.

As a final example, consider this study conducted among 934 employees, part of a total of 107 work units in a clothing store chain in Belgium by Zselyke Pap and her collaborators. The first insight that they discovered wouldn't be surprising for us by now: employees who perceived or experienced more customer incivility were less satisfied with their job, as they "go through an energy-depleting process when faced with sustained demands such as dealing with uncivil customers, which in turn affects outcomes like performance and work attitudes" (Pap, Vîrgă, and Notelaers, 2021). The authors went a step further, though, to uncover mechanisms that help prevent that, more specifically, they tested whether supervisor support (e.g., ("Can you count on your direct boss when you come across difficulties in your work?") and a participative climate in the work unit (e.g., "Can you consult satisfactorily with your boss about your work?"; "Can you participate in deciding what does and what does not pertain to your task?") can buffer the negative impact of customer incivility on job satisfaction. Indeed, both of these – supervisor support and participation – do help break the customer incivility–employee unhappiness relationship. In fact, as the researchers point out, "employees are satisfied with their job even in the case of frequent interactions with demanding clients when they perceive that their supervisor is offering sufficient support" (Pap, Vîrgă, and Notelaers, 2021). Quite similarly, "in work units where participative climate is higher, interactions with difficult clients do not relate significantly to satisfaction anymore" (Pap, Vîrgă, and Notelaers, 2021). This insight, of course, also refers us back to the empowerment section, where we saw how effective it is in buffering the negative impact of customer abuse.

So where does this leave us? During difficult encounters with abusive or even simply uncivil customers, employees experience a range of negative effects – like negative emotions and stress; to handle these, they expend more of their resources than usual, and even then, they might not manage to completely prevent more serious consequences, like burnout and its accompanying effects – lower job performance, lower job satisfaction, desire to withdraw, and the others we looked at earlier. To help employees in these circumstances, managers and organizations are well-advised to ensure that they offer them enough support – both social and organizational. This support can come in two basic forms – instrumental and emotional.

On the instrumental side of things, we already pointed out how critical it is to have a zero-tolerance policy for customer abuse, a well-defined process for managing such situations, systems for monitoring and reporting customers' aggressive behavior, and training programs designed to develop employee's skills for dealing with customer abuse.

On the emotional side, managers need to ensure that there is an open and honest line of communication between them and employees. The easier the latter find it to talk about their issues, the better, as this will give managers both knowledge into what is going on, and to what are the gaps in employees' skills, so they can assign appropriate training programs for them.

Furthermore, it is important for managers to create and maintain a team spirit or an organizational climate, if you will, of cooperation and mutual trust, both between them and the team members, and between team members themselves. Simple things like landing a sympathetic ear can help tremendously in these cases, but there needs to be enough time, space, and trust between people for this to happen. Creating a bond between team members with all the available tools is going to be very beneficial in this regard. If people believe they are pursuing a common purpose and if they believe that their manager is there to support them on the journey, nothing can stop them.

So far in this chapter we saw how many things managers can do to help their employees deal with the consequences of customer abuse. While the latter might never be completely eradicated, there are steps business leaders can take to support customer facing employees in this. To begin with, they can keep customer abuse always on their radar by establishing systems for monitoring and reporting it, and they can keep tabs on which employees might need support by making the most of technologies for recognizing emotions in real-time conversations. Next to this, they might help employees early on by giving them a glimpse of what the work actually entails; there is no point hiding it – customer abuse is part of their work life, and it is only fair and reasonable that employees know this. Furthermore, there are a number of practices managers can develop and foster within their teams that mitigate the damage done by abusive customers. Empowering employees to take decisions based on their own discretion has been proven to work really well, and so does social and organizational support (both instrumental and emotional). Both of these practices help by replenishing employee's resources drained from having to deal with customer abuse. Finally, behaviors such as ensuring a high level of interpersonal justice, servant leadership, and transformational leadership are also practices that help employees deal with the consequences of customer abuse.

The good news is that the number of practices that buffer against the negative impact of aggressive customers don't stop here. So far, we only saw what role managers can play in this process. The final piece of the puzzle brings us on the side of employees, what they can themselves do to safeguard their well-being after difficult interactions with customers.

What Can Employees Do to Mitigate the Damage Customer Abuse Causes?

As with many other things, so with customer abuse as well, nothing helps completely to repair the damage of bad behavior – there is always this little residue that leaves a mark on us. Yet, it would be equally wrong to just sit back and do nothing to help us recover. In fact, studies in this domain have shown that there is plenty of things employees can do. For clarity, we will have a look at them split into two sections – what employees can do on the short term and in the long term.

In the Short Term

Customer abuse is always painful, there is no doubt about it. Yet, what we've all seen in real life and what studies also show is that some of us are more deeply affected by it while others seem to recuperate more quickly and efficiently from it. It is worth, therefore, asking ourselves, why is this the case, and more specifically – what practices and behaviors can we adopt to become better at managing ourselves when we have been mistreated by customers. The answer to this lies again in the Conservation of Resources Theory of stress management, i.e., in the fact that what we consider stressful is that which either robs us of resources, or makes us expend more of them, or threatens the ones that we possess. Logically, then, in the short term the best defense against the negative consequences of customer abuse lies in practices that help us recover these resources or protect the ones that we have.

The first thing you can do, preferably not while you are at work though!, is, well, have a good sleep. We seem to often neglect it, but sleep is super critical for our proper functioning. For instance, the US Department of Health and Human Services reports that some of the benefits of good sleep include:

- Get sick less often
- Stay at a healthy weight
- Lower your risk for serious health problems, like diabetes and heart disease
- Reduce stress and improve your mood
- Think more clearly and do better in school and at work

- Get along better with people
- Make good decisions and avoid injuries — for example, drowsy drivers cause thousands of car accidents every year (Health.gov)

More closely pertaining to our topic here, one study shows that customer mistreatment is related to evening overeating (Liu et al., 2017), i.e., employees who were treated badly by customers in the morning tended to be in a negative mood in the afternoon (unsurprisingly!), and to consume more food than they needed in the evening. Importantly, though, the team also sought to understand if there is anything that can break this vicious circle. Sure enough, sleep does the trick! Under low customer mistreatment, negative mood was at a relatively low level for pretty much everyone. When customer mistreatment was high, though, those who were feeling less vigorous in the morning felt a much more negative mood, and while there was also an increase for those who felt more energetic in the morning, it was much less pronounced. A good night's sleep is the key that unlocks this whole chain of events, as it makes us feel more vigorous in the morning, thus protecting us against the perils of customer mistreatment.

Now, what makes for a good sleep is fairly easy to say: as a rule of thumb, we need about 7 hours of good sleep every night on a (relatively) regular schedule. Simple, right? Yet, as convinced as we might be of the benefits of a good night's sleep, a number of things in our daily lives derail us from this. Some of these you can't really control. Things like stress and pain and some health conditions like asthma can significantly impact how well do we sleep. Others, though, are by and large within our control, and that's where you play a role. Here are some tips:

- Create a good sleep environment. (Health.gov): electronic devices are out, sorry about that; ideally, you have a comfortable bed and pillow, and your bedroom is dark and quiet. Everything that has the potential to distract you from your one job must go.
- Try to keep a routine. That's quite difficult to do, I know, but you can at least give it a shot at going to bed at the same time and getting the same amount of sleep every night.
- If you exercise, avoid doing it right before going to bed. Yours truly, being a passionate long-distance runner, has some firsthand experience here and can testify to this. Exercising does a host of positive things to your body, but the one thing you don't want just before going to bed is to feel excited and pumped up on adrenaline. If you can, do your sports in the morning.
- Avoid caffeine six to eight hours before going to bed – if you plan to doze off around 22.00 or 23.00, you should be done with coffee and coke at around 15.00.

- Alcohol doesn't help good sleep at all, so either avoid it entirely, or at least don't have too many drinks, and try not to drink too close to bed time.
- Don't eat, or at least not big meals, close to bed time – an early dinner will give your body enough time to do the work so it (and you!) can relax before you go to sleep.

As you can see, sleeping well is not so much a matter of doing certain things, rather than avoiding them. In practice, your body knows what it needs to do, so just try not to make it hard on it and you'll be absolutely fine.

Further to sleep, another fairly obvious advice for replenishing your resources is to, well, take a break. It seems odd to say it, but when you feel that your batteries are down from having to deal with difficult customers, you'd better take a short break and change the environment, than stay and keep doing what you are doing but with less effort. How do we know this? Yes, researchers have examined that very question. Yue and his collaborators (2021) interviewed nurses in a hospital in Australia for ten days straight, three times a day. They wanted to know which strategy works better: on-task withdrawal, i.e., putting less efforts into ones' work, or off-task withdrawal, i.e., taking a short time out of ones' duties. Under low customer incivility, both nurses who took a lot of breaks and those who put less efforts in their work exhibited equal emotional exhaustion. Not so when there was a high level of customer incivility, though. In this latter case, the ones who didn't give it all in their roles were significantly more exhausted than those who simply took a time out to recharge.

The latter finding is, in my view, a crucial one, as it points toward a mistake a lot of us might be tempted to make. Slowing down and going at less than maximum power through the remainder of the day, after we have had a difficult interaction with an aggressive customer, is not the ideal solution – it doesn't help us recharge; all it does is make us withdrawn from work, most likely with consequences for the quality that we put into it. It is a much better advice to simply take a 10–15 minutes break, and importantly, to change the environment if you can. Going back to the emotional regulation topic we discussed earlier one of the tactics for handling stress we mentioned was distraction. Combine a short period of detachment from your tasks with a change in scenery to both distract yourself a bit and to recharge. This brief time will help you put in more energy afterward, thus increasing your productivity.

Research also shows that practicing mindfulness is also beneficial for tackling the effects of customer mistreatment. In a study among casino employees, Jang et al. discovered that, sure enough, those who were exposed to customer rudeness were not particularly likely to be engaged at work and to proactively try to address their customers' needs. Mindfulness practices helped buffer against that, as they replenish your resources. Broadly speaking, they are a

> type of meditation in which you focus on being intensely aware of what you're sensing and feeling in the moment, without interpretation or judgment. Practicing mindfulness involves breathing methods, guided imagery, and other practices to relax the body and mind and help reduce stress.
>
> (Mayo Clinic)

Here are three example exercises suggested by the Mayo Clinic that are quick and easy to do:

- Body scan meditation. Lie on your back with your legs extended and arms at your sides, palms facing up. Focus your attention slowly and deliberately on each part of your body, in order, from toe to head or head to toe. Be aware of any sensations, emotions or thoughts associated with each part of your body.
- Sitting meditation. Sit comfortably with your back straight, feet flat on the floor, and hands in your lap. Breathing through your nose, focus on your breath moving in and out of your body. If physical sensations or thoughts interrupt your meditation, note the experience and then return your focus to your breath.
- Walking meditation. Find a quiet place 10–20 feet in length, and begin to walk slowly. Focus on the experience of walking, being aware of the sensations of standing and the subtle movements that keep your balance. When you reach the end of your path, turn and continue walking, maintaining awareness of your sensations.

All of these take very little time and fit perfectly with the recommendation of taking short time outs from work and changing the environment to distract yourself a bit.

Last but not least, in the short term, you can also make good use of one of the most powerful strategies for replenishing your emotional batteries that exists – talk to other people. Who among us doesn't turn to friends and family in times of turmoil to seek advice and support? There is a very good reason we do this, of course, and it is because they could often be an excellent resource pool for us to tap into. The important caveat here is that you need to be very careful about the way you do this. Sharing your emotions with significant others is the productive approach here, but make sure that you don't end up ruminating, i.e., going over and over and over again through the same experience.

The latter can happen very easily, especially at work. You share something with someone, they recognize the situation and start sharing about that time when such and such happened to them. There is nothing inherently wrong in that – we all need to do it – but it can easily turn into an interaction which fuels your negative thoughts and emotions instead of helping with them. So yes, do share your emotions with others, but be mindful of the curse of rumination – the more you talk about something, the deeper it can get embedded into you. In a study by Baranik et al., for instance, "Social sharing of negative events was positively related to both wellbeing and emotional exhaustion" (2017, 1261). That is, sharing with others has a little bit of a paradoxical effect – it can leave us more drained than before, as we are going through the situation once again, but it can also leave us better off overall. In any case, do seek out to others and do share your feelings, as suppressing them is a counterproductive strategy. Just make sure that you don't get into a negativity spiral in which the conversation is more draining than anything else.

In the short term, then, it's all about recharging. If you can do it immediately after the customer abuse episode, do it – take a break, do mindfulness, talk to others, have a nice cup of tea, walk around, whatever rocks your boat. Just be sure that you don't get into a rumination mode in which you rerun the situation in your mind in an endless loop. Your goal is to give yourself a boost.

Further to these practices, and extending the time horizon a bit, taking good care of yourself – both mentally and physically – will also serve you well. Good sleep, good food, experiencing the little pleasures of life, doing sports – all of these things work in your favor to tackle the negative consequences of the stress you experience when a customer mistreats you. I don't know if it's clear, but smoking and drinking alcohol don't fit very well in this category. We often feel that they do, but their long-term effect on us is less than positive, so my recommendation would be to try and find more productive ways to recharge. Running – yes; cocktails – why not, but not too many and not too often; smoking and drugs are off the table.

All kinds of hobbies work well for recharging emotionally, too. Hobbies are characterized by a very strong internal drive to do things – when we paint, swim, photograph, do gardening or knitting, we usually do it because we like these things, and not because we need to. This freedom of expression is extremely valuable, as it promotes feeling of control and, put simply, pure joy. Go for them, especially when you are experiencing considerable stress. They also have the added benefit of distracting you from the source of stress and very often of giving you access to a diverse social circle. In a word, having a hobby is a very very good idea for managing stress.

What we went through so far is a host of practices that can help you recharge your batteries, drained from experiencing stress at work and particularly from abusive and aggressive customers. All of these you can take and start applying immediately to your life, and years of research have shown that they will work.

Before we close this chapter, and the book, we need to look at one final thing you as an employee can do to help yourself deal with customer mistreatment more easily. Unlike the behaviors we discussed so far, in what follows we will focus a bit more on a range of skills that you may want to look to develop. Clearly, you can't build them in a day, so these are long-term strategies that have been shown to have a wide-ranging positive effect on us.

In the Long Term

There are three skills that have been shown to effectively buffer against the consequences of customer abuse, namely, self-efficacy, resilience, and the ability to take another person's perspective. To be sure, there is a plethora of other skills that come in handy in this as well; we put emphasis on these four more to exemplify the type of abilities that promote productive coping with customer abuse episodes rather than do an exhaustive list of those. Our first stop is self-efficacy.

Self-Efficacy

Self-efficacy is a concept that is a critical part of the so-called social learning theory, the impetus for whose development came from the famed psychologist Albert Bandura in the 1980s. This broader theory is to a large extent part of the backlash in psychology against behaviorism and of the cognitive shift within the discipline. The goal of social cognitive theory is, as of many other psychological theories, to explain human behavior, and to do that it utilizes a number of key concepts. These include the behavior itself, of course; sociocultural factors, some of which promote and some of which impede it, e.g., living conditions, political and economic factors, personal circumstances, and so on; outcome expectations, be they physical, social, or self-evaluative, i.e., what do we expect that the behavior leads to, e.g., what will we experience when we do something and how would others evaluate it; goals, which "serve as self-incentives and guide decisions/motivation to participate in behaviors" (Luszczynska & Schwarzer, 2020, 35).

The latter concept, and one that plays a major part in the development of behavior and is our foci of discussion here is self-efficacy – the

individuals' beliefs in their capability to exercise control over challenging demands and their own functioning. It reflects a subjective estimate of the amount of personal control an individual expects to have in any given situation. As a result, self-efficacy beliefs are often labeled "I can" perceptions regarding future behaviors or tasks. If individuals hold strong beliefs that they can master an upcoming task, they are likely to invest the effort in engaging with it. Similarly, if an individual feels confident that they can overcome an imminent threat or challenge (e.g., an exam), they are more likely to approach rather than to avoid the threat. Self-efficacy, therefore, affects the amount of effort individuals will expend to change a particular behavior to obtain a particular goal and the extent to which they will persist in striving to attain that goal in the face of barriers and setbacks that may undermine motivation.

(Luszczynska & Schwarzer, 2020, 33)

It is very important that we distinguish self-efficacy from two related constructs and make clear why we position it as a skill that is very much worth developing. First, self-efficacy is not self-esteem. The latter refers to the level of regards that we have for ourselves, i.e., it's perhaps more accurately described as our sense of self-importance rather than anything else. Self-efficacy does not include an evaluation of whether what we can do is important or not, but simply that we have control and can do it. Second, self-efficacy is not self-confidence. The latter refers to a general personality trait indicating strength of belief, but not being specific about what the strength is about. Self-efficacy, on the other hand, is context- or task-specific, and captures the belief that one can successfully accomplish their specific goals.

The importance of developing self-efficacy for dealing with customer abuse lies in the fact that the higher the people are in self-efficacy in a certain domain, the higher the chances that they will engage and spend time and effort in it[2]; by proxy, employees high in self-efficacy related to handling abusive customers are better positioned to have the motivation to perform well in such situations and to exhibit the behaviors we described as part of the successful dealing with customer mistreatment. They act with confidence, remain calm, and show assertiveness, because they believe that they can handle the situation well.

There is plenty of evidence that higher self-efficacy helps deal with customer abuse. In 2012, Ruhama Goussinsky published the results of a study in which he sought to understand how negative affectivity and self-efficacy are linked to certain strategies for coping with customer aggression. What he discovered is that negative affectivity – negative worldview and pessimism – is associated with dysfunctional coping behaviors such as behavioral disengagement and venting. Importantly, employees with higher self-efficacy were significantly less likely to resort to venting, and although all employees feel emotionally exhausted after experiencing customer aggression, the relationship was much weaker among those with higher self-efficacy. Companies, the author concludes, "can foster their employees' sense of trust in their own ability to cope with customer misbehavior and consequently reduce reliance on dysfunctional coping strategies" (Goussinsky, 2012, 170).

In a similar vein, results from a study by Wang et al. published in 2011 show that, as we saw earlier, employees who were mistreated by customers are much more likely to sabotage other customers, i.e., to deliberately try to do a poor job in servicing customers. Importantly, high self-efficacy for emotion regulation, i.e., the confidence employees have that they can manage their emotions well, has a significantly moderating impact on this relationship. Among those who are low in emotion regulation self-efficacy, customer sabotage skyrockets under high customer mistreatment. Not so among those with high-self efficacy – as you can see, their intention to retaliate against customers remains low even when they are mistreated by customers. In a word, then, self-efficacy has been shown to be a very productive tool to have in general, and has been proven to work in the specific domain of handling abusive customers as well.

Importantly for us, self-efficacy is not a fixed entity, but something that can be developed in time. Social cognitive theory outlines four ways in which people can do that. These are mastery experiences, vicarious experiences, verbal persuasion, and emotional arousal, and we will have a look at each of them in turn.

The most powerful way for all people to develop self-efficacy, the feeling that they can do it!, is by achieving success themselves – this is what lies behind the "mastery experiences" concept. Graded tasks (or small wins if you will) are vital in this process. There is no need to jump too high, as that's more often than note a recipe for failure – you don't run a marathon on your second running session. Start small and build from there. Clearly, this needs to also happen in a fairly controlled environment, for example, during training sessions on the topic. In these settings, people can practice their skills without the looming risk of failure, and equally importantly, they can do it on piecemeal basis: today we do this, and then tomorrow we do that. This should all be supplemented by learning materials which allow people to study at their own pace the techniques for dissipating tension during difficult situations with customers. The combination of the two – "theoretical" or conceptual knowledge and real-life training will allow employees to experiment and hone their skills before they encounter aggressive customers.

The second important way to build self-efficacy is the so-called vicarious experiences. These, as psychologists Aleksandra Luszczynska and Ralf Schwarzer explain,

provide individuals with a "role model" that provides a "behavioral template" for the behavior and affects estimates of future confidence to do the behavior and, hence, individuals may form motives or intentions to do the behavior in future. When individuals witness other people (similar to themselves) successfully master a difficult situation, social comparison and imitation of the behavior can strengthen self-efficacy beliefs (Bandura, 1997). Similarly, imagery may enhance self-efficacy by presenting individuals with a "self-model" of the behavior…

(Luszczynska & Schwarzer, 2020, 38)

While with mastery experiences it's all about doing, with vicarious experiences the focus is on showing what good looks like and how can people make it happen. Furthermore, if the role-model is someone whom they can recognize as close/similar to them, they are more likely to think "Hey, if they can do it, then maybe I can, too." The role of these exercises is to instill confidence both by showcasing specific techniques and by making success appear achievable.

Next to these two approaches, self-efficacy can also be boosted externally, via verbal, also known as verbal, persuasion; for example, "a teacher could reassure students that they can prepare for a demanding exam, due to their effort, competence, and ability to plan" (Luszczynska & Schwarzer, 2020, 38) Clearly, this ties back to one of the practices that can help people deal with the consequences of customer abuse – receiving organizational and especially social support. Now, relying too much or only on verbal persuasion can be tricky. First, it is actually quite difficult to make others believe they can do something by only using words (but it is, unfortunately, quite easy to undermine it!). Second, building self-efficacy on the words of others alone can be quite misleading. Nevertheless, as an auxiliary tactic for boosting other people's sense of being capable to deal with customer abuse, verbal persuasion does have its place in our toolbox. After all, who doesn't experience a mood and morale boost after a kind word from their manager or a respected peer.

Finally, people also use somatic and emotional indicators to form judgments about their own abilities. This is most fully elaborated in the feelings-as-information theory in psychology, and the idea behind is that we use our reactions as an information into how do we feel about the case at hand. For instance, an increased heart rate signals to ourselves that we are frightened or anxious, while a relaxed bodily stance tells us that we are feeling confident. In a lot of ways, we are used to thinking that our mind determines what our body does, but there is strong evidence that this is a bidirectional relationship, so such practices are also instrumental in boosting self-efficacy.

Summarizing what we've just been through, then, one of the things you can strive to develop in the long term to help you deal with abusive customers is your self-efficacy, that is, a sense that you can actually do it. What works best for this is, perhaps ironically, to be exposed to such situations. Ideally, you would do this in a controlled environment, i.e., in something akin to a role-playing exercise. This gives you the comfort of being in a safe space, so you can explore and learn better. Next to this, such a setting is also ideal for employing the second tactic for boosting your self-efficacy – observing how others do it. Clearly, you can also do this in real life – just make sure that you are paying attention to what your colleagues are doing well. In a perfect world, the company would also be facilitating this process by organizing knowledge sharing sessions, for instance. And finally, managers are well-advised to provide verbal or social persuasion to employees, i.e., to try to boost their confidence. By the same token, don't forget that you can, as an employee, very well do this with your colleagues as well. Doing these things will help you become much more confident in handling abusive customers, which, as we saw earlier, is critical for managing tense situations well.

Resilience

Another skill that is extremely valuable for coping with the long-term personal consequences of customer abuse, and in life in general, is the ability to persevere in the face of difficulties, or what is known as resilience. The American Psychological Association defines resilience as "the process and outcome of successfully adapting to difficult or challenging life experiences, especially through mental, emotional, and behavioral flexibility and adjustment to external and internal demands" (American Psychological Association). People who display a high level of resilience are able to emerge from challenging situations stronger and more resourceful. Adversity even can be thought of as a fuel in these circumstances – unpleasant, for sure, yet also a catalyst for positive change. The reality is, we will all face difficult situations in which it seems like the whole world is against us. We lose a race, we don't get that promotion, we are being yelled at by customers; the list can go on and on.

One possible solution could be, of course, to try and avoid such situations. Yet, first, we are unlikely to succeed, as whatever we do, we never have full control over what happens to us. Second, and perhaps more important, not being exposed to potentially adverse circumstance means that we also lose opportunities for development and growth. After all, hiding might protect us from adversity, but it also doesn't build our abilities for cope with difficulties.

The better way, then, is to learn how to be more resilient, to emerge stronger from adversity, and to keep going. Research on dealing with customer abuse has unequivocally confirmed that higher resilience has a positive impact on how employees handle it. For instance, in 2018, a team of three researchers, Sommovigo, Setti, and Argentero (2019), conducted a study among more than 150 students working in retail sales or restaurants to understand whether customer incivility and other customer-related stressors like ambiguous or disproportionate expectations lead to burnout. Sure enough, they found sound evidence for such a relationship; burnout subsequently led to lower service performance by the participants, which is an unfortunate effect we discussed earlier on. Then, the researchers asked participants the 10 questions from the Connor–Davidson resilience scale, i.e., items such as "I am able to adapt to change" and "Coping with stress can strengthen me". Importantly, the relationship among customer incivility and lower job performance existed only among low resilience employees; among those high in resilience, there was no connection between whether customers treated them uncivilly and how well they did their job – they were shielded from the negative effect of customer abuse.

Similarly, van Erp et al. worked toward understanding how a very troubling phenomenon – bystanders getting in conflict with emergency care workers such as paramedics, policemen, and firefighters (yes, there are people who do that, and a lot!) – is linked to how well these people do their job. What they discovered is that "bystander conflict is negatively related to the affective, behavioral, and cognitive outcomes of individuals. Higher levels of bystander conflict were associated with more negative and less positive feelings …, unfavorable bystander appraisals …, and lower levels of performance …" (van Erp et al., 2015, 402). Importantly, among employees high in resilience, these effects were much less pronounced – they still existed, but to a much lesser extent, indicating that resilience buffers at least some of the negative impact of customer abuse (or in this case bystander conflict).

All in all, there are very good reasons to conclude that resilience is a major factor in tackling the consequences of customer abuse. And, it is vital to notice that in the definition of resilience we saw earlier resilience is not described as a trait, i.e., it's not so much a stable personality characteristic, but rather as something that can be learned and executed. There is no resilience gene that determines once and for all how well do you cope with adversity. You can become more resilient and deal better with challenging events by adopting certain mental habits and behaviors, and given that we are interested in how can you learn to better bounce back from customer abuse, it is imperative that we have a look at these practices.

One of the most helpful guidelines for this is provided by Diane Coutu in a brilliant article for Harvard Business Review. She outlines three characteristics that resilient people possess. First, they have "a staunch acceptance of reality" (Coutu, 2002). Optimism is certainly important if we are to be able to go through adversity. Yet, perhaps more vital to this is our ability to see and accept the situation we are in. We already touched upon a similar concept when we spoke about emotional intelligence. Awareness of where we stand right now, what is our baseline if you will, is paramount if we want to change anything in the world or in us. There is no use thinking, for instance, that only this particular customer was acting badly toward us – the fact is, this will keep happening. There is also no use in thinking that just because we've been through one (or ten) such episode(s) we will do better next time. We might, of course, but only if we develop our knowledge and skills to do it. Wishful thinking is an enemy when it comes to resilience; our ability to see the reality and our courage when facing it are much more helpful.

As Coutu puts it, "when we truly stare down reality, we prepare ourselves to act in ways that allow us to endure and survive extraordinary hardship. We train ourselves how to survive before the fact" (Coutu, 2002). The idea of training is another critical element that we need to point out. Resilient people (and organizations) don't just sit there and endure things – they learn how to handle them, and that is what makes them able to move on. And no learning can happen lest we know that there is something we need to learn. The first element that makes people resilient, then, is seeing and accepting the reality of things – some people are going to act aggressively, and our ability to deal with them might not be as high as we want it to be.

Facing down reality is not enough to be resilient, though. What we also need is a deeply held sense of purpose, or in other words – ability to find meaning in adverse circumstances. This might, of course, pose a serious challenge. It is not immediately clear how exactly does facing an aggressive customer relate to our sense of purpose in life, and this is true perhaps for most other difficulties we face in life. After all, as Harold Kusher points out in the preface to Viktor Frankl's stunning book *Man's Search for Meaning*, "Suffering in and of itself is meaningless; we give our suffering meaning by the way in which we respond to it" (Frankl, 1992, 10).

It is exactly this that makes it so difficult to discover the purpose behind our hardships, and one of the reasons why it's so easy to lose our sense of direction. The latter doesn't come from experience itself. There is nothing inherently meaningful in someone yelling at you or worse, in someone killing your loved ones in gas chambers. Yet, as Frankl, a concentration camp survivor and founder of logotherapy, poignantly describes, it is the lack of hope that is the true killer in camps. It is this insight that gave rise to his school of psychotherapy, which is centered on finding a sense of purpose in life. "One", writes Frankl,

> should not search for an abstract meaning of life. Everyone has his own specific vocation or mission in life to carry out a concrete assignment which demands fulfillment. … As each situation in life represents a challenge to man and presents a problem for him to solve, the question of the meaning of life may actually be reversed. Ultimately, man should not ask what the meaning of his life is, but rather he must recognize that it is he who is asked. In a word, each man is questioned by life; and he

can only answer to life by answering for his own life; to life he can only respond by being responsible.

(Frankl, 1992, 113–114)

It is this sense of a mission, if you will, that constitutes a large part of resilient people's ability to continue forward in the face of hardships. Things might be difficult, yet, they are no longer meaningless experiences; they become steps in a different and perhaps longer path to accomplishing "what life asks of us." Put in a broader context, facing abusive customers is clearly an unpleasant, not to say unhealthy and sometimes outright dangerous experience, which you will have an easier time going through if you can connect it with something bigger. It could be, for instance, akin to Frankl's own mission – to share about the experience with others and help them handle adversity better. It could be about learning the skills to deal with difficult customers. Or it could be about being able to better support your colleagues and friends emotionally when they are going through difficulties. This, as Frankl describes, can never be decided by anyone else but yourself, and I urge you to try and find it for yourself – it will help not only in going through customer abuse episodes but also in accomplishing your goals in life in general.

Finally, the third element that resilient people possess is the ability to improvise and make do with whatever resources you have at hand. The essence of a crisis, or a hardship, is that it ruptures the tissue of everyday life and exposes what's beneath. When was the last time you looked under the hood of your car? Most likely it wasn't on a random Thursday morning just because you had an itching sensation that you need to know what's going on there. In case you ever had have a look, it was when something went wrong – the engine refused to start or sounded off or was overheating; your car just stopped in the middle of the road; or you saw a suspicious patch of oily-looking substance under it. Similarly, crises draw our attention and make us look at things like you never did before. They make us ask questions on why and how are things like that. They make us explore what's out there as opposed to exploiting what we have.

And by breaking things up, crisis also opens opportunities for us to reassemble them in a new, perhaps better format. This is the reason, I believe, Rahm Emanuel memorably said that "You never want a serious crisis to go to waste." While painful adverse circumstances also open up opportunities to do things in a different way. That's where inventiveness comes into play. It's like having to build a castle with LEGOs, which all of a sudden it crumbles down. The pieces are still there, but now we are back to the drawing board, and it is our ability to make-do with what we have that will to a high extend determine how well we will do that. Those among us who are able to improvise in these difficult circumstances are the ones who are better positioned to learn from adversity as they muddle through it. They simply explore and invent new ways of doing things, and that, after all, is what growth really means.

Wrapping this part of the chapter up, next to self-efficacy, resilience is an important skill that you can develop in time to help you go through customer abuse episodes and tackle their negative impact on yourself. This ability to push through difficulties is learnable, and a good way to think about it is to see it as comprising of an ability to face down reality, to find meaning, and to improvise. Practicing these three pieces will make you more resilient in time, thus making it easier for you to handle difficult conversations, with customers and other people alike.

Take Another Person's Perspective

So far, we saw that deep-acting (as opposed to surface-acting), self-efficacy, and resilience are all skills and behaviors that can develop in the long run to help you deal with the consequences of customer abuse better. There is one more piece of the puzzle that we'll discuss here – the so-called ability to take another person's perspective.

It might seem obvious when we say it, but we typically see the world through our eyes and from our own perspective, and that's completely natural of course – after all, it's our own brains that are locked in our own heads, and their job is to navigate your own self in to the world. In a lot of ways, this is an ego-centric point of view, in which we evaluate things based on what they mean for us. For instance, when talking about TV series with others, we might, not necessarily consciously, consider their opinion from the perspective of finding something interesting to watch tonight.

We also possess, though, the wonderful ability to actively consider other people's point of view, and their own thoughts, motivations, and emotions, and the reasoning behind them. In psychology, this is also typically referred to as "theory of mind," that is, the ability to ascribe mental states to others, and holding in our minds the underlying assumption that these may be different from our own. As you will notice, this looks a lot like the much widely used these days term "empathy," and the two are indeed closely linked. There is, however, a subtle difference between empathy and perspective-taking, and it lies in the fact that the former is also linked to accepting the feelings of others, while the latter is about understanding them; as Healey and Grossman point out, "Affective empathy results from a combination of cognitive empathy and emotional contagion. Here, the perceiver not only models the other agent's emotion but also adopts it (i.e., affect sharing). Affect sharing thus distinguishes affective empathy from affective perspective-taking" (2018).

Perspective-taking, then, is a term that we will reserve for the "active cognitive process of imagining the world from another's vantage point or imagining oneself in another's shoes to understand their visual viewpoint, thoughts, motivations, intentions, and/or emotions" (Ku, Wang, and Galinsky, 2015, 95). The emphasis on "active" in this definition is important. While it might be that we automatically, without a guided effort, engage in perspective-taking, it will still be an active process in the sense that it is a conscious one – it's not something that happens behind the scenes, but something we are aware of. A corollary of this is that we can also control it much better, i.e., we can relatively easily engage in the process of taking another person's perspective (if we remember to do it, that is).

To those among us who are better at this, it brings a host of benefits. Studies show, for instance, that

> when you take on someone else's perspective, you start to see more of that person in yourself. This increases social bonds and reduces stereotypes. You also start to include the person whose perspective you're taking in your own sense of self, and features of the other person become more descriptive of yourself as well.
>
> (PsychologyCompass.com)

Not surprisingly, then, perspective-taking "leads to higher quality and more significant social interactions. It makes it easier to clearly communicate with others, and increases disclosure. People who are better at perspective taking even tend to have bigger social networks" (PsychologyCompass.com).

The benefits of being able to take another person's perspective have also been well proven in the context of customer abuse. Earlier on, we went through a couple of studies by Rafaeli et al. (2012), in which we saw that when customers act aggressively, employees pay cognitive costs and their memory gets impaired. This happens because they engage in processes, such as secondary appraisal, rumination, and arousal, which naturally drain their resources. As part of their investigation, the researchers also sought to see what might mitigate these negative effects. They reasoned that it might be the case that employees who are better at perspective-taking will engage in less secondary appraisal and rumination, because they are more likely to detach from negative events and exhibit enhanced social functioning.

These positive effects do indeed appear to be in place. Following interactions with aggressive customers, employees who were low in perspective-taking showed reduced performance on the Raven test, designed to measure general fluid intelligence and working memory. This was not the case for employees high in perspective-taking – there was simply no drop in their working memory after facing aggressive customers. Thus, as the authors point out, by promoting patience and understanding, perspective-taking appears to alleviate the negative effects of customer aggression on employees' cognitive functioning.

Relatedly, Rupp et al. (2008) investigated whether customer injustice, i.e., being treated unfairly by customers, has a negative impact on employees' work by making them engage in more surface-acting (as opposed to the more productive deep-acting). In a study among about 150 bank employees in Germany, they indeed found that there is such an effect, with employees who perceived customers to treat them unjustly tending to engage in surface-acting. Importantly, though, this is valid for those low in perspective-taking; employees who are good in perspective-taking simply don't experience this effect, and customer injustice doesn't make them more likely to engage in surface-acting.

Finally, Lee and Madera investigated whether perspective-taking can help mitigate the negative affect that employees experience after a difficult customer interaction, and if it can make them engage in more deep-acting and helping behaviors even after such situations. They conducted a diary study with employees working in US hotels for ten days; during the first five, there researchers did not intervene in any way, while in the latter five days they asked employees to do a customer perspective-taking exercise:

> Imagine yourself in the position of the customer. We do not often think about how customers can have a bad day and then take it out on us. For example, maybe his/her flight was delayed, or he/she is having marital problems, and this was his/her vacation to patch things up.
>
> (Lee and Madera, 2021, 5)

As hypothesized,

> participants experience less negative affect and more empathy towards customers on days they engaged in the customer-focused perspective-taking intervention than days without the intervention. The results also support a mediating effect of decreased negative affect and increased empathy on participant deep acting and helping behaviors on days they engaged in the customer-focused perspective-taking intervention than days without the intervention.

In simpler terms, when they tried to take the perspective of the customer, employees didn't feel that bad even after difficult interactions with them, engaged in more deep-acting (e.g., "I really try to feel the emotions I have to show as part of my job"), and were thus more likely to try to help the customer.

All the evidence, then, points toward the conclusion that perspective-taking helps alleviate a plethora of the negative effects that employees experience when customers act badly toward them. It serves as a kind of shield almost against negative emotions, cognitive impairment, and surface-acting, and promotes productive behaviors such as deep-acting and willingness to help customers.

Perhaps, the best thing about perspective-taking, other than the fact that it's a helpful thing to do in many areas in life, is that it's a very simple thing to do. It doesn't take a genius to do it, and it doesn't require complicated interventions that work in subtle ways. All it takes is a reminder and some practice. As the study by Lee and Madera shows, a very simple nudge toward looking at things from the customer perspective is often enough to make us feel better. Take the time to think how they might be feeling right now, and to look at things from their perspective. You don't necessarily need to be right – after all, you are unlikely to know whether the customer is having a backpain or if their flight was delayed. It does help, though, to consider these things. Who among us can say that we are at our best when these things happen to us? That's not an excuse, of course, to treat people badly, and that's not the goal here. Rather, it's to give you a sense of control in a way; knowledge is power, and knowing why a customer is acting aggressively already puts you on the path to handling it well.

What Did We Discuss in This Chapter?

We've been through a lot in this chapter, but unlike some of the previous ones I hope it was a much more positive journey, as we saw what you, managers, and you, employees, can do to help mitigate the negative consequences of customer abuse. Both can do a lot in this regard.

A sounds advice for managers is to first be able to identify which employees are facing considerable strain due to customer abuse. The reporting and monitoring systems in place in your organization should be able to help with this, and you can also make good use of technologies such AI, that unlock the opportunity to do real-time emotion recognition, for example. The latter makes it possible to build early warning systems based on the conversations employees and customers are having, so you can know immediately which of your people are involved in more heated debates with customers.

Empowering employees to take decisions on their own is another practice that helps them deal with the stress from customer abuse. It encourages them to take control and increases the level of autonomy they experience at work, thus making the work itself more motivating. In addition, it signals a level of trust by the manager and the organization that provides a further boost to their resources. Similarly, organizational and social support in its two forms – instrumental and emotional – is vital for buffering the negative impact of customer abuse on employees' performance. The key once again lies in providing employees with additional resources, in this case social and emotional ones. A number of studies have shown how working within a supporting environment are, at least to a certain extent, safeguarded against the consequences from dealing with customers mistreatment. Finally, on a leadership level, behaviors that ensure employees are treated fairly, and ones that characterize humble and transformative leaders have also been shown to help mitigate the effects of customer abuse.

Further to these practices, employees can do a lot of things to help themselves handle the stress that comes with customer mistreatment. In the short term, these boil down to practices that promote their well-being, including things like good sleep, mindfulness, seeking social support, taking a short break from work, and so on. And in the long run, employees can seek to further advance their skills and to work on some personality attributes to make them better in dealing with abusive or otherwise challenging customers. Deep-acting, developing resilience, growing self-efficacy, and learning how to better take another person's perspective are all qualities that have a positive impact on employees' well-being. These are not easy things to develop, but you are most certainly able to do it, given enough focus and persistence. What is more, they will do you good in many other areas as well, so I strongly encourage you to give them a try.

Notes

1 See Wang et al. (2013).
2 See Luszczynska and Schwarzer (2020).

References

American Psychological Association. Resilience. https://www.apa.org/topics/resilience, last accessed on January 13, 2023.

Baranik, L. E., Wang, M., Gong, Y., & Shi, J. (2017). Customer mistreatment, employee health, and job performance: Cognitive rumination and social sharing as mediating mechanisms. *Journal of Management*, 43(4), 1261–1282. https://doi.org/10.1177/0149206314550995

Bi, Yahua, Choi, Sooyoung, Yin, Jie, & Kim, Insin. (2021). Stress on frontline employees from customer aggression in the restaurant industry: The moderating effect of empowerment. *Sustainability*, 13, 1433. doi: 10.3390/su13031433.

Bromuri, S., Henkel, A. P., Iren, D., & Urovi, V. (2021). Using AI to predict service agent stress from emotion patterns in service interactions. *Journal of Service Management*, 32(4), 581–611. https://doi.org/10.1108/JOSM-06-2019-0163

Boukis, A., Koritos, C., Daunt, K. L., & Papastathopoulos, A. (2020). Effects of customer incivility on frontline employees and the moderating role of supervisor leadership style. *Tourism Management*, 77, Article 103997. https://doi.org/10.1016/j.tourman.2019.103997

Chan, K. W., & Wan, E. W. (2012). How can stressed employees deliver better customer service? The underlying self-regulation depletion mechanism. *Journal of Marketing*, 76(1), 119–137. https://doi.org/10.1509/jm.10.0202

Chen, J., Kang, H., Wang, Y., & Zhou, M. (2021) Thwarted psychological needs: the negative impact of customer mistreatment on service employees and the moderating role of empowerment HRM practices. *Personnel Review*, 50(7/8), 1566–1581. https://doi.org/10.1108/PR-06-2020-0489

Coun, M. J. H., Peters, P., Blomme, R. J., & Schaveling, J. (2021). 'To empower or not to empower, that's the question'. Using an empowerment process approach to explain employees' workplace proactivity. *The International Journal of Human Resource Management*. Advance online publication. https://doi.org/10.1080/09585192.2021.1879204

Coutu, D. (2002). How resilience works. https://hbr.org/2002/05/how-resilience-works, last accessed on January 13, 2023.

Frankl, V. (1992). *Man's Search For Meaning*. Ebury Publishing. Kindle Edition.

Gong, Z., Sun, Y., & Zhang, Z. (2018) The influence of customer's verbal abuse on turnover intention and job burnout of sales service staff—The moderating effect of organizational atmosphere and psychological capital. *Psychology*, 9, 2369–2383. doi: 10.4236/psych.2018.910135.

Goussinsky, R. (2012). Coping with customer aggression. *Journal of Service Management*, 23(2), 170–196. https://doi.org/10.1108/09564231211226105

Healey, M. L., & Grossman, M. (2018). Cognitive and affective perspective-taking: Evidence for shared and dissociable anatomical substrates. *Frontiers in Neurology*, 9, 491. doi: 10.3389/fneur.2018.00491.

Health.gov. Get Enough Sleep. https://health.gov/myhealthfinder/healthy-living/mental-health-and-relationships/get-enough-sleep, last accessed on January 13, 2023.

Ku, Gillian, Wang, Cynthia, & Galinsky, Adam. (2015). The promise and perversity of perspective-taking in organizations. *Research in Organizational Behavior*, 35. doi: 10.1016/j.riob.2015.07.003.

Lee, Lindsey, & Madera, Juan. (2021). A within-level analysis of the effect of customer-focused perspective-taking on deep acting and customer helping behaviors: The mediating roles of negative affect and empathy. *International Journal of Hospitality Management*, 95, 102907. doi: 10.1016/j.ijhm.2021.102907.

Liu, Y., Song, Y., Koopmann, J., Wang, M., Chang, C. D., & Shi, J. (2017). Eating your feelings? Testing a model of employees' work-related stressors, sleep quality, and unhealthy eating. *Journal of Applied Psychology*, 102(8), 1237–1258. doi: 10.1037/apl0000209.

Luszczynska, A., & Schwarzer, R. (2020). Changing behavior using social cognitive theory. In M. Hagger, L. Cameron, K. Hamilton, N. Hankonen, & T. Lintunen (Eds.), *The Handbook of Behavior Change* (Cambridge Handbooks in Psychology, pp. 32–45). Cambridge: Cambridge University Press. doi: 10.1017/9781108677318.003

Mayo Clinic. Mindfulness exercises. https://www.mayoclinic.org/healthy-lifestyle/consumer-health/in-depth/mindfulness-exercises/art-20046356, last accessed on January 13, 2023.

Pap, Z., Vîrgă, D., & Notelaers, G. (2021). Perceptions of customer incivility, job satisfaction, supervisor support, and participative climate: A multi-level approach. *Frontiers in Psychology*, 12, 713953. doi: 10.3389/fpsyg.2021.713953.

Park, Y., & Kim, S. (2019). Customer mistreatment harms nightly sleep and next-morning recovery: Job control and recovery self-efficacy as cross-level moderators. *Journal of Occupational Health Psychology*, 24(2), 256–269. doi: 10.1037/ocp0000128.

PsychologyCompass.com. 3 counter intuitive ways to take on another person's point of view. https://psychologycompass.com/blog/point-of-view/, last accessed on January 13, 2023.

Rafaeli, A., Erez, A., Ravid, S., Derfler-Rozin, R., Treister, D. E., & Scheyer, R. (2012). When customers exhibit verbal aggression, employees pay cognitive costs. *Journal of Applied Psychology*, 97(5), 931–950. doi: 10.1037/a0028559.

Rupp, D. E., McCance, A. S., Spencer, S., & Sonntag, K. (2008). Customer (in)justice and emotional labor: The role of perspective taking, anger, and emotional regulation? *Journal of Management*, 34(5), 903–924. https://doi.org/10.1177/0149206307309261

Schat, A. C., & Kelloway, E. K. (2003). Reducing the adverse consequences of workplace aggression and violence: the buffering effects of organizational support. *Journal of Occupational Health Psychology*, 8(2), 110–122. doi: 10.1037/1076-8998.8.2.110.

Sommovigo, V., Setti, I., & Argentero, P. (2019). The role of service providers' resilience in buffering the negative impact of customer incivility on service recovery performance. *Sustainability*, 11(1), 285. https://doi.org/10.3390/su11010285

Spreitzer, G. M. (1995). Psychological empowerment in the workplace: Dimensions, measurement, and validation. *Academy of Management Journal*, 38(5), 1442–1465. https://doi.org/10.2307/256865

van Erp, K. J. P. M., Rispens, S., Gevers, J. M. P., & Demerouti, E. (2015). When bystanders become bothersome: The negative consequences of bystander conflict and the moderating role of resilience. *European Journal of Work and Organizational Psychology*, 24(3), 402–419. https://doi.org/10.1080/1359432X.2014.904290

van Jaarsveld, D. D., Restubog, S. L. D., Walker, D. D., & Amarnani, R. K. (2015). Misbehaving customers: Understanding and managing customer injustice in service organizations. *Organizational Dynamics*, 44(4), 273–280. https://doi.org/10.1016/j.orgdyn.2015.09.004

Wang, M., Liao, H., Zhan, Y., & Shi, J. (2011). Daily customer mistreatment and employee sabotage against customers: Examining emotion and resource perspectives. *Academy of Management Journal*, 54(2), 312–334. https://doi.org/10.5465/AMJ.2011.60263093

Wang, M., Liu, S., Liao, H., Gong, Y., Kammeyer-Mueller, J., & Shi, J. (2013). Can't get it out of my mind: Employee rumination after customer mistreatment and negative mood in the next morning. *Journal of Applied Psychology*, 98(6), 989–1004. https://doi.org/10.1037/a0033656

Wang, X., & Wang, H. (2017). How to survive mistreatment by customers: Employees' work withdrawal and their coping resources. *International Journal of Conflict Management*, 28(4), 464–482. https://doi.org/10.1108/IJCMA-11-2016-0089

Yue, Y., Nguyen, H., Groth, M., Johnson, A., & Frenkel, S. (2021). When heroes and villains are victims: How different withdrawal strategies moderate the depleting effects of customer incivility on frontline employees. *Journal of Service Research*, 24(3), 435–454. https://doi.org/10.1177/1094670520967994

Chapter 8

Recap

In the beginning of this book, and in the process of writing it, I had two goals for myself. First, I wanted to learn more about customer abuse, share what I know, and put it firmly on the agenda of business leaders. Second, I wanted to arm manager and employees alike with tools to prevent, deal with, and tackle the negative effects of customer abuse. It is not up to me to decide how successfully I've accomplished this of course. One can only hope that if nothing else, the very existence of this book and the fact that you've read it and have a good overview of the field is enough to move the proverbial needle in the direction of eradicating customer abuse, and more naively, that it contributes to making the world a better, kinder place.

Given that we have been through quite a lot of content, it is perhaps worth noting in an almost telegraphic style what did we learn about customer abuse in the course of this book.

What is Customer Abuse?

Customer abuse is part of the broader phenomena of customer-deviant behavior, which could be profit- or nonprofit-driven. Examples of profit-driven customer deviant behavior include shoplifting, piracy, deshopping, making false claims, fraud, switching price tags, and many others. Nonprofit-deviant customer behavior can be directed at the company – for instance, vandalism; at other customers – for example, jumping queues, or acting in such a way that it ruins the experience of other customers; or at the company's employees. The latter – nonprofit-deviant customer behavior directed at company employees is what we called throughout the book customer abuse.

Exact definitions of customer abuse abound, but for the sake of having practical, working knowledge, we can think of it as customer behavior that is directed toward company employees and that goes against the accepted social norms of behavior, be they social or company ones. It takes two major forms: verbal and physical.

DOI: 10.4324/9781003402565-9

Examples of verbal customer abuse include customers using condescending language (van Jaarsveld et al., 2015), customers yelling at employees (van Jaarsveld et al., 2015), making insulting comments, shouting, cursing, speaking rudely, speaking with sarcasm, speaking with a strong voice, arguing forcefully, sexist comments (both explicit and implied), racist comments (both explicit and implied), irrelevant personal remarks (e.g., about your appearance), threats (e.g., I'll have you fired), intimidating silence, accusations of various sorts (e.g., calling you a racist), comments about your competency, knowledge, dedication[1].

Examples of physical customer abuse include standing in your personal space, starting at you (long eye contact), table pounding, throwing things, leaning over you (using height advantage), fearsome facial expressions, loud sighing, pointing, other offensive gestures, shoving of personnel, slamming a phone down, attacking employees, unwanted physical contact[2].

How Widely Spread is Customer Abuse?

Customer abuse affects most painfully people who are exposed to frequent communication with customer, of course, and according to the World Bank, in 2019, for the first time in human history more than half of the world's population works in the service sector, thus worldwide, one in every two employees is at risk of experiencing customer abuse. In markets such as United States, United Kingdom, and the Netherlands the share of people working in the service sector reaches more than 75%.

As with many other things in the social world, exact numbers about the share of people who are have been abused by customers don't really exist. We still know enough, though, to conclude unequivocally that it is reaching pandemic proportions. Here are three facts to give us an idea of its spread: in a call center study in 2004, researchers discovered that "The average number of customer aggression events per day was 10 (about 15–20% of total calls per day), and 60% reported that such an event had occurred already that week or that day." (Grandey, Dickter, and Sin, 2004, 408); in 2017, homecare workers reported being on the receiving side of each the following in the last year: "verbal aggression (51.5%), workplace aggression (27.5%), workplace violence (24.7%), sexual harassment (27.6%), and sexual aggression (12.8%)." (Glass et al., 2017, 641); and the annual "Freedom From Fear" survey by the UK Union of Shop, Distributive and Allied Workers shows that 90% of service workers reported verbal abuse in 2020 and 2021, up from about 65% in the preceding three years; and in 2021, 12% of the workers said they have been physically assaulted by customers, up from about 4% in the 2017–2019 period (USDAW).

Why Should We Care?

In a word, we should care because when customers act abusively, both employees and companies pay a high price.

Customer Abuse Hurts Employees

As can be expected, when customers act abusively, employees experience higher stress and more negative emotions, accompanied with all the detrimental effects of both. These are unpleasant and often times outright unhealthy experiences on their own right, but the situation is further exacerbated by the fact that employees, being in a professional setting, must actively manage their performance. The stress and negative emotions further create an emotional dissonance – a tension between the emotions employees feel and the performance they should put on ("Service with a smile"). To tackle it, employees need to engage in active emotion regulation, which on the one hand they are not necessarily well-equipped to do (and might thus use unproductive strategies), and on the other, drains their cognitive and emotional resources. The latter leads to emotional exhaustion and burnout, with all the negative psychological and physiological affects of the latter.

Customer Abuse Hurts Companies

I strongly believe that the negative effects of customer abuse on employees are reason enough for business leaders to take action. But these negative consequences are not only limited to employees; indirectly, they have a significant impact on organizations as well.

When put in stressful situations, employees have a number of options for managing it (just like any of us): they can fight it, they can freeze, or they can try to run away from it. Freezing and running away in a work environment indicates lower employee engagement, more surface-acting, and higher turnover intention. Simply put, when customers act abusively, employees either become disengaged at work, start faking emotions, or, in in the worst-case scenario for the company – quit.

As for the fighting part, there are productive and unproductive ways for employees to do this. In the worst-case scenario, customer abuse leads to customer-directed employee retaliation, i.e., employees simply start taking revenge on their customers. The productive way to deal with customer abuse would be, unsurprisingly, to push through it, remain engaged, and try to improve your skills in managing difficult situations. The issue here is that even if employees are highly motivated to do their job well, employees might not be able to do this, as a plethora of studies show that customer abuse hampers cognitive abilities like memory, for instance. This worsened performance quite logically leads to lower customer satisfaction, thus creating a viscous circle, given that poor customer experience is very often the major reason behind customer abuse.

When and Why Customers Act Abusively?

Given all these major negative consequences of customer abuse, fighting it appears, I hope, to be a mission worth embarking on. To do that, it's worth reviewing the factors that lead to customer abuse. Research has identified three groups of factors that create or trigger customer abuse: situational, personal, and societal ones.

Situational Factors

Situational factors are perhaps the strongest reason why customers act abusively. A nonexhaustive list of those includes:

- An uncivil or rude employee – as the title of one paper on the topic succinctly puts it, "Catching rudeness is like catching a cold" (Foulk, Woolum, and Erez, 2016)
- Customer abuse is also very often triggered by poor service recovery. This could be caused by employees doing a poor job in solving customer issues, but it could also be that the company itself hasn't designed and implemented good service recovery practices.
- Employees who surface-act also experience more mistreatment by customers, that is, customers can recognize when employees fake emotions and punish them for this.
- Finally, simply observing other people acting aggressively sends us a message that this is an acceptable behavior and we are more likely to go along.

The second group of situational factors is not related to the social environment but to the physical one – there is a host of things in the service setting that makes customer abuse more likely to occur. For instance, too high temperature, too loud or aggressive music, and crowdedness have been shown to have a direct impact on customer aggression.

Personality Factors

Further to the situational factors that we reviewed, the key to customer abuse often lies in specific personality traits of either the customer or the employee.

On the customer side, research has linked a host of personality characteristics to higher likelihood to be aggressive or abusive. These include:

- Narcissism: people high in this trait have an exaggerated sense of self-importance, a strong sense of entitlement, being "preoccupied with fantasies about success, power, brilliance, beauty or the perfect mate" (Mayo Clinic), taking advantage of others, an insistence of having nothing but the best, manipulative behaviors, belief in their superiority, and expectation for this to be constantly recognized, among other things.
- Machiavellianism: the tendency to manipulate others to achieve one's goals and disregard of morality.
- High neuroticism/negative affectivity, i.e., people who experience sudden and large shifts in mood, feel anxious, get upset easily, and struggle to recover from stressful events (Cherry, 2022).
- Low agreeableness, i.e., those among us scoring low on behaviors like cooperativeness, kindness, and altruism.
- Low conscientiousness.
- Biases and prejudices.

And then of course, there are certain personality characteristics that make employees more likely to be the subject of customer abuse. High neuroticism and low agreeableness are personality factors that influence how often employees subject to aggressive customers (just like they influence how likely a customer is to exhibit aggression). Furthermore, employees higher in self-esteem also feel the impact of customer abuse more acutely and their willingness to go the extra mile, which is under normal circumstances higher compared to low self-esteem employees, diminishes. Finally, younger employees and those with lower job tenure are also more likely to feel the impact of customer abuse more strongly and/or to have lower coping abilities.

Societal Factors

The last group of factors that drives or triggers customer abuse is related to the broader social environment that we share. The Customer Is King philosophy and the sense of entitlement and power it creates is the major factor in this set of factors. As companies try to win in the market place by delivering better and better products/services and customer experiences, they also increase customers' expectation. Supported by the customer-is-king philosophy, this creates a feeling of entitlement and power in customers, both of which ultimately make customers more likely to act aggressively when their demands are not met.

Armed with this knowledge, we are now in a much better position to propose actions to fight customer abuse. As discussed previously, there are three broad sets of practices companies and employees can employ to achieve this mission: they can try to prevent customer abuse from happening; they can try to handle abusive customers better; and they can work toward mitigating the negative consequences of customer abuse when it happens.

How to Prevent Customer Abuse?

Improve Customer Experience

Defense is the best attack, and similarly, preventing customer abuse from happening is the best way to deal with it. Given that a major driver behind customer abuse is poor customer experience and poor service recovery, it makes very good sense to start from these two (very closely related) elements. By now, the fact that customer experience can make or break a company's business is, fortunately, common knowledge, and organizations invest a lot in measuring and improving customer experience. The scope of this book doesn't permit a more extensive discussion, but it's worth noting that good customer experience:

- "encompasses every aspect of a company's offering—the quality of customer care, of course, but also advertising, packaging, product and service features, ease of use, and reliability." (Schwager and Meyer, 2007). Everything, every interaction between a company and a customer, contributes to a customer forming an impression of the company and its products and services, thus creating a customer experience.
- Great customer experiences are coherent: they leave nothing to chance and every interaction is designed and executed in a way that matches every other interaction to contribute to the creation of a coherent experience.
- Great customer experiences are easy and effortless. We, as customers, don't stumble all the time in our customer journeys, but there is a smooth flow from one stage to another, from purchasing, through delivery, to servicing, etc.
- Great customer experiences are very reliable – we get what we expect, and we get it consistently. There might be surprises, of course, but these need to be minimal and positive, if any at all.

Improve Service Recovery in Particular

A specifically painful part of the customer experience is when customers face an issue with the product or service and need to resolve it. The key issue here is again that people experience a loss of resources or a threat of losing them – we paid for something (invested resources) and we are not getting a return on our investment (because the product is not working). What a good recovery process does is to restore justice into the world along three dimensions: procedural justice (how well the process of recovery worked out), interactional justice (how well the employees handled the interaction), and distributive justice (how happy customers are with the outcome they got). Poor execution of the recovery process means a higher chance of customer abuse, so a very good practice for preventing it is to put in more efforts in a good, seamless, and satisfactory damage control.

Do Predictive Personalized Post-Sales Service

Going a step further, the leading companies are less and less relying on customer complaints to manage customer satisfaction, and actively look for ways to get engaged with customers. In the more common shape of this process, they reach out to customers to seek their feedback, and then act on it accordingly. The ever-growing amount of customer data available to companies means they can start going a step further and proactively engage with customers – instead of waiting and doing it on a smaller scale, organizations, especially the data-rich ones, can predict customer needs and deliver proactive personalized post-sales service at scale. The latter means that organizations can now get engaged with customers proactively, thus addressing any potential issues before they arise.

Other Ways to Prevent Customer Abuse

Going beyond these, there is a plethora of other actions companies can take to prevent customer abuse. Running campaigns that increase the awareness of the issue and trying to communicate appropriate norms of behavior will help in increasing customers' sensitivity toward the issue. Companies might also consider adopting a zero-tolerance policy toward customer abuse, and communicating it clearly to customers both in physical premises and via digital channels. Furthermore, the presence or at least the easy access of management to potentially heated situations will also help in tuning emotions down. This can be supported by early warning systems applied on either customer level (knowing which customers are more likely to act aggressively) or interaction level (monitoring conversations for emotional words).

All of these actions – from campaigns, through early warning systems, to better customer experience and better service recovery – will contribute to reducing customer abuse. Unfortunately, just like with anything else in the world, eradicating it completely is unlikely to ever happen; no matter what we do, some customers will still act aggressively toward our employees, and that leads us to the critical question of how to deal with customer abuse as the situation unfolds.

How to Deal with Customer Abuse in the Heat of the Moment?

Zero-Tolerance Policy and Good Processes

First things first, companies can help employees manage customer abuse by adopting zero-tolerance customer abuse policies and processes that guide employees on how to go through these interactions. Ideally, these would cover the company's intention (the policy's goal), roles and responsibilities, and the specific process that employees can follow to notice, handle, report, and monitor customer abuse. The policy and the process of handling aberrant customer behavior serves as one piece of additional resource for employees in their toolbox, and ensures that they know the company has got their backs, and that they don't invent the wheel every time.

The four Ingredients of Successfully Diffusing Tension

There are four key ingredients to successfully diffusing a situation of tension between a customer and an employee, and all of these can be trained and practiced upfront so that when a situation happens, the latter knows how to react. First, do your best to remain calm. Try to remain as calm as possible, keep your posture, control your tone of voice, and avoid abrupt bodily movements and nervous gestures like touching your hair; if you are typing on a computer, avoid pounding on the keys; remain polite during the whole interaction and show respect – this is what leading by example is. If you are in a physical space, maintain the appropriate social distance to avoid provoking the customer further. Show the customer what an appropriate behavior looks like and convey in all possible ways that they cannot intimidate you.

Next, you need to act with confidence. Talk in a way that shows the customer that you are in control and although you want to do your best to meet their needs, a deviation from the socially acceptable behavior wouldn't be tolerated. Don't interrupt them and don't patronize them. Maintain appropriate eye contact instead of averting your gaze – this shows that you are not scared (which I hope you are not!). Don't get defensive, don't start explaining yourself, and don't show the clear signs of withdrawal like crossed arms and shrugging your shoulders. Your goal is not to show that you can fight them, but it's also not to show you are a second away from fleeing the scene. It is your territory, it's your company, and it's your right to be treated well – show it.

Rule of thumb number 3 says that you need to try to establish a connection with the customer. Ideally, you would have done this even before the customer became abusive of course, but if not, it's absolutely critical to do it now. You've seen this done in negotiation situations in dozens of movies, and it's included there for a reason – people are significantly less likely to hurt people they know and feel somehow connected to. Your goal is to show the person that this is not a fight but a collaborative effort in finding a solution. You are one the same side; you are a team! Show it to them. Asking questions is absolutely the best advice there is for building a connection; it is vital that you couple this with listening carefully to what the customer is saying and trying to clarify things. Try to establish common ground by finding something you share. This is surprisingly simple to do, as studies show we feel closer to people who share absolutely accidental characteristics with us, like the first letter of our names or the same place of birth. A smile and some positive attitude can also do miracles of course.

And finally, rule of thumb number 4 is, as can be expected, to solve the issue at hand. Adopt a problem-focused approach that brings better results than focusing on the emotions that are unfolding. This requires two elements to be in place. On the one hand, they need to have the skills and knowledge to do it, e.g., to be able to understand the issue at hand, and to be aware of the company's policies and processes for doing it. On the other, the company holds a significant responsibility on this end, as after all, an employee can only do as much as the company has empowered them to. Being flexible is critical in this regard. It is a good idea to embed a considerable amount of adaptability in this process, so as to give employees the space of maneuver during difficult interactions.

All these four – remaining calm, acting with confidence, building rapport, and solving the issue – are learnable things. It might be true that some people are better at them than others, but it's also true that everyone can become better with practice. During the more detailed discussion on these elements earlier on we provided a host of suggestions, which hopefully provide a good guidance for doing this.

How to Alleviate the Negative Consequences of Customer Abuse?

Finally, even if handled well, customer abuse will still have a detrimental impact on employees and organizations, so further to trying to prevent it and to learning to deal with aggressive customers, companies and employees will do well to try and mitigate these negative consequences. There are things managers (or organizations, more broadly speaking) can do, and there are things employees themselves can add to the mix

What Managers Can Do?

Knowing Which Employees are Most Affected

The first question managers can do is to identify which employees suffer from more customer abuse and/or which feel its impact the most. The monitoring system that we advocated for earlier helps in this regard, and so do recent advances in artificial intelligence, which make it possible to monitor interactions in real time to identify high level of negative emotions and stress. Next to this, it's also a good idea to offer potential employees a good idea of what the job they are about to take on entails. While it is clear that some candidates might be put off by what they see, it is better to have it this way, rather than hire an employee with the wrong expectations only to have to replace them shortly after.

Empower Employees

Empowering is one thing that research has unequivocally shown to decrease the negative impact of customer abuse on employees. Empowerment means, psychologists suggest, that employees experience these four things in their work:

- First, they consider the work as fitting what they strive for and their beliefs and values. Meaning is about the sense and enjoyment that stems from doing what we believe makes sense and is worth doing in this world.
- Second, empowered employees have a high sense of competence or self-efficacy. They feel they can do their job well. It's not about self-esteem, which rather refers to how highly we regard ourselves, but about whether we can cope with whatever the world throws at us or whatever we want to push forward.
- Third, self-determination reflects the aspect of autonomy in starting and continuing doing work-related activities. This is perhaps the most commonly known element of empowerment – being able to select the goals and the means by which to pursue them.
- Lastly, the concept of impact reflects employees' feelings and perceptions that they can influence what is happening in their workplaces.

Social and Organizational Support

Social and organizational support boils down to employees' perception about the degree to which the organization, including peers and managers, pays attention and cares about their well-being. This can manifest itself in a large variety of ways, ranging from lending a sympathetic ear, through the provision of policies and processes for handling customer abuse, to providing encouragement in the face of adversity. What is important, given that customer abuse drains employees' resources or threatens to do so, is that managers and organizations try to replenish those, and that's exactly the purpose of social and organizational support – to supply employees with emotional or functional resources to deal with the process.

What Employees Can Do?

Next to the role of managers in the process of alleviating the negative consequences of customer abuse, employees can help themselves in this as well. There are two broad groups of things they can do – ones that can be adopted in the short run, and skills and practices whose development will likely take considerably more time.

Quick Wins

In the short term, the keyword is recharging. If you can do it immediately after the customer abuse episode, do it – take a break, do mindfulness, talk to others, have a nice cup of tea, walk around, whatever rocks your boat.

Further to these practices, and extending the time horizon a bit, taking good care of yourself – both mentally and physically – will also serve you well. Good sleep, good food, experiencing the little pleasures of life, doing sports – all of these things work in your favor to tackle the negative consequences of the stress you experience when a customer mistreats you. All kinds of hobbies work well for recharging emotionally, too. Hobbies are characterized by a very strong internal drive to do things – when we paint, swim, photograph, do gardening or knitting, we usually do it because we like these things, and not because we need to. This freedom of expression is extremely valuable, as it promotes feeling of control and, put simply, pure joy.

Go for them, especially when you are experiencing considerable stress. They also have the added benefit of distracting you from the source of stress and very often of giving you access to a diverse social circle. In a word, having a hobby is a very very good idea for managing stress.

Skills that Help Alleviate the Negative Consequences of Customer Abuse

Finally, there are three skills that employees can try to develop to help them better mitigate the negative impact of customer abuse on their lives.

First – self-efficacy. The idea refers to the beliefs we hold that we can control challenging situations and we can cope with them; you can think of it also as an "I can" perception about what we are about to encounter.

The higher the people are in self-efficacy in a certain domain, the higher the chances that they will engage and spend time and effort in it; by proxy, employees high in self-efficacy related to handling abusive customers are better positioned to have the motivation to perform well in such situations and to exhibit the behaviors we described as part of the successful dealing with customer mistreatment. They act with confidence, remain calm, and show assertiveness, because they believe that they can handle the situation well. There are four ways to develop self-efficacy: mastery experiences, i.e., achieving success themselves; vicarious experiences (having a role model to observe); verbal persuasion; and techniques to reduce stress.

Next to this, growing your level of resilience will help, too, and not just for dealing with customer abuse. Resilience is defined as "the process and outcome of successfully adapting to difficult or challenging life experiences, especially through mental, emotional, and behavioral flexibility and adjustment to external and internal demands." (American Psychological Association), and people who display a high level of resilience are able to emerge from challenging situations stronger and more resourceful. There are three behaviors that resilient people exhibit: they face down reality, they find purpose in hardships, and they improvise relentlessly.

Finally, the ability to take another person's perspective, i.e., ability to actively consider other people's point of view, and their own thoughts, motivations, and emotions, and the reasoning behind them, has also been shown to help alleviate the negative consequences of customer abuse. All the research evidence points toward the conclusion that perspective-taking helps alleviate a plethora of the negative effects that employees experience when customers act badly toward them. It serves as a kind of shield almost against negative emotions, cognitive impairment, and surface acting, and promotes productive behaviors such as deep acting and willingness to help customers.

Final Words

My hope is that this book contributes to creating momentum toward fighting customer abuse, an ugly and harmful behavior no one benefits from. There is a lot we can do about it: we can try to prevent it, we can learn to deal with it better, and we can alleviate the negative consequences. First and foremost, though, I feel we need to start talking about it. Dealing with abusive customers is some employees' daily life, and that is simply not OK. It is not OK to be yelled at, threatened, insulted, or physically attacked at work. It is not OK to go home after hours of completely avoidable stress and negative emotions. It is not OK to feel so drained as to not have the energy to engage with your partner or play with your kids because customers were annoyed and aggressive. We can stop all this if we act now.

Notes

1 Except for the first two items on this list, for the rest I'm indebted to Robert Bacal's excellent book If It Wasn't For The Customers I'd Really Like This Job: Stop Angry, Hostile Customers COLD While Remaining Professional, Stress Free, Efficient and Cool As A Cucumber (Bacal, 2011).
2 The majority of this list is compiled following Robert Bacal's book (see Bacal, 2011).

References

American Psychological Association. Resilience. https://www.apa.org/topics/resilience, last accessed on January 13, 2023.

Bacal, Robert. (2011). *If It Wasn't For The Customers I'd Really Like This Job: Stop Angry, Hostile Customers COLD While Remaining Professional, Stress Free, Efficient and Cool As A Cucumber.* Bacal & Associates. Kindle Edition.

Cherry, K. (2022). What are the big 5 personality traits? https://www.verywellmind.com/the-big-five-personality-dimensions-2795422, last accessed on January 13, 2023.

Foulk, T., Woolum, A., & Erez, A. (2016). Catching rudeness is like catching a cold: The contagion effects of low-intensity negative behaviors. *Journal of Applied Psychology*, 101(1), 50–67. doi: 10.1037/apl0000037.

Glass, N., Hanson, G. C., Anger, W. K., Laharnar, N., Campbell, J. C., Weinstein, M., & Perrin, N. (2017 Jul). Computer-based training (CBT) intervention reduces workplace violence and harassment for homecare workers. *American Journal of Industrial Medicine*, 60(7), 635–643. doi: 10.1002/ajim.22728. Erratum in: *American Journal of Industrial Medicine* 2017 Sep, 60(9), 840.

Grandey, A. A., Dickter, D. N., & Sin, H.-P. (2004). The customer is not always right: customer aggression and emotion regulation of service employees. *Journal of Organizational Behavior*, 25, 397–418. https://doi.org/10.1002/job.252

Mayo Clinic, Narcissistic personality disorder. https://www.mayoclinic.org/diseases-conditions/narcissistic-personality-disorder/symptoms-causes/syc-20366662, last accessed on January 12, 2023.

Schwager, A., & Meyer, C. (2007). Understanding customer experience. https://hbr.org/2007/02/understanding-customer-experience, last accessed on January 12, 2023.

USDAW, Freedom From Fear, https://www.usdaw.org.uk/freedomfromfear, last accessed on January 10, 2023.

van Jaarsveld, D. D., Restubog, S. L. D., Walker, D. D., & Amarnani, R. K. (2015). Misbehaving customers: Understanding and managing customer injustice in service organizations. *Organizational Dynamics*, 44(4), 273–280. https://doi.org/10.1016/j.orgdyn.2015.09.004

Index

Printed in the United States
by Baker & Taylor Publisher Services